Ulick Joseph Bourke

Pre-Christian Ireland

Ulick Joseph Bourke

Pre-Christian Ireland

ISBN/EAN: 9783337027162

Printed in Europe, USA, Canada, Australia, Japan

Cover: Foto ©Lupo / pixelio.de

More available books at **www.hansebooks.com**

PRE-CHRISTIAN IRELAND.

BY

CANON U. J. BOURKE, P.P., M.R.I.A.,

EXAMINER IN KELTIC AND IN IRISH HISTORY, ROYAL UNIVERSITY OF IRELAND.

BROWNE & NOLAN,
NASSAU STREET, DUBLIN,
𝔓rinters and 𝔓ublishers.
1887.

BROWNE AND NOLAN, PRINTERS, DUBLIN

CONTENTS.

CHAPTER I.
Certainty of Early Keltic Settlements in Eire — — — 1

CHAPTER II.
The Kelts of Europe—Descendants of Japhet — — — 4

CHAPTER III.
The Firbolg or Belgae — — — — — 9

CHAPTER IV.
The Fate of the Firbolg — — — — — 17

CHAPTER V.
The Tuatha De Danann in power contrasted with the Firbolg—
The Fomorians — — — — — — 36

CHAPTER VI.
Fomorians Defeated—Danann Dynasty continued — — 53

CHAPTER VII.
The Eponymous Character of the Danann Chiefs — — 64

CHAPTER VIII.
Sources of Historical Truth regarding the Danann People—They certainly built the Palace of Aileach, and perhaps, most of the Round Towers — — — — — — 69

CHAPTER IX.
Other Proofs—Manuscripts—Monumentary Mounds—Sites selected by the Conquered Danann Chiefs, known to-day as "Faery Hills," are footprints on the sands of the past period of Danann Power — — — — — — 82

CHAPTER X.
Had the Danann Tribes and Pre-Christian Gael any knowledge of Letters?—What Character or Alphabet did they use? — 89

CHAPTER XI.
Ogham—What it was—Material for Writing—Origin of this Secret Art—Proofs of Pagan Parentage—Christian Ogham Inscriptions—The Letters—General Character of the Danann Race — — — — — — — 97

Chapter XII.

Fable and Fact—Mythology reduced to a System—Three views—The Danann an intelligent Pagan People—Their form of Government — Clan System — Kings — Laws — Religion—Druidism—Social Habits—Music—The "Caoin"—Marriage—Arts—Public Gatherings—Dwellings—How they lived - 113

Chapter XIII.

The Defeat of the Danann Dynasty by a Colony of Kelts from the South of Europe—Certainty of a Keltic Colonisation—Uncertainty of the record contained in Irish Manuscripts—Heroic deeds of Milesians recounted by the Bards - - 124

Chapter XIV.

Mission from Spain to Ireland—Ith—His death—Preparation for the Invasion of Inisfail—They come—Strange details—Story of the Milesian landing - - - - 138

Chapter XV.

A Storm—Queen Scota unfurls the Sacred Banner—Battles of Mis, of Tailtean, of Druimlighean—Defeat of the Danann Tribes—How the Leaders of the Danann Clans select the "Sidhe" or best sites throughout the land—They finally settle amongst the people—Stories relative to that age - 144

Chapter XVI.

Stories and Romances regarding the Early Irish Period - - 149

Chapter XVII.

Fate of the Children of Turenn—A story relating to the early Danann Period - - - - - - 156

Chapter XVIII.

A new Dynasty—Heber and Heremon—Division of Ireland—New Possession—A falling out—Battle of Geashill—Death of Heremon—Names of places tell to this day of the Milesian Dynasty - - - - - - - 161

Chapter XIX.

The Families descended from Heber Fionn—From Heremon—And from Ir, or Heber, son of Ir—The leading princely Milesian families of Ireland trace their descent from those three princely Houses of Heber Fionn, Heremon, and Ir—Length of time does not destroy certainty of connection—The chief Monarchs up to the time of Conor Mac Nessa—A Kingly Government existed in Eire for over two thousand years, "Eire apo, Inir na Riġ," Noble Eire, Island of Kings - 166

CHAPTER XX.

Ireland's Royal Backbone—Her line of Kings reaches nigh three thousand years—The nature and character of the Brehon Laws, best test and proof of the Social State and Manners of the Irish in the far past—The Clan System—The Rights of the Clan and of the Chief—Elective Power—Tanistry—Gavelkind—Moral and Physical characteristics of the Irish People ... 177

CHAPTER XXI.

The Question of the Round Towers of Ireland—Three leading opinions regarding them—The Christian Theory, as it is called, advocated by Dr. Petrie and his followers—The Pagan Theory—A third Opinion, that many of the Towers were erected in the Christian Period, that others had come down from Pagan times, but in all, the figure and form of the edifices, and the purposes for which they were first erected were of Pre-Christian origin and growth—Reasons for the different opinions—The controversy not yet closed—The Towers described --Their probable number—Their durability- 192

APPENDIX I.

A Summary of Dr. Petrie's History and Antiquities of Tara Hill - - - - - - - 205

APPENDIX II.

A list of the Best Hundred Irish Books - - - - 211

PREFACE.

Before the time of Copernicus, Canon and Priest of Frauenberg. (A.D. 1473-1543), and for some years after his death, a variety of problems, difficult then to be solved, regarding the sun, the planets and the stars, presented themselves to those who made the science of the heavens their study. The power of solving all the difficulties that arose to the minds of intelligent scholars, appeared then to be beyond the limits of human understanding. This was of necessity the outcome under the Ptolemaic teaching.

Directly that the system of astronomy taught by Copernicus was established, these difficulties, like filmy clouds before the noon-day sun, vanished. The discoveries made by Sir Isaac Newton (A.D. 1642-1727) over a century later, simplified other problems which at one time appeared as if they could never be solved.

At a still later period, say one hundred years ago, few indeed could tell what is lightning or thunder which accompanies it, or the northern lights, or how it is that a magnet possesses the property of attraction and repulsion, and in every part of the globe points in the direction of the poles. The discoveries in the walk of electrical science have made these things now-a-days quite plain; those questions are known at present by ordinary college students.

The science of comparative philology is to the historian and antiquarian of the present time, what the correct system of astronomy has been to those who wander in safety and certainty amidst the stars. Things that before appeared difficult and uncertain to the antiquarian to-day are plain and pleasant.

Take for instance amongst the ablest historians of the early past Livy as an example. He could not account for the beginnings of the first inhabitants of Latium, or the Sabine territory; or for those who had flourished some centuries anterior to the period when Romulus and Remus are supposed to have lived. The ancient Etrurians were a people of whom the earliest Roman writers knew very little; yet they at one time enjoyed power, and a civilisation not inferior to that possessed by the Romans during the age of the Gracchi. The ancient writers could not tell who were the Pelasgi, the Egyptians, the peoples of Niniveh and Babylon, or what connection existed between the Greeks and the inhabitants living east and west of the Appennines.

Those primitive states taken separately were to our ancient historians what the severed joints and members of an organised body appear to an uneducated boy—a perfect puzzle. The earth and the different peoples that dwelt upon it were to them a complete mystery. No one could rightly tell what the earth was, or where the people first came from who dwelt on its surface. At a later period, even our own Dr. Keating—the author of the History of Ireland in Irish— knew very little of the geography of the earth, and much less concerning the languages which the different nations in the past had employed as a vehicle of thought. It was not his fault: he was up to the teaching of the period in which he lived (16th century). The modern science of comparative philology makes those ethnical and lingual difficulties which historians or antiquarians, in past centuries, were unable to solve, regarding individual nations, plain and clear.

This science shows that we have all come from one primitive and primeval habitat, separating as the earliest emigrants proceeded westward into different clans or large families, and settling down in some new territory, efformating there in process of time a new race and a distinct people. Had Livy had any idea of this scientific view of early mankind, apart from any knowledge furnished by Hebrew writers, he would have known that all European tongues are sister languages, that Latin, so called, had in its beginnings the start of Greek, not only in the race westward, but in its more robust and unaffected phonetic forms of speech which Romulus and those who flourished in the eighth century before the Christian era, had used as a language on the banks of the Tiber and the Anio. If he had had any notion of the light which comparative philology throws over the map of Europe two thousand years before the coming of the Christian era, he would not have thought that the earliest inhabitant of his own beautiful Italy had grown out of the soil of that charming country; and if our own Irish historian, Dr. Keating, had any forecast of such a science, he would not have written so readily, or copied the unmeaning views of earlier annalists in their vague statements regarding the primitive languages of mankind, and the geographical relations that existed between the kingdoms and nations of the world as known to the ancients.

While a youthful student in college the writer had a longing to learn thoroughly the history of his native land from the earliest period. Again, and again he read the ancient story connected with the beginnings of our people; and although it was his wish to believe the traditions recorded in our manuscript history, yet there were statements in them regarding, for instance, the primeval progenitors of the Milesian race that did not appear in harmony with other historic events told of the outside world.

It is true that the connexion of Ireland in remote times with the East was pointed out by Dr. Keating, and by the annalists of ancient Eire, but the narrative in the stream of facts thus flowing down did not seem to fall in with the clear current of historic truth gathered together from other known sources of the world as a whole. Hence like many sons of Eire and others not Irish, but who have studied our early national history, he was obliged to look upon those early records as partly imaginative or mythic, with some groundwork of fact on which the edifice of fable and myth had been erected.

Outside the region of history, so-called, and, as a result of comparative philology and comparative ethnology, it is now certain that the substance of the story contained in ancient Irish manuscripts is true. Ancient Irish writers erred in the manner and in many of the details connected with what they have related; that the ancient Milesian forefathers of the Irish people came from the East—that is true; that they had journeyed by sea, and journeyed by land—that is true; that there were several migrations from the east—that is equally true; that all the early inhabitants spoke a generic Keltic speech—that also is true; and that they brought with them the manners, the social and national customs special to the East—is likewise true. The manuscript records tell all this. The statement is confirmed by those modern sciences that deal in comparing languages and races of men. The light derived from the luminous sources of comparative philology and ethnology presents the records of the ancient Gael of Ireland in a favorable view, showing that the leading facts are in substance correct, and are like writings of a kindred kind regarding Rome, Greece or Egypt.

Accordingly it is not a matter of surprise that there were two classes of readers of ancient Irish history quite opposed in their estimate of its value; one class regarded the early Irish records as mere romances or myths; the other gave credence to everything recorded in Eire's story, and believed, for instance in the wanderings of the forefathers of the Milesian invaders, just as firmly as they believed in the wanderings of the Hebrew people under Moses in their passage during forty years from Egypt to the Promised Land.

The following view of the history, or story of the earliest inhabitants of Ireland is presented to the consideration of Irish students at home and abroad. It is derived from a three-fold source, (*a*) from the record contained in Irish Annals; (*b*) from the monumental remains that still abide in the Isle of Destiny, correcting that record by the light, which extrinsic evidence from other nations and other lands furnishes; (*c*) lastly, from the facts which modern investigators supply.

The nomenclature of the countries of Europe such as Albion, Helvetia, Iberia, Gallia; of the great towns as Lugdunum, Rome; of the rivers, as the Rhine, Rhone, Seine, Garonne, Danube; show that a people kindred in language at one time inhabited the most of Europe. It is morally certain that a people, known as Kelts, dwelt in southern and western Europe in what may be termed the remote period: that they had emigrated from the East; that all did not emigrate at one time, but that there had been successive waves of emigrants from Asia to southern and north-western Europe; that some of those, for instance the Belgae, or Firbolgs, found themselves making use of a language which was a dialectic variety of the primitive Keltic; that the new shoals of emigrants steering through Spain and south-western Europe came in the rere of the more ancient colonists carrying with them a language—called from them Gaelic—differing little from primitive Keltic, spoken at a time anterior to the coming of the Belgae from Eastern lands; that the tongue of the Milesian race and of those who had retained the primitive Keltic is still living in the Gaelic speech heard amongst the peasants of the west of Ireland, or in Argyle and the islands along the coast of Scotland. This latter is known as Scotch-Gaelic, and is a branch of Irish-Gaelic, spoken by those who in the early centuries went from Ulster to Albion. Further, that the language once spoken in the Isle of Man, and at one time even in Britain, is only a phonetic form of the same Gaelic, or primitive and unaffected Keltic. It is true also that affected Keltic found a home amongst the ancient Belgae and the Gallic and the ancient Firbolg of Ireland—amongst the Kimbri of Wales, the Britons of Cornwall, and the Bretons of West Normandy.

Taking, then, primeval Gaelic as spoken at one time in the south of Europe, among the Sabines for instance, to be the basis of the Latin speech—an opinion held by many philologists—affected Keltic, which survives in modern Welsh and Bas-breton, must have been the basis of Greek, which in phonetic features are so like.

Supposing those views to be correct, then the ancient Kimric speech brought first to northern Europe by the Belgian Kelts, was anterior to Greek; and consequently one must go back a good many hundreds of years till he has reached the far off time when the races who spoke affected Keltic came from the motherland in Asia. Changes in language spoken by a race of people do not arise suddenly or in a few hundred years. They took a much longer period. And next, if Gaelic, as an unbroken language, must have been earlier still, one can form some idea of the great antiquity of the language of Eire.

There is a school of *savants* and antiquarians who at present wish to show that all those dialectic varieties arose in a few hundred years. It was no such thing. Before the development of geology as a science—or, as far as it is known scientifically, one was taught to think that the alluvial earth, and all beneath the surface, was only some few thousands of years in existence. Geology tells a different story; and even the inspired word of God confirms that truth when it says: " In the beginning God created the heavens and the earth." The words, "in the beginning," bring us a great way back. The stratifications of the earth help to bring the thoughts of the student a great way back: so the series of linguistic growth, and phonetic falling away—in the long line of languages from the present Gaelic to the Aryan tongue spoken at one time in Asia, bring one's thoughts back to a period of several thousand years. What are three centuries or four compared to such a length of bygone years!

Lastly—in the present volume, it has been the desire of the writer to put before the modern student, all those races who spoke Keltic from a time at least two thousand years before the Christian period up to the first year of our Lord's coming. They were a living reality, not a myth, nor an abstract conception; they had a name, they were a chosen people, a gifted race; they were endowed with intelligence and knowledge, they were warlike, and brave to a fault, capable of heroic deeds of heart and hand, trained to the directive influence of laws, they were children of civilisation, holding the rights of others and their own in due regard, they fostered learning, they loved their kith and kin, as their descendants do to-day. Looking back into the past, our ancestors bear a favourable comparison when put in line with the primitive progenitors of the other nations of Europe—the Roman, the Greek, or the Teuton. What a long array of ancestry the Irish people see rising before the mental eye in the area of History, back two thousand, aye, four thousand years and longer, to the days when Abraham left his Chaldean city.

The tale of the pagan patriarchs of the Keltic clans, lighted up for the first time under the lamp of science, is presented to the reader in the following pages.

Father Lockhart in a lecture delivered some years ago said :—
"Ireland was a nation long before England came into existence. And long even before Britain was known, Ireland had already been a colonised and famous country. Ireland was a colonised and a civilised nation 1,400 years before Christ's coming. For nearly 3,000 years one dynasty reigned upon the Irish throne; the dynasty was unbroken save twice. Again, parliaments which have only been known and introduced into England and other countries in recent times, formed an institution in Ireland one thousand years at least before Christ."

"Before the empires of Greece and Rome were founded, representative legislation existed in Ireland."

Again; "Long before either Germany or Britain was known as a state, Ireland had been the university and seat of learning for the civilisation of the world."

In the introduction to the manuscript publication—the well-known Book of Leinster, given to the literary world a few years ago by Robert Atkinson, M.A., the Editor says; "The real historic gain is to be sought by the skilled investigator in the endeavour to shape out from those curious records some consistent conception of the social life of the Irish Nation, for a period extending back centuries from the time when the manuscript itself was written."

It was copied before the Anglo-Norman invasion.

At the Council of Constance which was held in the year 1417—the English representatives would not be allowed to vote, as a nation and in the priority of position to which they laid claim. The Canonists were clear that the English were included in the nation of Germany, for they had been subdued by the Germans, who, at the time, were the subjects of the Emperor. But the English directly put forward the plea that their King was Suzerain, or Lord of Ireland, which kingdom always held the third rank amongst the nations of Europe. On this head the position of honour sought, with liberty to vote, was granted, because they were connected with Ireland, which, at that time, was allowed to be the third in dignity amongst the nations of Europe.

U. J. B

PRE-CHRISTIAN IRELAND.

CHAPTER I.

CERTAINTY OF EARLY KELTIC SETTLEMENTS IN EIRE.

Q. 1. Where did the earliest races who first reached Ireland come from?

A. From the East; from the high table-lands reaching from Mount Ararat in Armenia, by the Caspian Sea, south and east; from the present Persia and the country stretching eastwards to the Hindu Kush Mountains, and to the River Hindus.

Q. 2. What proofs exist to show that the first settlers in Ireland came from this eastern land?

A. Apart from the proofs presented by the native Annals published, or yet in manuscript unpublished, of which there are many—convincing reasons are furnished: (*a*) by the science of comparative philology; (*b*) by the similarity of manners, customs, laws, that exists between the ancient Eastern races and the early Irish people; (*c*) proofs are at hand if one compares the state of the arts and sciences as known in the East, and shewn to exist in days of old amongst the races of the far off "Isle of the West;" (*d*) proofs are present when one regards their poetry; their building powers; their taste in music and painting; their patriarchal rule, similarity of land tenure in times past, social habits, love of imagery; above all, from their language, which, to this day, has left its impress on the lands through which they journeyed from Aria to Ara, from Iberia to Eire. A knowledge, therefore, of the ancient languages and laws; of the pagan religious rites, social state, modes of thought, and manner of life; civil government and literary advancement; of the ethnological character of the races, leads to the conclusion that the early progenitors of the Irish race came from the East.

"It is now a recognised fact in science," says W. K. Sullivan, vol I., p. 4., *On the Manners and Customs of the Ancient Irish*, "that from the Hindus to the Atlantic Ocean, and thence across the American continent to the shores of the Pacific, the descendants of one primitive, blue-eyed, fair-haired race, divided into several branches, and speaking dialects of what was once a common language, held sway."

Q. 3. By what name are the early settlers or immigrants known in Irish Annals?

A. The earliest are the followers of (a) Partholanus, who, it is stated, came to Ireland two thousand two hundred years before the Christian period; next in succession came (b) the Nemedians; and the pirate races (c) the Fomorians, who at all periods loved to plunder the land rather than to settle in it; (d) the Firbolg or Belgæ; (e) the Tuatha De Danann and lastly (f) the Milesians; in all, including the Fomorians, six separate settlements.

Q. 4. How is it certain that these came from the same Eastern regions, though they made their migratory incursions at periods quite different and remote one from the other?

A. Because, as a matter of fact, all spoke the same Gaelic language, differing at most in phonetic or dialectic variety.

Q. 5. Do the Irish Annals state about what time Partholan and his followers came to Ireland,* "the Island of the Remote," as they called it?

A. Yes: about the time that Nachor, the grandfather of Abraham, lived at Ur of Chaldea in the East,—Partholan with his followers

---

* ınıꞃ na b-ꝼuıneꝺaċ; ꝼuınn means end, or extreme part—found in the Latin *finis*.

"Il faut donc bien se contenter de partir du fait incontestable de cette dispersion déjà accomplie *plus de deux mille ans avant notre ère*; car à cette époque, la race que nous appelerons Arienne étendait ses rameaux depuis l'Inde jusqu' aux limites extrêmes de l'Europe à l'Occident, et formait, d'un bout à l'autre, comme une longue chaine de peuples sortis d'un même sang, mais ne se reconnaissant plus comme frères." *Les Origines Indo-Européennes, ou les Aryans Primitifs*, p. 2, par Adolphe Pictet, Paris, 1859.

came from Iberia, between the Black and Caspian seas, or from Macedonia, through the Mediterranean, to the Isle of the West.

Q. 6. Where did they land—and how long did the people survive their leader ?

A. At Kenmare, in the county Kerry. That lovely bay was the scene of the landing of the first colonists that came to Eire. It was known afterwards as Inver Skené, either from Skené wife of Amerghin the Milesian who some centuries later was drowned there, or from Scéıne (gen. *Skené*), meaning " wild beauty," that is, " the frith of wild beauty."

From Kenmare they went by sea to the estuary at Ballyshannon, another beauteous strand or estuary, through which pass the tumbling waters that rush down from Lough Erne. Partholan and his wife and companions came ashore there at " Inis Saimher," which lies in the estuary. " Saimher " is from " so," pleasant, and " muir," sea.

After some time Partholan settled at " Sean-Mhagh," *old plain*, subsequently known as " *Magh n-Ealta*," *plain-of-flocks*, that stretch of land from Howth to the foot of the Dublin Mountains. Partholan died there thirty years after he had obtained possession of Ireland for himself and his descendants. Soon, however, his followers had to contend with pirate invaders.

Many lakes, such as Conn, Cullen, Mask, in Mayo; Gara, in Roscommon; Cuan (or Strangford), in county Down, became known in Partholan's time.

In three hundred years the followers and descendants of Partholan had multiplied, yet their numbers were often reduced by the attacks of pirates. Eventually they were all swept away in a week by famine, pestilence, and plague, at Tallacht, near Dublin—caused by the foul air which the bodies of the unburied slain had produced.

Q. 7. Is there any monument to tell succeeding generations where those plague-stricken colonists found a tomb ?

A. Yes; the name of the well-known village and district called Tallacht;* famous in modern as well as in early Christian and pagan

---

* τáṁ means sleep, rest, trance ; leaċt, a monument.

times, tells the philologist that the mounds there once form monuments for those who on that occasion "slept in death," struck down by plague or by the plundering sea-pirates—the Fomorians.

CHAPTER II.
THE KELTS OF EUROPE—DESCENDANTS OF JAPHET.

Q. 1. When was Ireland peopled again?

A. It is stated that, within thirty years after the time the followers of Partholan had perished, another leader, by name Neimheadh, or Nemedius,—pretty much about the same period that Abram had left Ur of Chaldea and settled in Haran of Mesopotamia,—started from Thrace or the territory south of the Balkan range, the present Roumelia, close by the Black Sea; that he and his followers wandered north-westward by the Danube, the Dnieper, and the Vistula, through a territory well known afterwards as the Kingdom of Gallicia, the land of the Gauls, south of the present Poland, and forming the northern part of the Empire of Austria; that some of those tribes went onwards, dwelt for a time to the south of Denmark, and passed by Belgium, and Alba, as Britain was at first called, into "the Isle of the West."*

Q. 2. Did the third colony, the Firbolg, come from the East?

A. Yes.

Q. 3. And the Tuatha De Danann tribes?

A. Yes; for both these peoples, though rivals and enemies, were only tribal communities,—offshoots of the same Nemedian stock.

An instance of tribes of the same people being bitter rivals will be found in the 10th century, A.C., when the Danes or "Black foreigners" attacked, defeated and plundered the Norwegians or "White foreigners" who before them had reached Ireland. See "Cogadh Gaedhil re Gallaibh."

Q. 4. What do the Annals of Ireland state on this point, regarding the dispersion of the Nemedians and

---

* The chronology of the Sepuagint, adopted by the Four Masters, is here preferred, as safer and nearer the truth.

the coming of the Firbolg, of the Tuatha De Danann, and of the Milesians?

A. They tell us that the posterity of Nemheda dwelt nigh two hundred years in Ireland; that, from time to time, they like their predecessors, the followers of Partholan, were attacked by a sea-roving race, known at that remote period by the name Fomorians, which is a Keltic term, meaning sea-robber (" ꝼoꞅ" plunder, and " mᴀꞃᴀ" of the sea); that in consequence thousands of the settlers, near Cork, in the south of Ireland, perished from plague and pestilence; that the Fomorians held strong towers of defence along Donegal and Derry, and chiefly in Tory Island, or the Island of Towers; that the native Nemedians made there one grand united attack on them, unlike not the effort made by the Irish in the eleventh century against the Danes at Clontarf; that the Fomorian forces were aided by the arrival of other pirate invaders; that in the battle thus renewed, and fought with savage fierceness on the strand of Tory Island, the Nemedians and their foes perished in thousands, either by the sword or in the rolling billows of the angry Atlantic, rushing in to appease, as it were, the fierce wrath of such merciless contending foes. The surviving Nemedians, after a time, forsook the Irish shore, and sailed, under three independent leaders, from the land of their fathers; some under Briotan Maol, to Britain; some to Scandinavia or Northern Europe; others under Simon Breac, or the *Speckled*, to South-eastern Europe. During a space of two hundred years, the Sea-robbers and a few Nemedians had the "*Noble* Island" completely to themselves. Then we are told that under a new name, that of Firbolg or Belgæ, the descendants of the colony which had gone to the south-east of Europe, returned in their numbers, like the children of Israel under Moses, to the land of their forefathers. They re-conquered Ireland from the Fomorians; joined their newly-acquired power with that of the primitive Nemedians, their own kindred, and settled in the island. They divided the country into five great divisions, which exist almost in the same form to this day. A king was appointed over each respective "Cúigë" (*a fifth*), or province, and a supreme monarch or Ard-righ appeared for the first time at Tara. After a few years—say, thirty-seven—the other Nemedian colony returned from the north of Europe with a new name, that of "*Tuatha De Danann.*" Finally— about two centuries later—another race, from the Keltic territory of Iberia or Gallicia in Spain, known in Irish annals as Milesians, or descendants of the warrior Gollamh (surnamed *Miledh, i.e., Miles*, soldier, warrior) came by the Atlantic wave to Inisfail, their "Island of Destiny." They in turn conquered it some fifteen hundred years before the Christian era, and since then they have virtually been the dominant party in Ireland.

Q. 5. How can one be sure that all this is substantially true?

A. First, from the discoveries made within the past half-century by the sciences of philology, ethnology, and kindred sources of knowledge, it is certain that some people came, at least four thousand years ago, from the East, from the land that lies between the Euphrates and Hindus ;* that from time to time for centuries afterwards migratory bands came from the same Eastern lands, and took up their abode in Southern and Northern Europe, and that some of the same communities proceeded by different routes to Ireland; some shoals of immigrants, like the followers of Partholan and Milesius, reaching the far west by the Atlantic wave; others, like the Nemedians and their kindred tribes, coming to their new home through Gallicia in Austrian Poland, Gallia, Germany, Belgium, and Britain.

It is now a well-known fact, proved by the language these migratory races spoke, and the footprints that point out to this day the land through which they trod, that the Keltic area extended, in the remotest times, from the southern shores of Italy to the north of Gaul, and from Iberia in the west of Portugal to Greece in the east of Europe.†

The national tradition, then, of the Keltic races, and above all, of the early Irish settlers, comes in to lend special support to the discoveries effected by philology and European antiquities; thus aiding the student in identifying the migratory bands who had come to the Western shores, and pointing them out under the title of Nemedians, Firbolg or Belgæ, Tuatha De Danann, and Milesians.

---

* It is in keeping with the meaning and history of the word to call this river "*Hindus*" rather than "*Indus*," because as Max Müller shews, its primitive name was *Sindus* or Sind, and "*h*" represents the affected sound of "*s*." The word should therefore be "*Sindus*" or its affected form "*Hindus*," and not *Indus*, as the phonetic "*h*" gives the affected value of "*s*" which is completely and wholly lost in "*Indus*."

† See *Eastern Origin of the Keltic Nations*, by Pritchard. Edited and enlarged by Dr. Latham. London: Quaritch, 1857.

Q. 6. Were the early Keltic races, Turanian or Scythian, descended from Japhet, the youngest son of Noah, or from Ham or Cham, his second son?

A. This is one of the vexed questions amongst Irish historians and annalists. The native writers quote those authors who have written before their own times respectively, but they have not, up to the present, attempted to reason the question into any semblance of certainty. O'Flaherty will have it that all, including the Fomorians, were descendants of Japhet, and therefore all must have been, in the sense of modern anthropologists, Turanian.

At the remotest period, long before that of which Livy had any notion, or Herodotus, in Greece, conceived any idea, Southern, Western, and even part of Eastern Europe, were peopled by Keltic races. All these were confessedly Japhetians. Hence, the earliest colonists of Ireland are, as Kelts, descended from Japhet, Noah's youngest son.

On the other hand, many writers maintain that Ireland was inhabited by Cuthites, or descendants of Cush, son of Cham; that, therefore, in their ethnological character, they were not Turanian but Scythian. Not a few of the old school, and some one or two amongst moderns, maintain that the Kelts of Ireland are descendants of Sem.

The science of languages proves the contrary, that not only they are not Semitic, but they are children of Japhet. This science has set at rest for ever the question regarding the Gaelic language. It is Aryan or Japhetic; nay, more, the Semitic speech has no relationship whatever with the Keltic dialects. There are a few primitive roots that have similarity of sound and meaning, but as languages the Semitic cannot be put at all in the same class with the Aryan languages, of which the Keltic is a primary branch. Hence, the Gael, or Irish, whose inheritance that language has been for four thousand years and more, are not sons of Sem, but are sons of Japhet, and consequently Turanians and not Scythians.

Q. 7. Were the Fomorians descendants of Japhet?

A. Some authors—O'Flaherty is one—say that even the Fomorians, judging from their language, were descended of Japhet. It is likely, however, that they were sons of Canaan, son of

Cush; if one credit the authority of writers whose opinion ought to be respected: and many extend this view even to all the Gaels.

This opinion is at least probable, on account of the authorities who support it; and chiefly, because, like the Canaanites of Phœnicia, the Fomorians were powerful at sea, and they never ceased to hate and harass the Aryan tribes—Japhet's descendants.

Q. 8. How is it shown that these early Keltic colonies, the Firbolg for instance, or the Milesians, had come to Ireland at a period so long before Rome was founded—say, at least, one thousand years?

A. Strong extrinsic evidence exists to confirm the statement of native annalists on this point.

The date of the building of Rome is allowed by all writers to be beyond doubt. Now, the chief inhabitants of Rome were made up of Sabines, Volscians, Etrurians, Samnites, and Latins. The Latins* were over a thousand years in Latium before Rome was thought of; they built large cities, and formed a series of united republics, not unlike those of the United States of America. But the Latins themselves were only a mixed race of Umbrians, Oscans, and Siculians.† The Oscan ruled and efformated into one confederation the various peoples

---

* Varro, *De Initiis Urbis Romæ;* and Dionysius.

† "The extent of the Latin coast, from the mouth of the Tiber to Circeii, is about fifty miles; the breadth of Latium, from the coast to the Sabine hills, thirty miles. Within this area, before the dawn of history, many Latin cities flourished in more than one confederation. Even at that period many mixtures of population had occurred." *Regal Rome.* By Francis W. Newman. London: Taylor, Walton, and Maberly.

"Two nations are mentioned as dwelling in the earliest times to the north and south of Latium—the Umbrians and the Oscans. The Umbrians were regarded by the Romans as a truly primæval Italian race, who at one time held possession of all Lombardy and Tuscany, reaching into Latium. The Oscans, including the Volsci and Aurones, or Auruncans, were the principal people of South Italy. The Oscan language and Umbrian were sister tongues; Oscan sides with Greek and Welsh; Umbrian with Latin and Gaelic. The Sabine race were a branch of the Umbrians." *Regal Rome.* By Newman, pp. 3, 4.

"The only point left uncertain is whether the oldest Latin itself, or only some of its affluents, was the Keltic influence. . . . . . On actually comparing the Latin vocabulary with that of Greeks, Germans, and Kelts, a far greater similarity to the Keltic shows itself. The Sabines spoke a form of Gaelic." *Regal Rome.* Newman.

south of the Tiber to the Lucanian coast; the Umbrian ruled north of the Tiber, as far as the Alps and Venice, including Etruria. The Umbrian spoke a language akin to Gaelic; the Oscan a speech like that of the Welsh of the present day. Both people were Kelts. Their power and that of the Etrurians had extended over a period of twelve hundred years beyond the time when Rome started first into existence, and before her sons depurated the dialects of the Etrurian, the Volsci, the Sabine, and the speech of the Umbrian and the Oscan, into that in which the laws of the Twelve Tables were subsequently inscribed, and which in due time became the magnificent Latin language of Cæsar, of Cicero, and Tacitus. The works of art left us from the hands of the Etrurians are proof positive of the extraordinary knowledge which at that remote period those people possessed; and it is fair to infer that the higher classes amongst the Umbrians had no small share of that intellectual inheritance, which the higher classes of the Keltic nations throughout Europe retained. The Keltic races in every clime enjoyed the same kind of laws, privileges and government; and their Druids and lawgivers, and the upper classes, had the same facilities for acquiring learning. Hence the Kelts of Spain, say those in Gallacia or in Iberia, were a skilled and a powerful people sixteen hundred years at least before the Christian period. From Spain the Milesians sailed to Inis Fail.

CHAPTER III.

THE FIRBOLG OR BELGÆ.

Q. 1. Why were the descendants of those Nemedians who first returned to the mother country, called Fir bolg?

A. Because they were a pastoral people, for "bolg" in Keltic means a cow-herd or drover.

Q. 2. What light does the history of the period throw on their character?

A. The name "Firbolg,"* like the term "Greek," applied to the Hellenes, or "Scoti," to the Irish of the early Christian centuries, was evidently given to this race not by themselves but by other Keltic tribes, in accordance with a well-known custom, existing from the earliest times amongst them, of designating a place or person or people by a name expressive, in their own tongue, of the characteristics or special qualities that strike others as peculiar in the locality or in the people. Gaelic names of places and persons fully shew that the earliest colonists in Eire exercised this æsthetic faculty. This practice was common amongst the Semitic as well as the Japhetic races. Adam called all the beasts by their names, and all the fowls of the air and all the cattle of the field, just as he " saw " or knew the special properties of each kind, and the ends for which they were suited.

Observe for what the Firbolg, on their return from the south-east of Europe, were remarkable. They had flocks and herds in their journey to the northern coast by the south of the Vistula, the Oder and modern Belgium.

After some of the warrior chiefs had regained the home of their forefathers, the rest of the Firbolg tribes came, as colonists usually come, not in a body, but by degrees, and as people progress and multiply.

The Keltic tribes attended to the culture of cattle and crops, rather than to seafaring pursuits.

On the other hand the Canaanites, or descendants of Cham, had secured by their skill in naval affairs dominion over the seas, known at the time to the merchants of the East and West.

The Firbolg, as Keltic clans, preserved their tribal traditions, their national learning, language, laws, government. The term "bolg," then, in the language of neighbouring Kelts, helps to show that the people were, in journeying through Europe, and perhaps on their passage through Britain, "drovers." They had cattle and herds, and "drove" their flocks with them wherever they went.

Q. 3. Does the name "bolg" accord with this view, which history, as far as can be known, furnishes?

A. Yes: this meaning of "bolg" is now for the first time presented to readers of Irish history. "Bolg," like many other Irish

---

* "He (the Fear-bolg) was a shepherd and an agriculturist." Words of Sir William Wilde in his lecture at Belfast in the presence of the British Association.

words of one syllable is a compound term. It is made up of bu (cc..), and ᚈelᚷ (to drive), or bó-ᚈelᚷ: "s" in composition loses its natural sound and receives an affected one, that of "h," thus bo-helᚷ and in one syllable, boelᚷ. The vowel "o" is found in the Gaelic, while "e," the second vowel, is retained in the continental term *Belgæ*. The derivation, taking the component elements as Irish-Gaelic, is very plain and natural. But it is plainer still, if the student bear in mind that the Belgæ, or Firbolg, were a Kimric, rather than a Gaelic colony, as O'Mahony states in his Annotations to Dr. Keating's Ireland, and in that remote period that they had, it is likely, adopted the affected sound of "s" (namely "h") rather than its natural sound.*

The opinion of O'Mahony, that the Firbolg were a Kimric colony, is confirmed by the traces known of the language which they spoke during their intercourse with the Aryan races north and south of the Danube, who at this time, while the Pelasgic period was in a transition state, were, like the Hellenes, efformating a new but affected pronunciation of many primitive terms commencing with "s," and "f," for example: Greek, $\xi\xi$ for *sex*; $\xi\pi\tau\grave{\alpha}$ for *septem*; $\tilde{\upsilon}\varsigma$ for *sus*, &c.

Some may say that "seilg" means to *hunt* simply. The primary meaning of "seilg" is *to drive*, its secondary is *to hunt*. That it means *to drive* is clear from the kindred words (*a*) "*seol*," to lead, to conduct, to direct, to drive, to steer; and (*b*) "*sealbh*," a herd, possessions.

The derivation and meaning of "bolg," as just presented, is not the less certain because it is new, for its value rests on the historic character of the people (the Belgæ); and on the primitive meaning which Irish-Gaelic root-words still possess. They present to-day to the Keltic scholar the same meaning that they expressed four thousand years ago, as in the words *Tamhleacht* (Tallaght), *Fōmoraigh* (sea-pirates).

Some will reject the meaning, because to them it is new; others will rather be pleased at the discovery, for the name "bolg" is a fossil-term now, after ages, presented with its primeval significancy.† It

---

* *To hunt, to drive together*, is "seilg" in Irish, in Welsh "helg:" and in general, words beginning with "s" in Irish-Gaelic, in Welsh commence with "h" as Irish, *sean*, old; Welsh *hen;* Irish *sealbh*, possessions; Welsh, *helw*, possessions.

† The meaning of the term "ferbolg" (*fer* means *man, fir*, plural *men*), or

will be asked why did not the old word-interpreters, King Cormac of Cashel, or Ænghus Ceilé-Dé, or O'Davoren tell its meaning long ago? Why? Because they were not philologists. They knew nothing about linguistic science.

Objection—But there remains still the narration, graphically told by Dr. Keating, that these Firbolg had gone under a certain leader all the way to Thrace; that they were brought under bondage there, were obliged to carry earth in leathern bags from deep valleys to bleak hill-sides, and cover the barren rocks with earth, thus changing the cheerless waste into a smiling and fertile garden? It is true that Dr. Keating narrates this strange story as history, but neither he, nor the bards before him, who had penned the tale, could tell why these Belgian colonists were called "fir-bolg," for "bolg" means, as they understood the term, either "leather bag," "sack," "quiver," "pouch," or "belly." To account for the name the story was invented. Not one of the ancient Irish historians or *Seanachaidh* knew anything about the state of Europe at that early period—eighteen hundred years before the Christian era. The term "bolg" suggested the idea, that the people so called had special developments of body. But that too was a mere fancy.*

Belgæ, just presented is strengthened by the following note copied from the Irish version of Nennius, edited by the late learned Dr. Todd:—

Text:—*Viri Bullorum, i.e.*, Firbolg iardain, agus *Viri Armorum, i.e.*, fir Gaileoin, agus *Viri Domnioum, i.e.*, fir Domnann: síl Nemid ann sud.—p. 44.

Translation:—The *Viri Bullorum, i.e.*, the Firbolg afterwards, and the *Viri Armorum, i.e.*, the Fir-Gaileon, and the *Viri Domnium, i.e.*, the Fir-Domnann: these *were* the race of Nemed.

We see that the Latin form in which the *Firbolg* are named by Nennius is *Viri Bullorum*. *Bullum*, says Dr. Todd, in the Latinity of the middle ages, signified, according to Du Cange, *Baculum Pustoris*, which suggests a derivation of the name Fir-Bolg, that the editor has not seen noticed. So far Dr. Todd in his Commentary on the Text.

The derivation given in this work is that which Dr. Todd in his time would have wished to see.

* "The tale that Keating here recounts from the Seanachies was manifestly coined in order to account for the forgotten origin of the national name."—*Keating's Ireland.* By O'Mahony, p. 130. New York: published by P. M. Haverty. 1857.

"A fanciful derivation." Note by Dr. Todd; *Irish Version of Nennius*, p. 45. Dublin, 1848. Printed for the Irish Archæological Society.

"Keating's work consists of nothing more than a compilation of those materials as many as he had by him in his wanderings; and he seems to have done nothing but abridge and arrange such accounts of historic facts as he found in them."—*O'Curry, MS. Materials*, p. 442.

Q. 4. Were the Firbolg of Ireland and the Belgæ of Gaul of the same race?

A. Yes: their ancient language, their ethnological character, and their common Keltic origin, their early names or customs, and the præ-Christian history of the two races tend to prove, almost to a certainty, that both are descended of the same primitive Aryan* race.

Q. 5. Does not St. Jerome say that the Belgæ and the Galatians of Asia Minor were the same?

A. He does: it is true, speaking generally, that all the Kelts are of the same Aryan family; St. Jerome says, moreover, of the Galatians of Asia :—" *Galatas propriam linguam habere,*" that the Galatians had, apart from the Greek which they spoke, a language, such as the Welsh or Irish have to-day, peculiarly their own; and he adds that it was almost identical with the language which the Treviri spoke in the north-east of Gault† : now—the Treviri, according to Cæsar were Belgians, and their country—part of the present Belgium, between the Meuse and the Rhine.

Q. 6. What position did the Galatians and kindred Kelts hold in Asia long ages before the Christian era?

A. On the authority of Varro, Lactantius, St. Jerome and other writers, they were very powerful in the East; all the cities of Asia were alive with them, as the towns in England and in America are to-day with the Kelts of Eire and of Caledonia. The destinies of kingdoms were then as now in their hands, and their power reached at one time from Susa to Sardis.

---

* "The Firbolg were evidently a portion of the nation of the Belgæ, so renowned for their valor amongst the ancient inhabitants of Gaul and Britain, who were of Kimro-Keltic and not of Germanic origin."— *O'Mahony's Keating's Ireland*, p. 130.

† " Unum est quod inferimus et promissum in exordio reddimus Galatas, excepto sermone graeco, quo omnis Oriens loquitur, propriam linguam, eamdem poene habere quam Treviri, nec referre, si aliqua exinde corruperint, cum et Afri phœnicam linguam non nulla ex parte mutaverint, et ipsa latinitas et regionibus quotidie mutetur et tempore." Prolegomena of the Commenta y by St. Jerome on the Epistle of St. Paul to the Galatians, iv. p. 430.

He cites Lactantius as his authority :—" Lactantii *nostri*, quæ in tertio volumine de sua gente opinatus sit, verba ponemus."

Q. 7. And in Europe, what was their position, say one thousand seven hundred years before the Christian era ?

A. According to Dr. Latham, they filled almost all Europe. They spread over Helvetia (modern Savoy and Switzerland), Rhætia or the Tyrol, Styria, Carinthia, Illyria, Dalmatia, the Lower Danube, the Bastarnæ and the kingdom of the Galatæ, Würtemberg, Bavaria, Bohemia, Thracia, Macedonia, Græcia, Belgia Prima and Secunda, the Middle Rhine; the Ligurians, the Spanish Peninsula, Italia, Gallia, Britannia, Hibernia, Caledonia or Alba, the Isle of Man, and the Islands north and west of Scotland, all the Western Continent, from the Euxine to the Atlantic.

Q. 8. Were the Firbolg an intelligent race?

A. Yes: judging from what they achieved, they must have been a brave, a civilised, and a cultivated people.

Q. 9. How is this seen?

A. (*a*) They defeated the Fomorians and became masters of the island; (*b*) they laid the foundations of that magnificent palace at Tara* for the use of Ard-Righ and parliament (feis), and built its chief edifices; (*c*) they divided the island into fifths, or "*cúiyés*," (pronounced *kooigé*), known to this day as provinces, each having a king subordinate to the Ἀρο-ριξ or sovereign-in-chief; (*d*) it was the Firbolg who formulated and established the Pentarchy in Eire—a form of government that continued to the twelfth century of the Christian Era—fully three thousand years; (*e*) they had a standing army intended for the defence of the palace and the support of the dignity of the supreme monarch; (*f*) they possessed a code of laws and had them duly enforced; (*g*) they had a knowledge of architecture,

---

* "In any attempt to treat of the early or primitive buildings or habitations of Eirinn, we must, of course," says O'Curry, in vol. iii. of *Manners and Customs of the Ancient Irish*, edited by W. K. Sullivan, p. 5, "give the first place to Tara, which, according to all our ancient accounts, had been first founded by the Firbolg, the third in the series of the early colonists of Ireland. In the ancient account of the battle of the first, or Southern *Magh Tuireadh*, we are told that the Firbolg, who had been dispersed into three parties, on their approach to the Irish coast, by a storm, had, on their landing, repaired by one consent to RATH NA RIGH (*i.e.* the Rath or Palace of the Kings) at Tara.

and as Kelts, they cultivated poetry and history. There is no direct mention made in Irish annals that they or their predecessors, the Nemedians, practised any religious rites or ceremonies in adoring the Deity—either, as the true God, or, like the Gentile world, having lost a knowledge of the true God,—in the worship of false gods. It is certain they had amongst them Druid priests, Brehons, poets, like other Keltic clans; they must therefore have had some religious rites— in woods or wolds, in groves, or by wells and streams—as was then the custom in the East, but temples or towers they did not erect; worship of Bel or Beal did not prevail.

Proofs from MSS. and Ruins.

When Breas goes out from the camp of the *Tuatha De Danann* to meet Sreng, the Firbolg warrior, whom they saw coming towards them, *Breas* asks *Sreng* where he had slept the night before, and *Sreng* answers, that it was at *Rath na Righ* (the Rath of the Kings) at Tara.

This "Rath na Righ" was, therefore, built before the battle of Magh Tuireadh, or before the victory of the Danann.

It is stated in an ancient poem on Tara, that the "Rath of the Kings" was first founded by Slaingé one of the Firbolg chiefs. . . . "RATH NA RIGH was the most conspicuous, and by far the most extensive, upon or round the Hill of Tara; it was within its ample circuit that the palace of Cormac Mac Airt (213, 266, A.D.) was (subsequently) erected." See Dr. Petrie, *History and Antiquities of Tara Hill;* and the map of the ruins of it, drawn under the direction of the Ordnance Survey, published 1839.

IMMENSE PROPORTIONS OF RATH NA RIGH.

Now, the greatness and the immense proportions of this *Rath na Righ*, which was actually erected by the Firbolg, become known, when it is stated (from p. 6 of O'Curry, vol. iii., *Manners and Customs of the Ancient Irish*, and from Dr. Petrie's history just alluded to), that it contained, besides other edifices, *Teach Mor Milidh Amus,* the Great House of the Thousand Soldiers. O'Curry adds, the "Great House of the Thousand Soldiers was the particular palace of the chief monarch; it stood *within* ' Rath na Righ,' and it was called 'Tigh Teamrach,' or the *House of Tara.*" And of this Tigh Temrach he states, on the authority of the Book of Leinster (MS.) folio 15—"The Rath was nine hundred feet in Cormac's time. His own house was seven hundred feet. There were nine mounds around the house. There were three times fifty—that is, one hundred and fifty—compartments in it."*

This view suggests the immense size of the *Rath na Righ* and the other buildings connected with the palace of the Ard-Righ.

It must be added, in the words of O'Curry—" The enclosure of the *Rath* of the Kings, when measured in 1839 by the officers of the Ordnance Survey, was found to measure across, from south-east to north-west, *within* the ring only, 775 feet."

Raths often contained more than one house—

> " Seven Duns in the *Dun* of Teamur,
> Seven score (140) houses in each *Dun*,
> Seven hundred warriors in each *Dun*."—vol. iii., p. 8.

Regarding Tara, Standish O'Grady, the latest writer of Irish history (one who goes back to the pre-Adamite period, and takes for certainty the fanciful theories of anthropologists—those who treat of man—not of geologists who in the main are right), says, regarding Tara in the time of the Firbolgs—

" Through all displacements and expansions of beaten or triumphant tribes and tribal confederacies, that one spot upon the plains of Meath gleams brighter and brighter as day advances ; and mighty Rome, the sun of our northern regions, rolls up from the underworld. In the waning night, it glitters like the morning star before the eye of the historian.

. . . .

Starlike now, it will itself be one day a sun. All the tribes shall look to it for light and heat, for justice and order. All Eiré, from sea to sea, shall be convulsed for its possession."—p. 47, vol. i.

" To the great customary Feis of Tara, more than to actual conquest and downright superiority in arms, is to be attributed the

---

* " In ancient Erin, we find at Tara a spot for ever sacred, the locus of the plastic and formative principle, the centre upon which the chaos of the septal struggles was destined to subside. A palace, a strength, a city ; a place of rude parliaments, and conventions of the justest law, and the wisest brehons; the most frequented fair green ; best place for the jeweller to sell his rings and brooches, the armourer his weapons; where the harper found his art best judged and best rewarded ; where the chronicler could best display and best correct his dry antiquities; the bard find the most liberal and appreciative audience. Who can tell the number of brave men whose blood has reddened those green plains, warring to keep or gain for their own chief those sacred and king-making Raths?"

power and dignity of the Irish Ard-Righ. Yet there was action and counteraction. The power of the chieftain enhanced the dignity and authority of the fair, and the importance of the fair extended the influence and renown of the chieftain. Accordingly, it is with the strife of contending factions, eager to secure for their own candidate the possession of this coveted honour, that Irish history begins—the crash of contending armies for the possession of Teamur, is the first striking event in the records of Irish history."—*History of Ireland*, p. 42, vol. i.

CHAPTER IV.

THE FATE OF THE FIRBOLG.

Q. 1. Were there not other tribes known as Fir-Domnann* and Fir-Gaileonn?

A. Yes: but these three powerful tribes have, in Irish history, come under one generic name of Fir-bolg, for they were all governed by one supreme monarch; and in reality, they constituted only one national body. The Fir-Domnann effected a landing at, and subsequently gained possession of, Erris, in the north-west of the present County Mayo.† The *Fir-Gaileonn* landed on the coast of

---

* *Fir-Domhna* (pr. Downa), *i.e.* the men of *Domhnann*, were, it is manifest, a sept of those known as *Damnonii*, who resided in Gaul, in Britain, and in Ireland. They are called *Damnii*, and perhaps *Daunii*. In Britain their chief seat was in Devonshire, near Cornwall, a well-known habitat of the early Keltic tribes. Domhnain is genitive case of *Domhna*, and in sound or phonetic value is equivalent to *Devon* in modern English.

The Fir-Galeon, or *Galenii*, were manifestly a sub-tribe of the Belgæ, or Firbolg. The name *Galli*, of ancient Gaul, and of the *Galatians* of mid-Europe; the *Galatoi* of the Greeks, the Galatians of the East in Asia Minor, and of the West in Spain, is plainly traceable from this noun; also, *Gwalia*, Wales; and *Corn-wall* (wall, phonetic for *Guall*).

The terms Fir-bolg, Fir-Domnann; and Fir-Gaileonn, *Belgian-men*, or *Gaul-men* is a form of address like that in use by the Greeks, ἄνδρες ἀθηναῖοι, Athenian men.

† Erris is correctly written Iar-rus from *iar*, rear, after, or western; and *rus*, or *ros*, a portion of land nigh surrounded by water, either inland as "Ros-"common, and "Ross," in England, or, by the sea, as in Iar-rus, Ros-trevor; Ross in Munster, Ross in the Highlands.

Leinster, and hence, according to some, is derived the old Irish name for Leinster, ɢaιlean. According to Dr. Keating and Dr. O'Brien, the name is *Laighean* Leinster, frɔm Laιgean, a special kind of spear employed thirteen hundred years later than this date by the soldiers of the Milesian King, *Labhraidh Loingseach*.

The Firbolg proper landed at Wexford, and the name of the river Slaney, rising in Wicklow, and commingling its waters with the sea in Wexford Haven, bears to this day the name of the Firbolgian chief who landed there, and became the first monarch of Tara.

Q. 2. Does any authentic record exist giving an account of the Battle of Magh Tura Conga, and the defeat of the Firbolg: any monuments still standing?

A. Yes: amongst authentic MS. remains, a tract, written over fourteen hundred years ago, tells the history of the battle, its cause, and its consequences. In it we are told, when Eochy, son of Erc, the ninth of the Firbolgian dynasty, was reigning at Tara, that he and his people were surprised to learn that the island contained other inhabitants whom they had not hitherto seen. Those, it seems, soon became known as the *Tuatha De Danann*—the descendants of one of those chieftains of the Nemedians and his followers, who, over two centuries before, fought the Fomorians on the strand at Tory Island, and escaped the destruction which had, from the spears of the sea-robbers and the surging billows of the Atlantic, overwhelmed their companions. This chieftain's name was *Iobath, death-healer* (*ioc*, balm, or healing; *bath*, death, drowning) son of Beathach, (reviver; root, *beatha*, life). Only a few of his clan came safe from that disastrous fight. Those who survived he determined to save in a foreign land, the home in after times of the Kimri, and of the Dani—modern Jutland. Another chieftain, as we know, sailed, after that overwhelming disaster, to Gaul, and made his way to the south-east of Europe. The followers and descendants of the latter were the *Firbolg*, at this time in peaceable possession of the sovereignty of Ireland, the new-comers, the *Tuatha De Danann*, were the posterity of Iobath and his people. Like the Irish race in Canada and in the United States—the one known as "Irish-Canadians," the other as "Irish-Americans," both descendants of the same stock, so the *Tuatha De Danann* and the *Firbolg* were of the same Nemedian race; both had pretty much the same form of government; both spoke the same language, the Belgæ, a modified form somewhat, like the Gaelic spoken to-day by the Highlanders, compared with that spoken by the natives of Ireland.

The Danann tribes had landed on the north-east coast of Eire. Directly, on coming to the shore, they destroyed their boats and ships; a habit not unusual among the Keltic races, as Cæsar, in his *Commentaria de Bello Gallico*, narrates. From the north they advanced with great caution till they reached the hilly portion of Leitrim, and settled in a place known as Magh Rein. There they erected temporary works of defence. There they watched and waited to see what advance the *Firbolg* would make in their regard, to receive them as friends or to banish them from the country as enemies.

Q. 3. What did the Firbolg do?

A. Eochy, the King of Tara, wiser than some of his people who thought, it seems, that the invaders had come to the island on the wings of the wind,—seeing that he had powerful and skilled tribes to deal with, took counsel with his wise men what was right to be done in the circumstances. All agreed to send one of the best and bravest of their warrior chiefs to reconnoitre the settlement at Magh Réin, and to report what kind of people those strangers were. The name of the chief chosen for this arduous duty was one named SRENG, that is, "overreacher." Armed like a warrior champion, he sets out. The Danann sentinels perceive his approach; and they send directly one of their own chieftains, by name BREAS, to meet him and to talk to him. "Both warriors approach with great caution until they come within speaking distance of each other. Each of them plants his shield in front to cover his body, and with inquiring eyes views the other over its border. Breas, on the part of the new settlers, was the first to speak, and Sreng, one of the old stock, was delighted to hear himself addressed in his own language, for to each the old Gaelic was mother tongue. They draw nearer, and after some conversation discover each other's lineage and remote consanguinity."

Next they examined each other's spears, swords and shields, and in this examination they discovered a very marked difference in the shape and excellence of the spears; Sréng, the Fearbolg, was armed with two heavy, thick, pointless, but sharply rounded spears; while Breas, the Danann hero, carried two beautifully shaped, long, slender sharp-pointed spears. Breas then proposed, on the part of th*Tuatha De Danann*, to divide the island into two parts, between th two great parties, and that they should mutually enjoy and defend it against all future invaders.

Next, they exchange spears for mutual examination, on the part of their respective hosts; after forming vows of future friendship, each returned. Thus the interview came to a close in the happiest way. Breas returned to his own people on the heights of Leitrim ; Sreng directed his steps to " Rath na Righ," or, " fort of the kings" within the precincts of Tara.

The Tuatha De Danann must, however, have pondered over all that was said and done with greater thought and foresight than appears on the surface. They all came to the resolution of abandoning the settlement which they had made at Leitrim, and to make further to the west, both for greater security, if any encounter with the Firbolg should ensue, and to have larger facilities for making their escape to the western or southern shores, if disaster should be their lot in the final struggle. Accordingly, they abandon Magh Réin, and, pursuing their way westward, take up a strong position in that " narrow neck " of land, known from its *narrow* character *Cong* (Ir. Cumang, a strait, or " Cuing," a tie, a strait), between Loch Mask and Loch Corrib, on the mearing of the two counties, Galway to the South, and Mayo to the east, west and north.

They form a temporary settlement on and around Mount Belgedan, the modern Benlevi. Their camp extended from the southern shore of Lough Mask to the northern shore of Lough Corrib, and from Benlevi to that mound known to-day as Fair Hill. Thus they are entrenched between two hills and two lakes—Benlevi to the west, and " Fair Hill" to the north east;—with Lough Mask to the north, and Corrib flanking them to the south. No better position could be selected by a military commander.

Meantime Eochy, the Firbolg sovereign, assembled a council, and with his wise men deliberated, at Rath na Righ, what course should now be pursued. Should he wage war against the newcomers, or should he not, that was the question. The council was divided:— Sreng was for peace, and a quiet settlement of the matter;—for war, King Eochy. As is usual, the majority sided with the king: war was decreed. Next the chieftains from all quarters were summoned. The four provincial kings, for the first time, were called to aid the "Ard-Righ," or supreme sovereign. Troops from every part of the kingdom began to arrive at Tara. After due preparation, all things are now made ready. King Eochy Mac-Erc, monarch of Eire Uile, brave certainly, and dauntless, even in those days, leads his army forth from Tara, in East Meath, crosses the Shannon, enters the western province, and takes up his position on the eastern side of Knock Ma* in the county Galway, some five miles south-west from the town of Tuam.

From Knock Ma the country stretches out to the west one continued level, as far as the eye can behold, to Cong. This flat was known at that time as "*Magh Nevi*," or "plain of Nemhedh," the former leader of that immigrating band who came to the "*Isle of the West*" after the death of Partholan's people. The plain extends from Knock Ma to the fertile fields of Kilmaine in county Mayo, onward to Cong, and to the rising slopes fronting Sliabh Belgadan. On Nevy's plain, westward from Knock Ma, the monarch's troops bivouac. They number at least ten thousand fighting men, besides women, and sutlers, and a great army-following that must needs have come to minister to the wants of the myriad warriors. The two Munsters and Leinster, if at the time known by that appellation, and Ulla to the north, had sent forward their due number of warriors lead on by courageous chiefs. That the Firbolg had reached

---

* "Ma" is supposed by some to be a contraction for magh (pr. *mawh*, in which the *h* final has an explosive sound, as in *cath* (*kawh*) a battle; by others "Ma" is for *Madbh* (pr. *Mauve* or *Maw*), the name of the famous queen of Connacht in the first century of the Christian era, who reigned long, and with such power and fame, that her name has been by the people identified in Ireland and in England, under the name Mab, with the beings of fairy land. Those who derive the name from *magh* a plain,—call "Knock Ma" *the hill of the plain*;—while in the other acceptation, it is "Mab's hill." There is a third name *Meadh* by which the hill was known before the Milesian Kelts landed in Eire. It is likely a man's name. The defeated *Tuatha de* Danann to defy and elude their Victors selected for residences the most remarkable hills in Ireland. Finnbharr one of their chieftains obtained the *Sidh* or *site* of *Meadh*, within five miles of Tuam. See Atlantis, p. 386, Vol. III. The interpretation of "hill of the plain" does not convey the idea of any special and peculiar trait, for every hill can be named "hill of the plain." In the tumulus erected on the top of this hill, lady Kesair, the granddaughter of Noah and the guide of an antediluvian colony into this western island, is supposed to be interred;—antiquity quite sufficient to surround the hill with mythical associations. The present *carn* on the summit is of modern date.

Knock Ma, became soon known to King Nuada of the Danann, through his active and ever watchful scouts.

Surrounded by his sages, his counsellors, and chiefs; by his druids, bards, poets, and physicians, he is entrenched in safety on the eastern slopes of Benlevi, called Sliav Belgadan.

King Nuada, desirous only of obtaining a place for his people and himself wherein to settle, has from the commencement been opposed to bloodshed. He is still anxious for peace. Accordingly he sends an embassy to Eochy mac Erc, King of the Belgæ, across Nevy's plain. By this time the order for advance from their position near Knock Ma had been given to the troops, and they were already beyond Kilmaine, and close to that district known at present as the village of Cross, but in the second and third centuries, up to the time of St. Patrick and later, as part of the territory of Conmaicne Culaid Tolad. Here they presented their master's demands to the Firbolg king. Eochy at the head of troops—monarch of Eire Uilé—proud, naturally undaunted and brave—accustomed to rule, to have no equal—Ard-Righ of four sovereigns who yield to his majesty implicit obedience; his people devoted to his cause—eleven battalions of soldiers in all their martial glory advancing to fight his battles, could not brook any newcomer to reside in the island, his equal, or in any way independent of his power and jurisdiction. Flushed with the notion of his greatness, and with the idea of success, which, at the time, he regarded as certain, he would listen to no terms. The Danann must leave the land, remain as slaves, or fight to the death. The members of the embassy retire. The challenge is accepted;—war declared. All prepare for the coming struggle,—" to be, or not to be," possessed of the plains, of the fair hills and fertile valleys of this " Noble Island." A struggle, like that which is now about to begin, has from that time to the present been often renewed.

The Firbolg pitch their camp on that tract of territory which has to the south the north-eastern shore of Lough Corrib, stretching fully three miles to the south-east of Cong, and bounded on the north by a line extending from the village of Cross, to the river at Ashford, which forms the mearing line of the counties Mayo and Galway.

The Danann troops advance from Benlevi eastward towards the present Fair Hill, in the direction of Ashford House, the seat of the present Lord Ard-Oilean (lately Sir Arthur Guinness), to the plain of *Nia*, the ancient name of MAGH TURA.

Curious enough, instead of commencing the fight, both armies agree to have first of all a trial of strength. Three times nine warriors on either side are selected.

The game at which they are to try their relative prowess is "hurling." The valley or glen selected is that to the south-east of Nymphfield, in the direction of Kilmain road and the heights towards Knock Má, extending fully an English mile. The valley is known in history as *Glean-mo-Ailleam*, "glen-of-men-athletes." The game ended in the defeat and death of the twenty-nine Danann hero-youths; over them was erected the great carn or stone monument known as *Carn na Cluithe*, or, the "heap-of-the-game," to be witnessed to this day. How like in its way the erection on the plain of Marathon, pointing out the spot where the Athenians fell beneath the spears of the Persians!

Q. 4. Why narrate so much of this history?

A: Because the account of the Battle of Magh Túra has never before, as a matter of history, been put in full before the student; because the whole record of events that then transpired is true; because the details throw fresh light on the manners and customs of a race once powerful, and even to this hour, great in their descendants.

Moreover, the Irish tract which presents this account is authentic. and, according to O'Curry, of such value, that he says :—" I am bold to assert that I believe there is not in all Europe a tract of equal historical value yet lying in manuscript—considering its undoubted antiquity and authenticity;" and of the battle he says: "it is the earliest event upon the record of which we may place sure reliance." —O'Curry, Lecture xi. pp. 243-7, *MS. Materials of Irish History*.

In addition, it is time at last to put the history of this battle not only fully, but also *clearly*, before the students of Irish history. The compilers of the *Annals of Ireland*, and even Dr. O'Donovan, did not give the account of the Battle of Magh Tura Conga in full. O'Curry in his lectures proposed to give a full account, yet he succeeded only partially, for he, too, confounds the history of the Battle of MAGH TURA of the *Fomorians*, fought twenty-seven years later in Tír-Erril, the eastern barony of the Six, in the county Sligo, with the Battle of MAGH TURA CONGA; he makes it appear that King Eochy fled from Cong to Balysadare, on the sea-coast of Sligo. The encounter between the Fomorians and Danann, on the strand at Ballysadare, was in connection with the second battle of Magh Tura, which, to distinguish it from that now about to be described, was called Magh Tura of the Fomorians; that fought on the isthmus between lakes Mask and Corrib, is known as the Battle of Magh Tura Conga. These are reasons quite sufficient to give. in detail the events of that fight, which is no ordinary occurrence, but which forms rather an epoch in the history of Ireland.

Q. 5. Can you give an account of the battle?

A. Yes: next day, June 11th, the battle commenced. It lasted four days. The warriors on both sides were armed with swords, spears, darts, and shields. It is not stated in the manuscript account that the soldiers made use of bows and arrows, or availed themselves of the sling; although, in the second battle, that known as Magh Tura of the Fomorians, fought twenty-seven years later, the conquering Danann made use of the sling for firing off stones against their foes in fight. Balor, the Fomorian leader, was laid low by a stone penetrating the eye and piercing the brain with a force which the nerve of the human arm, unaided by mechanical power, could never have imparted. There is no record, that at the Battle of "Magh Tura Conga" slings, or bows and arrows, were instruments of warlike attack.

On the other hand, it is worthy of note, that each army had its military physicians, who prepared what in those days was called a "sanative pool," or a "healing bath," made of the juice of the choicest healing herbs mixed in new milk. In this warm preparation the wounded warrior was bathed, his wounds bound, his wants, as far as was possible, attended to, and many thereby were restored to health and strength. Modern philanthropy, for wounded and dying heroes, cannot claim to itself alone all the glory which such wisdom and intelligent sympathy must certainly win, from all who have a heart to feel for suffering and self-sacrificing brothers.

The trumpet note ordering the attack is heard over the plain. The mountains around take up the terrible call, and in echoes fling it back over the waters of lakes Corrib and Mask. The hearts of the young warriors are moved. Their martial spirit is roused to action. They form into line. The Belgian forces rush to the fight, led by their king Eochy, by Kerb the son of Buan, and by Nearchu. Fathach the poet incites them to battle, and with his fellow-poets recites the Rosg Catha, or Eve of Battle.

On the other side, the Danann come calmly and resolutely to the fight, commanded by King *Nuada*, and the potent and clever *Dagda*, and Adleo. Edana the poetess chants the song of war, accompanied by the poets and songsters of Danann clans.

Their line of battle extends from the right side of the river, at Cong, flowing through Ashford into the Corrib, on to the north-east, towards the district known as Nymphfield, having Lough Mask some two miles or so in the rear. The Firbolg drew up along the line, which the road at present from Cong to the Neale points out, having the Corrib on the left.

Each army had erected a rath intended for a stand for the king, a place of security for the women and for the sutlers of the host, and likely too, in the caves made within its borders, a place for the cattle intended for victualling their respective troops. From the days of the *Firbolg* and the Danann conquerors, these raths are found in Ireland. The royal stand on the Danann side was known as " Rath Fearainn," or the " fort of heroes," that on the Firbolg side, as "Rath-Cro-porta," "fort-of-fold-like defence." Each of these raths remains but not identified, that of King Eochy is likely adjacent to Cross;—Rath Fearainn, near Fair Hill. The note of battle is heard again. Both armies move forward to the attack. Darts are flung ; the air is darkened with the shower of flying lances. Shields are raised. The warlike spirit of the men bounds within them. They rush to the encounter ; shield strikes against shield ; hostile swords cleave the flesh of foes; limbs of living heroes are strewn on the plain. The ground is red with streams of gore. The air resounds with the moans of the dying, and the cries of the maddened hosts. It is a man to man encounter. Hero slays hero, and chieftain slays chieftain, as in Troy at a later period. The fall of each mighty chief is described, but it is enough for the historic student to know that the Belgæ were victors in the first fight, and at the close of that eventful day each victor carried with him to present to the king at the rath the head of one of the enemies slain, along with a stone to raise a carn to commemorate the victory achieved.

An old chronicler, Conall Maceochegan, says of this terrible battle : " Here was committed the greatest slaughter that was ever heard of in Ireland, at one meeting" of hostile armies.

Second Day's Encounter.

The warlike spirit of the troops, or their taste for slaughter, had been excited by the terrible carnage of the first day's fight. The

Firbolg were anxious to complete quickly and at once the victory which they had already partially achieved. The troops of Nuada were fighting for their lives, and they were determined to sell them at the cost of the lives of their fighting foes. They were more intelligent too, and depended not so much on mere animal strength, and mere bodily prowess, as on coolness and plan. The Firbolg were victorious until the sixth hour. In the evening, the tide of battle began to turn with the sinking sun. They were driven back to their lines, yet they managed to bring with them for the second time heads of their slain enemies, and each a stone to raise a carn as a sign of the day's success.

THIRD DAY'S FIGHT.

The Firbolgs arose at earliest dawn on the morning of the 13th of June. In crossing the plain of Magh-n-Eithrigh, that to the right side and to the left of the way which at present leads between the villages of the Neale, Caherduff and Cross, the Belgian warriors filed into squares, and held their shields joined over their heads, making as it were a "Scell" *i. e.*, Scátall, a high shade; (Scát signifies shade, "ál," huge, prodigious), to protect themselves from the darts. They placed their battle spears, like trees, at intervals between the shields, and thus marched across the field of battle in "Turtha," or columns, and hence, says the narrator or the copyist, the plain was called by the Danann the "Field of Columns," or "*Plain of the Shield-shell.*" O'Curry, however, says the field was called Magh Tura, from the *piles or towers* of stones erected there after the battle, to commemorate the death of heroes, or chieftains. Besides, the name is not *Magh Turtha*, it is Magh Túra (towers, heaps).

Nuada and Dagda commanded the Danann hosts. They ordered their men to form circles of defence made of large flag stones. The field to this day abounds in circular areas of defence of this kind; a body of men took their stand within them, covering themselves with their shields against the darts and swords of their enemies. The fighting men received help from those upright flags, standing so high that one could lean against them for support, or take his stand behind them for defence. This practical plan lent great support to the Danann in the third and fourth day's fight.

King Eochy, Sreng, and Fintan, King of Leinster, were the chief leaders of the Firbolg on the third day: Nuada, and Dagda, and Ogma were the most distinguished among the leaders on the other side. There were several brave personal encounters of heroes and chiefs.

The most remarkable, because of the heroes engaged and of the history connected with the event, is that recorded to have occurred between Sreng of the Belgian host, and Nuada of the Danann. Sreng singled out Nuada, and with a blow of his great sword, smote the rim of the king's shield, and cut off the royal arm. The king was rescued by " Aengabla," his northern ally. The wound was soon healed by his physician, Diancencht (*i.e. Dia*, God, *'nceacht*, for " nA ıceAċt, root ıc, balm ; and ıceAċt means power of healing): *Credne Cérd*, or Credné, the artificer, made for him a silver hand. Hence, this monarch is known in history as " Nuada of the Silverhand"—ⁿuAoA Aıŋsıⱺ-Láṁ. The arm cut off was buried on the plain, and a monument raised over it, on the spot where the royal blood was shed upon Cró-Ghaile, that is, the " enclosure of the foreigners."

The Belgæ moved north-east, fighting fiercely on towards the village of the Neale and Knoc nag-Cuach " the hill of the cuckoos." Sreng, the general-in-chief, and King Eochy fought with astounding bravery and valour, and directed and encouraged their men : nevertheless, the skill and cool tact of the Danann prevailed. The Firbolg were forced for the second time to retire at the close of evening to their lines, leaving the Danann victors.

Fourth Day's Fighting.

On the fourth day, Slainge the son of King Eochy, and Slainge's four sons with the Ard-Righ, their grandfather, and the general Sreng, gifted with prudence and prowess, determined to recover the loss inflicted on them during the second day and on the third. The fourteenth of June was one of intense heat. The king had been engaged in battle now three days. He had taken a part in two engagements consecutively. And during the early part of the fourth day he fought like a lion let loose in a fold. His lips became parched. His blood was hot and fiery. He was dying of thirst. The fight at the time was where no wells or watercourse even to this day exist. The water known and named as Mean-Uisge (middle-water) was not near at hand. The flower of the Firbolg army was cut off. Eochy was gasping from thirst. He entrusts the sole command to Sreng, and with a hundred chosen men endeavours to cut his way across the plain from near the Neale, in a north-western direction, towards Lough Mask. The king's flight and his fainting condition is perceived by the three sons of Nemed Mac-Badhrai. They call around them a band of one hundred and fifty brave clients, and pursue the king and his hundred men. Before the shore of the lake is reached, those are overtaken. Another encounter ensues. The hundred warriors are forced, after a desperate encounter, to yield to the one hundred and fifty Danann troops. Eochy slays his three youthful assailants with his own hand, and now, himself, expires. "Thus fell," says the chronicler, "the mighty Eochy, only a few days ago so proud as not to yield or listen to any man; now stretched lifeless on the strand, cut down by the invaders, and dying of wounds, and want of water to cool his burning tongue." A lofty cairn was raised by the victors over his body. It is to this day to be seen. It is called Carn-*Eochaidh* from his name. "The most extensive and remarkable cairn in the West of Ireland," says Sir William Wilde in his treatise on Lough Corrib, " stands to this hour on the grassy Hill of Killower, a carn about a mile distant from Lough Mask." Sir William is of opinion that this is the carn which, after the battle, was raised by the Danann victors over the remains of King Eochy Mac Erc, the last of the Firbolg Kings of Erin. At the western extremity of the same strand, still exist the monuments of his slayers, called "Leaca Mac-Nemedh," *the flags of the sons of Nemedh*. In after times the carn was regarded as one of the *mirabilia* or wonders to be seen in Eire; not unlike the huge pile raised over Absolom, who fought in battle against his own father, King David; or like that pile raised over Achilles and Patroclus on the Sigean shore. A rampart, the top of which is 2,500 paces in circumference, crowns the very summit of this singular structure, standing still to strengthen the story of this strange struggle.

"Both parties withdrew after the fourth day's fighting: the dispirited Firbolg to their camp along Corrib shore, and the Danann to their mountain fortress. Both parties interred their dead—the Firbolg raised *Dumhas* or *Tumuli* over their nobles; *Leaca*, or flag-stones over their heroes; *Ferthas* (graves) over the soldiers, and *Knocks* or hillocks over their champions."

Three thousand men out of eleven battalions survive. Sreng and his wise men hold a council of war. They agree to send a challenge boldly to the victor host, to fight them in single combat. According to the rules and practices of chivalry and public warfare in those days, their opponents could not, with honor and safety, decline to accept it. Instances like this narrated are presented by Homer, in the single combat fought between Menelaus and Paris; in the battles between the Sabines and Romans, and to this time it is the practice in Abyssinia. Such heroic courage on the part of the survivors secured for them, if not all their own, at least a select portion of the kingdom, and the very best terms that the victorious invaders could have offered.

King Nuada and his counsellors were, from the commencement, opposed to bloodshed and battle; and accordingly, on their side, they now proposed terms of peace, and proffered the undaunted Firbolg chief and his followers their choice of the five great divisions of Eire. Sreng selected that which he and his people knew best—the western province—which from him was known, up to the time of Conn of the "hundred fights," as *Cúigeadh* Sreing—Sreng's Province. To this day their descendants, distinguished from the Milesian and Norman races, by well marked form and features, and their peculiarly defined physical and cranial character, so well described by Duald Mac Firbis (A.D. 1650), possess in the west a permanent habitat. "Their descendants, and those of their conquerors, the Tuatha De Danann, constitute to-day the great mass of the peasant people of Connacht."

Q. 6. Are there not many who will say that accounts such as these are inventions of the ancient bards?

A. First, in regard to all historic accounts, such as those of battles, handed down to the present time in our national manuscripts and penned generally by Ollamhs or professional teachers in Ireland, it must be remembered, that there existed a most stringent law requiring those *Ollamhs* to tell the truth and nothing but the truth, and if it were found that they had invented, or did tell what were not facts, they were directly deprived of all their privileges for life. Men holding a position in the learned professions were Ollamhs. Every judge or Brehon should have obtained the degree of Ollamh ; all and each were bound by law, by position, by fear of losing caste, to tell nothing but the truth in these narrations regarding battles. "I beg to assure you," says O'Curry " of the historical authority of all the substantial statements respecting these ancient battles." He states, we are assured of their authenticity on the highest authority. Again, " these historical tales the Ollamh was bound, unless by hazarding the loss of dignities and privileges, to have for recital to the people."

Secondly—There is a poem by Columkillé, in the Book of Lecain, in praise of Eochaidh Mac Erc, in which the most of the foregoing account is given.

The tract, from which Dr. O'Donovan and O'Curry translated the history of the battle is, in its present form, over fourteen hundred years old. This fact brings us up at once to the time when St. Patrick was in Ireland. Even then it was a transcript of a tract more ancient still.

Thirdly—From internal evidence the account bears the impress of truth.

(a) "The story is told with singular truthfulness of description; there is no attempt," says O'Curry, "at making a hero, or in ascribing to any individual or party the performance of any incredible deeds of valour."

(b) From the position and course of proceeding of the bards before the battle, and during its action.

(c) From the origin of the name, "Magh Tura" *plain of towers*, which must have had a reason for the term : there must have been some cause of the *leachts*, *cromleacs*, and *mounds* which abound there, and carns and pillar-stones—all matters of such antiquarian importance, and wound up also with the historic records that describe these places and events. It is impossible, therefore, that the substance, at least, of all that has been here narrated, should not be true.

(4) Moreover, the whole account, in a condensed form, has been presented in the Annals of the Four Masters ; in the Book of Leinster, a MS. of the highest authority, published lately by order of the British Government ; in the Books of Lecan and Ballymote ; in the writings of St. Columba, King Cormac, Keating and MacFirbis.

Hence there is no suspicion of the undoubted authenticity of the Irish tract from which this narration has been taken, and of the antiquity of the work itself there is no question. If Homer had never written the *Iliad*, the mounds of ancient Troy, excavated within the past few years, would tell the tale of the greatness of that ancient city of Asia Minor, the certainty of the triple town built there, and the antiquity of the people who dwelt within its walls, and of the distant period when and before Priam was its king.

Q. 7. Is there any proof like that in favor of Troy at hand in favor of Magh-Tura, showing for certain that a battle was once fought there between the Firbolg and the Tuatha De Danann ?

A. There is : the late Sir William Wilde has furnished such a proof. He told the present writer the following facts. One day in the autumn of the year 1863, Sir William was reading, in

Dublin, the Irish tract containing an account of the famous battle of Magh Túra. He noticed in the original, that on the morning of the second day of the fight, King Eochy went, as was his custom, to take a bath, on this occasion, into a well or stream deep down in a ravine, known as "Mean-Uisgé" (or middle water), that flows in those underground channels which convey, at Cong, the waters of Loch Mask to the Corrib; that while performing his ablutions, three Danann warriors coming suddenly over the spot, beheld the king. He looked up, saw overhead three of the enemy, asked for quarter, and demanded a fair fight. They were determined not to give quarter, nor to accept a fair fight, but were about to descend to seize his person alive, or to have his body dead. At that moment a single but faithful guard came to the rescue of his royal master. He drew his sword, fought the three champions on a mound quite adjacent, slew them, and, from the number of wounds which he had in turn himself received, expired on the spot where he had defended the king and saved his sovereign's life. The three Danann were interred in the mound, and on the top of it, as emblematic of the victory achieved by the King's faithful body-guard, a " carn " or huge stone-heap was piled by the hands of his warrior comrades. The mound to commemorate the event was called *Tulach an Triuir*, and the stone-heap on top Carn-an-aoin-ḟir, "*the heap of the one man.*" The *tumulus* and the carn received those names to honor the brave soldier who fought the three and conquered. The name of *Tulach an Triuir* kept alive the recollection of his heroic exploit. " This record of so remarkable an event struck me very forcibly," remarked Sir William. It was a beautiful episode, well worthy of record in the history of any country or any people. But was it true? " I happened " continued he, " to be proprietor at the time of some of the lands on which the battle had been fought, some three thousand six hundred years ago. I resolved to test the truth of the admirable record, and to search for proof on the spot where the men were said to have fought and fallen, to find the well and the mound and the " carn." I came with tract in hand to the spot. I saw the well and the mound and the stone-heap. The *tumulus* is to this day known by the peasants as *Tulach an Triuir* (mound of the three), and the " carn," 176 feet in circumference, crowns its summit. Most of the heap of stones had been some time ago removed. I conceived the idea of digging the *Tulach* in order to see what was within it. For that purpose, with the permission of the then occupier of the field, I engaged on a suitable day a number of workmen. They delved and dug for some time. I thought the work was somewhat a heavy undertaking; so I pondered how best to achieve the end in view, with the least amount of labor. The thought struck me that the Druids were in the habit of turning to the east, and of having in that quarter an opening to their *tumuli*. I directed the men to try a certain spot on the eastern slope. There, after removing a few spade-fulls of earth, they soon came upon a large, smooth, horizontally placed, gritstone flag. On raising which another somewhat larger in size was discovered. The latter remains *in situ*, and covers a small square chamber, twenty-eight inches high and thirty-seven wide, the walls of which are formed of small stones. On removing some of these, on the western side, we found embedded in the soft, black, powdery earth, that had fallen in through the apertures and mixed probably with charcoal, or the dried dust of organic remains, an urn which contained the incinerated remains of human bones." It is now to be seen in the Museum of the Royal Irish Academy.

Here, no doubt, the body of the loyal Firbolg youth was burned, and his ashes collected and preserved in this urn.

Perhaps a more convincing proof of the authenticity of Irish, or of any other ancient history, has never been afforded.

If the "towns-of-the-dead" the "Nekropoles," are proof of the wonderful civilisation and refinement of the Etrurians, at a period long before Rome was founded—say a thousand years at least ; if the royal remains, with their costly golden ornaments, found at Mykenæ, are proof of early Grecian riches, refinement, and advancement in art ; if the discoveries at Troy are proof of ancient Trojan greatness, then the discovery made by Sir William Wilde at Magh-Tura, is proof of much that the writer contends for in these pages, and new to many of his readers.—*See O'Flaherty's Ogygia, Part* III, *chapters* 10, 50.

The account of this event has been published by Sir William Wilde himself, both in his work on "LOUGH CORRIB," and later still, in the Address read by him, as Chairman of the *Anthropological Department*, before the BRITISH ASSOCIATION at BELFAST, some seven years ago.

"With respect to the authenticity of the early chronicles and legends that relate to the history of these immigrations,—so much sneered at by one set of inquirers, and so faithfully believed in by another,—let me make two observations, one chronological, and the other topographical, ...
. . . of a portion of Irish chronology there can, however, be little doubt ;—for in recording cosmical phenomena, such as eclipses of the sun or moon, the approach of comets and the like, they scarcely

differ by a year from that great astronomical and chronological work, *L'Art de Vérifier les Dates*, computed by the French philosophers, hundreds of years after these annals were last written or transcribed. .

. . . .

The other incident is of equal authenticity, in confirmation of the historical statement of our early records. Long, long before the Christian era, it is there said that a battle took place on a certain plain in Mayo; and an incident connected with the fight is thus told:—

" A king or chief was surprised in early morning, while performing his ablutions at a deep well, by three warriors of the enemy, who came upon him unawares. By the prowess of one of his attendants he was saved, who killed his three assailants, and then died upon the spot. Hundreds of years passed by, the locality around had been cultivated and grazed upon again and again; still the valley, the well, the subterranean watercourse with its fairy legends, the hurling-field, the cairns, circles, pillar-stones, and other surrounding topographical features remained. The gallant soldier who laid down his life for his royal master, was buried where he fell; and as the army (stated to have been thousands strong) passed by, each man, as was the custom of the day, threw a pebble on his grave, then called, and still known, as the Carn-of-One-Man" (Carn-an-aoin-ḟir).

" Not long ago, with the written story in my hand and possessing a full knowledge of the locality, and accompanied by a few stalwart Connachtmen, I proceeded to the spot, told my incredulous auditory the tale of their ancestors; dug and lifted stone after stone until we came upon a smaller chamber under a large flag, wherein we found deposited a beautiful cinerary urn, containing some black earth and fragments of burned human bones. The sepulchre, with its surrounding stone circle, still exists on the battle field of Moytura Conga, and the decorated urn is in the Museum of the Royal Irish Academy."
—From the Address by Sir William R. Wilde, M.D., M.R.I.A., &c.

Q. 8. Tighearnach, Abbot of Clonmacnois, who lived in the eleventh century, and whose name stands amongst the first of Irish annalists, states " that all the records of the Scoti, that is, the Irish, up to the time of Kimbaeth, who flourished four centuries before the Christian period, are uncertain." Thomas Moore in his

D

"History of Ireland," Dr. O'Donovan in his early writings, A. M. Sullivan in the "Story of Ireland," the latest historian of Ancient Eire, Standish O'Grady, and Robert Atkinson, author of the introduction to the *facsimiles* of "The Book of Leinster" Irish MS., speak of the events before Kimbaeth's time as uncertain and blended with fable : the question is, are these authorities worthy of credit, and if so, how reconcile their statement with that just put forward in these pages ?

A. First—Tighearnach styles the records not "*falsa,*" or "*fabulosa*" (fabulous), but "*incerta,*" uncertain. To him they had been uncertain in date, in consecutive arrangement, in the matter of many of them. But the great features of early Irish history that have left indelible impressions on the national memory, and upon the physical appearances of the country, are not uncertain in their origin, in the record that has transmitted them, in the results that have arisen from them.

Secondly—Owing to the wonderful achievements of Irish archaeology, many things uncertain in the eleventh century are in the nineteenth made quite certain. This truth is evident.

Thomas Moore confessed to Dr. Petrie, in presence of O'Curry, that he was himself ignorant of early Irish history ; that he had never seen the ancient manuscripts of Ireland until, in 1839, he opened the leaves of a few in the Royal Irish Academy.

"Petrie," cried he, " these huge tomes could not have been written by fools, or for any foolish purpose. *I never knew any thing about them before*, and I had no right to have undertaken the History of Ireland." And O'Curry declares in p. 440 of his *MS. Materials*, that "it is *in these manuscripts chiefly* that the materials for the ancient history of the country are to be sought." Sullivan does not profess to write regarding the ancient period of Eire's story. O'Grady, although very learned in the Gaelic lore of Scotia Major, and fond of her antiquities, does not strengthen his position by availing himself of the great advantages offered (*a*) in the history of pre-Christian Europe, Asia and Africa ; (*b*) in the ancient languages, sciences, arts and civilisation known to the early inhabitants of Asia and Eastern Europe, and in Africa from the mouths of the Nile to

Abyssinia; (c) in the laws, manners, customs and religious rites practised in those remote periods. Dr. O'Donovan declared to the present writer that he, too, at the commencement of his career as antiquarian, joined in the common opinion. Time and reading corrected the false notion. Men with a reputation for learning, scholars from the halls of Cambridge, Oxford, or Trinity, gave expression to that view; they were ignorant of Irish History. Their presumed knowledge was taken for learning, and their nescience gave the tone to literary thought. Dr. O'Donovan declared that if allowed by the publisher Smith, to revise the second edition of his noble work, the ANNALS OF THE FOUR MASTERS, he would have corrected his early notions on these points, and have given the primary meaning of some Irish ecclesiastical terms, which at times he rendered into English to please his friends, rather than to express fully the faith and practice of the early Irish Church. He told the present writer, that his simplicity and want of courage in early life often gave him pain in his riper years and his hours of thought. (See pp. 37-38, further on.)

Q. 9. After the Battle of Magh-Tura where did the surviving Firbolg and their descendants make a settlement?

A. Chiefly in the west of Ireland. They retained possession of the province of Connacht. Some held large possessions between the rivers Suir and Slaney; others again, probably the warriors and soldiers, immediately after the battle sailed across the Corrib, proceeded to the Islands of Aran in the west, where to this hour are to be seen the work of their hands, those stupendous barbaric monuments, the admiration of antiquaries and historians, the most extensive and the oldest structures of their kind in Europe. Some sailed to Aran in the north, to Rathlin, and to the Isle of Man; others proceeded in a course more northerly still, to Caithness, Ross and Sutherland, to the Hebrides and Orkneys. The descendants of some emigrants returned centuries afterwards to the "old country."

Q. 10. What certain historic marks of their presence at one time in this island can be pointed out to the eye of an inquiring Irish student?

A. (a) The Irish Pentarchy; (b) Tara and its monuments, the

history of which is as certain as that of Carthage or Rome of old; (c) the Battle of Magh-Tura Conga just described; (d) the cyclopean piles at present in Aran, and others that had been in existence some fifty or eighty years ago—for instance, between Cong and the Neale in Mayo where the glebe is now erected there stood eighty years ago a great Caher, built by the Firbolg, "and which," says Sir William Wilde, "was perhaps one of the largest in Ireland, and resembled Dun-Aengus or Dun-Connor, and others in Aran."—(*Wilde's Lough Corrib*, p. 238); (e) the raths and caves so numerous in Ireland are the work of the Firbolg and the Danann; not a few, however, were erected by the the Fomorians; Rath-na-Righ within the precincts of Tara was certainly founded, and in part erected, by the Firbolg. That noble work is a proof of their advanced knowledge and early architectural skill. It is not stated that they adored the sun. Like all Keltic and Aryan nations they were acquainted with poetry, rhyme, laws, and certainly with letters. They practised in some instances cremation.*

CHAPTER V.

The Tuatha De Danann in Power Contrasted with the Firbolg; the Fomorians.

Q. 1. What race succeeded the Firbolg in acquiring supreme dominion of Eire?

A. The Tuatha De Danann.

Q. 2. How can a student of history be certain that a statement, such as that just made, is true: perhaps it is like the story about Romulus and Remus, regarding the early beginnings of Rome?

A. The sources of certainty on this point are five: (a) tradition, written and oral, together with historical manuscript authority,

---

* Niebhur says:—The Belgæ and Kymry were the same, and that the Firbolg were of the Kymry (see p. 11 supra), who with the Teutones defended the north of Germany against C. Marius.

handed down from the earliest times; (*b*) monuments; (*c*) philology; (*d*) numismata and antiquities; (*e*) hermeneutical harmony found to exist on this subject in Irish history, topography, ethnology, language, national customs, and the folk-lore of the Gael.

And first as to (1) Tradition—that of the fullest and amplest kind, oral and written, attests the fact. (2) Antiquities come in to corroborate the same statement. The mounds on the battle-field of Magh-Tura Conga, in Mayo County, and of Magh Túra of the Fomorians, in Sligo, point to it clearly. "These very curious mounds," says O'Donovan, "are still to be seen on those battle-fields" And in his MSS. (Ordnance Survey) marked $\frac{14}{x\,19}$, R. I. Academy, he states: "I must believe that a battle was fought there at a very remote period, even though I should not be able to calculate the year, or go within five centuries of it."

The grand discovery made by Sir William Wilde in one of those mounds, known as " *Tullach an Triúir*," near Cong, is very striking, and certainly convincing to any unprejudiced mind. Of that discovery Sir William himself writes:—" Perhaps a more convincing proof of the authenticity of Irish, or of any other history, has never been afforded."

(3) The Gaelic historic titles of persons and of places, rendered famous by deeds worthy of record, are to the philologist, like fossils to the student of geology, a proof of civil, social, or political change. These terms, owing to the insular character of the country and conservative nature of the people, as fresh now in their meaning as they were nigh four thousand years ago, tell their own story, and in their own way. (4) Then we have yet standing, if not the towers and palaces which those people erected at Aileach, or Tara, at least, the tombs on the banks of the Boyne, where the remains of their kings, leaders, physicians, poets, and poetesses lie interred.

(5) The cinerary urn, the specimens of spears and swords, made use of in warfare by some such people, are to be seen in the Royal Irish Academy, or in the Museums of Dublin, or the British Museum, London.

Now, one can reason thus on the historic character of the Tuatha De Danann, even if no history respecting them were ever written.

The Necropoles or " Cities of the Dead," in Etruria, proclaim at once, without the aid of written history, that a people flourished north and south and east of Latium, and within its borders one thousand years at least before Romulus or Remus thought of laying the first foundations of the city of Rome; and, what is more, that this ancient people were highly civilised, wealthy, and thoroughly skilled in the arts and sciences known at the time; that they had a literature of their own, and a fostering government under which they advanced in social greatness, and amassed wealth. The proofs regarding the existence of the Danann race in Ireland, furnished from the sources named above, are equally convincing. They show, at all events, the general truth, that some people or other existed at the time, no matter by what name known, who fought and conquered the Firbolg races, and whose descendants are found to this day in Ireland. Then (6) the native annals, and (7) the uniform harmony found on this point to exist in topography, ethnology, philology, the national customs of the Gaels, and their folk-lore, in which they tell tales of Danann spirit-power, confirm the minor proposition in the argument, that those who then flourished were the Tuatha De Danann.

One must add: it is opposed to the use of right reason to lean upon an hypothesis of one's own choosing, in order to suit preconceived notions, and to object to, or, at least, not to adopt the substance of those facts furnished by our ancient records. All these hundreds of volumes, still in MSS., could not have been pure inventions; "they were not written," as Thomas Moore said to O'Curry "by foolish men, or for any foolish purpose." Such hermeneutical harmony, too, could not have grown in the past by mere chance or any inventive process. And, lastly, if broken in part, like a beautiful vase, the whole fabric of history regarding the Danann race, must be completely destroyed—and their existence denied, in the face of heaps of evidence to the contrary. Who can say that no such people ever found a residence within the shore of Eire; that the works attributed to them are figments, and that the buildings still extant were not built at all? To assent to such a proceeding, or to adopt such a course, is repugnant to intelligent or rational minds. They cannot assent to it. Therefore, the history, at least in substance, regarding the Danann is true.

Q. 3. Who were the Tuatha de Danann?—and in what respects were they superior to the conquered Firbolg ?

They were Kelts. As a race they came somehow from the East. The Irish annals state, that they were descendants of Nemheadh and his people—the second great migration that had reached Ireland. The story already known is this,—that their progenitors suffered defeat from the Fomorian pirates, assembled on the strand opposite Conaing's Tower, in Tory Island; that some few of the surviving Nemedians, under a leader known as *Io-bath*, "survivor of drowning," sailed away till they reached the mouth of the Elbe : that two hundred and thirty-five years afterwards their descendants, who, like the children of Jacob in Egypt, had now grown into a great, a skilled, and powerful people, returned to the land their forefathers had left. They came by Caledonia, and, after a time, effected a landing on the coast of Antrim. They made their way quietly to the west of Ireland as far as West Brefni, that district in Leitrim which became known in the first century of the Christian era as Magh Réin, situate to the east of Lough Allen; they entrenched themselves safely on and around the "Iron-Mountain," or *Sliabh an Iaruin*, as that high hill is called, which serves as a boundary between the counties of Leitrim and Cavan. They feared a coming battle with the inhabitants—the Firbolg, and with the Nemedians resident in the island,—and, therefore, for greater security they moved further west, till they reached that narrow neck of territory lying between Loughs Mask and Corrib ; where the present counties of Mayo and Galway meet, called, from its position, by the Gaelic name Conga (Cong), that is, narrow. After the hard-fought battle of Magh Tura Conga, they became lords and masters of the island. They ruled it, as their predecessors had done, in accordance with the laws common to all Keltic nations. They have left the impress of their genius and power on the soil of Ireland, by their buildings made of stone, at Aileach, in Donegal, at Tara, at New Grange, Dowth, and Kowth, or Cnoghda ; at the Brugh on the Boyne near Stackallen Bridge, and at Naas ; by their raths and cromleachs at southern and northern Magh Tura, Cruachan, Sliabh-na m-ban, Ballysodare, and other parts of ancient Eire ; by their superior skill in arts and sciences, the shadows of which are traceable in the "sidh" (fairy) stories of the Gael up to this day. Their leading men and women were famous for their knowledge of the healing art, and of the medicinal properties possessed by herbs, and how to apply them to the wants of the sick and wounded. They were skilled in music, according to the times ; in the art of mixing colors ; in writing, drawing, dyeing and in carving in wood or stone. All that remains to the present day as the work of these tribes, goes to shew the truth of these statements. And if one reflect that the Etrurians, and, besides them, the Pelasgi in eastern Europe, at the time that the foundations of Argos and of the "Wideway" Mykenæ were laid, were wonderfully skilled in many arts wholly unknown to people of a later age, he will not feel surprised at the knowledge and skill possessed by the Danann races in this remote period.

The theory connected with the science of anthropology—of

dividing the ages of mankind into the "stone" age, "bronze" age and "iron" age—is a mere "fancy," and rests on no solid foundation. The presence of peace or war, of plenty or want, of law or disorder, of learning or ignorance, made man a child of the bronze, or iron, or golden age. No thoroughly intelligent man advocates the "iron or bronze age" theory now-a-days. It pleases a few who cling, right or wrong, to what they have once been told was true.

Regarding the superiority of the Danann as a race, compared with the Firbolg, it must be admitted that the latter were beaten, and that success attended the former, both on account of their bravery, intellectual skill, energy, and by making use in battle of mechanical helps which the Firbolg neglected or despised.

It must be borne in mind, however, that all conquering nations, regarded in their character as conquerors, possessed at the time of power, and holding greater sway, are superior to the conquered. The Persian races were superior to the nations whom they ruled from the Tigris to the Nile; the Grecians were in turn superior to the Persians; the Romans to the Greeks; the Franks under Charlemagne, and in the present century the French people, to the rest of Europe, until in turn their very success became the cause of their defeat, both under Napoleon I. and Napoleon III. The Danann dynasty conquering the Firbolg, were compelled to yield two hundred years later to another Keltic race, fresh for fight and vigorous in the manly exercise of mind and muscular development; while the Firbolg, who had formerly been conquered, partially arose again to the position and privileges which they had previously possessed. The two peoples, therefore, the Danann and Firbolg, equal in family origin, differed only in fortune, training, energy, and skill.

Q. 4. What are the special traits of character of the Tuatha De Danann compared with the Firbolg?

A. As far as can be gleaned from Irish annals, they differed (*a*) in features; (*b*) in intellectual power, or rather in its higher developments; (*c*) in religious rites, or in the expression of that highest adoration due by man to the Supreme Being. (*d*) The civilisation of the Danann was more developed, but not of a higher kind, than that cultivated by their Belgian predecessors. (*e*) In language, laws, social state, and in their form of government the Danann differed very little from the Firbolg. Each of the two peoples was Keltic in kith and kin; each descended from the same Nemedian stock.

PROOFS:—(*a*) The testimony of Duald Mac Firbis (1580-1670), taken from the Book of Genealogies, goes to confirm the statement that the two races, the conquering and the conquered, differed in features and form. "This is the distinction," says this distinguished genealogist, "which the profound historians draw between the Firbolg and the Danann : every one who is large and fair-haired is a descendant of the Tuatha De Danann : those who are dark or black-haired are the descendants of the Firbolg in Eirinn."

(*b*) Again, in reference to their intellectual powers, he says:— "Musical persons, those who profess musical or entertaining performances; those who are adepts in druidical or magical arts—they are the descendants of the Tuatha De Danann." So far, Mac Firbis. It would be exceedingly illogical, however, to infer that all not skilled in music in times past in Eire were not of the Danann race ; or that all who were musical had been Danann. Mac Firbis states only what, in the moral sense, the people supposed to be the case; neither does he state that the converse of the proposition which he makes is untrue. Nevertheless, he goes very far in putting that illogical view before the student of Irish history ; for, he says, " the non-musical, and the churlish and the inhospitable were of the Firbolg race." The traditional rhyme of some irate bard is stamped by Mac Firbis as history. The true meaning of the effusion is, that some few not gifted with a knowledge of the fine arts, as then known, were of the Firbolgian race. At the present day, it is well known that knowledge and skill in music, and in the fine arts, depend on early training as much as on intellectual power. It must also be borne in mind, that in times past trades and professions of the same kind were usually and nearly always confined to the same families. The Danann were very careful to cause such arts to be heir-looms in their respective clans.

Whatever may be said of the non-musical powers of the Belgian race, it is quite certain that the effect of their *martial* training was, each succeeding century, felt in all parts of Ireland, and even on the continent of Europe. The Gamanraidhi, or Belgic tribe of Erris, Mayo, were athletic, brave, and warlike. The Clanna Morna of Connacht, under their chief Goll son of Morna, celebrated in Irish annals, were famous warriors in the third century: rulers of the Firbolgian line, these held sway in Connacht down to the third century of the Christian period.

At the present time, nineteenth century, the intermingling of races has been such that the descendants of the Danann cannot well be distinguished from those of the Milesian, a later race; both bear a striking resemblance one to the other, in form and figure, in the colour of hair; and in the style of physical features. "It is likely," says O'Mahony in his notes to *Keating's History of Ireland*, "that the majority of the Irish people are to this day, maternally at least, sprung from the Belgic and Nemedian Kelts, and that their language is that now known as Gaelic." The Belgic race as a class preserve their primitive dark complexion. Individuals are found fair-skinned and of good figure.

The Gaelic character of the nation's speech was settled at least under the Danann dynasty. The names and terms used by them are to this day plain, unmixed, and unaffected Irish Gaelic.

Q. 5. Of the eight Firbolgian kings how many have made a name that deserves a place in history?

A. Only one—the last and the greatest, king Eochy MacErc, who died on the shore of Lough Mask, fighting in defence of his crown and his life, on the fourth day of the battle at Magh Tura Conga. By nature he was clever, intelligent, intrepid, ambitious, a man of high purpose and great resolve, but like Saul, the first king of Israel, he was proud and self-willed. He imbued his hands in the blood of his predecessor. He could not brook the presence of the Tuatha De Danann in Eire. He would not give ear to the sage counsel of Sreng, who preached peace, and that the two races should in amity share between them the same "Noble Island." War he should have. He waged it, but lost his crown and his life; his people lost their country and a right to hold sovereign sway in their own land. A foreign adventurer, Nuada, leading tribes famed for their skill and energy, succeeded to the sovereignty and became the supreme master of ancient Eire.

Q. 6. Of the nine kings that ruled the Danann race for nigh two hundred years, who were the leading sovereigns?

A. (1) Nuada; (2) Breas; (3) Lugh, or Lughaidh, called "Lárh-ꜰᴀᴅᴀ," *long-hand*; and "ıoʟ-ᴅáɴᴀ," *many arts*; (4) Daghda, known also as oʟʟ-ᴀᴛᴀıꞃ, or the *great-father*, that is *president*; these were the chief men amongst a host of heroes.

First.—Nuada, known by the nickname of *Airgead-lamh*, or silver hand, who fought and won the battle of Magh Tura Conga (in Mayo); and, again, twenty-seven years later fought the battle of Magh Tura of the Fomorians. In the former he conquered the Firbolg, won the crown of an Ard-Righ, and founded a dynasty; in the latter he overcame the Fomorians, but, in achieving the victory, he lost his life, at Tir-errill in the county Sligo. He was slain by Balor of the Evil Eye, known too as "the hero of mighty blows,"—lord of the Northern Isles.

Second.—Breas, who reigned for a time in place of Nuada, till the maimed king was fully restored to his usual vigour. He was remarkable for his skill, strength, and courage. As sovereign or Ard-Righ, he was mean, parsimonious, autocratic; as ruler, partial and one-sided, and therefore unfit to govern. In the first satirical poem ever composed in Gaelic, *Cairbré*, the princely poet, son of a gifted poetic mother, Etana, exposed the royal failings, chiefly his tyranny towards the nobility and his lack of hospitality; consequently, the people, unable to bear any longer one devoid of kingly virtues, deposed him from the sovereign position which for seven years he had held. He fell in battle at Northern Magh Tura.

Third.—Lugh, famous for his wonderful talent, great knowledge, prowess, skill in planning and putting his plans into execution. This last quality is apparent in the record of what he achieved for the reigning Ard-Righ Nuada, when commissioned to make preparation for the great battle of Magh Tura of the Fomorians; also by the splendid character of the games which he established, when elected to the position of Ard-Righ. These sports were truly national, and in their kind not unlike the Olympic games, so well known to students of Grecian history. The princes and nobles, men and women of position, from all Ireland came to witness their celebration annually, which lasted from the fifteenth of July to the fifteenth of August. This gathering continued to be held each year for a period far beyond two thousand years after the time of Lugh; for we know that St. Patrick preached at Tara during the Easter week A.D. 433, and that, after preaching the truths of the Christian faith there to thousands, he proceeded, the July following, to Tailltenn (Telltown), where the public games were being celebrated. In fact, the fair continued to be held more or less regularly up to the time of |Ruṗᴀı O'Connor, the last King of Ireland. The month of August in the Irish language is known as the month of *Lugh's games* mi nᴀ Luᵹ-nóṛᴀ (mi means month; nóṛ, a custom, a practice, an exercise repeated). All the great marriages amongst the noble ladies and chiefs of the nation were celebrated here. What gave rise to the institution of these public sports, and the great "Aonach" or fair at Telltown, is told in the following:—

Taillte (daughter of Magh Mōr) was wife and queen to Eochy

Mac Erc, the last of the Firbolg kings. Eochy was slain at the great battle of Magh Tura Conga. Taillte had become the foster-mother and tutoress of Lugh, the most gifted by far, and the most talented of all the Danann. The ex-queen, now married to a Danann chief, took particular care of her foster-child, and had him taught in all the then known arts and sciences, like Peter of Russia in times comparatively modern. Lugh became Ard-Righ. He held his royal court at Nas (now Naas), in the present county of Kildare. Taillte died; King Lugh had her remains interred in a great plain near the river Boyne, in the present barony of Kells, in county Meath. He erected over her grave a large sepulchral mound, which, with others, remains to be seen to this day; and around this mound he ordered that public games and sports, in honor of his beloved Taillte, should, after the manner of eastern countries, be celebrated for ever. Cuan O'Lochain (ob. A.D. 1024), chief poet of Malachy II., has written a poem on this subject.

Lugh's reign was illustrious. He was slain by MacCoill, at Caen Druim, "the fair ridge," the more ancient name of the Hill of Uisneach in Westmeath.*

Fourth,—Eochaidh, called Oll-athair, *great-father*, or Daghda Mór—(as if "dóigh-da," *hope-god*; or "dógh-da," *fire-god*). He was the hope and stay and strength of the Danann people. As a

---

* The following anecdote told in Irish annals regarding Lugh, when, having finished his education, he came a young man to Tara, to see the king, will give the reader an idea of the ability of the young chieftain, of the customs of the period, and of the kind of training considered necessary for chief and nobles in those days. Lugh's character is not unlike that of Cyrus the Great, the conqueror of Babylon.

The story of Lug, as a man skilled beyond all others of the time in the arts and sciences, is as follows:—When he came first to Tara, he introduced himself as a young man possessed of all the arts and sciences then known at home and abroad; and, hence it is, that he was afterwards called the SABH ILDANACH, that is, the "*stock (sabh) or trunk of all the arts.*" When first he came to the gate of Tara, the door-keeper refused to pass him in, unless he was the master of some art or profession. Lug said that he was a *saer*, that is, a carpenter or mason, or both. The door-keeper answered that they were not in want of such an artist, as they had a very good one, whose name was *Luchta*, the son of *Luchad*. The young artist then said that he was an excellent smith. "We don't want such an artist," said the door-keeper, "as we have a good one already, namely, *Colum Cuaellemeach*, professor of the three new designs" [*Greisa*]. Lug then said that he was a champion. "We do not want a champion," said the door-keeper, "since we have a champion, namely, *Ogma*, the son of *Eithlenn*." Well, then, said Lug, "I am a harper." "We are not in want of a harper," said the door-keeper, "since we have a most excellent

general, or military chief, he was like fire, ever active; vigilant as a ruler, and as a law-giver, a shining light amongst his kindred and people. He was, while alive, patron of poetry, music, and the arts. After death, he was regarded as the Apollo of the Keltic tribes. Like the *Pythian*, he was the father or founder of necromancy; a *foreteller* of things to come. The name *Dagh-da*, interpreted as *fire-god*, tends to confirm the notion that the worship of the sun by means of fire was a practice amongst the Danann people; and that, like other practices, civil, social, political, or religious, they had brought this custom from the East.

This opinion appears to be the one held by the Most Rev. Dr. O'Brien, author of the Irish Dictionary, and by O'Mahony, editor and annotator of *Keating's History of Ireland*. He observes:—" He (Dagh-da) might have got this name from having been priest of the '*Great Good Fire*,' that is the sun."

---

one, namely, *Abhcan*, the son of *Becelmas*." "Well, then," said Lug, "I am a poet and an antiquarian." "We do not want a man of these professions," said the door-keeper, "because we have already an accomplished professor of the sciences, namely, *En*, the son of *Ethoman*." "Well, then," said Lug, "I am a necromancer." "We are not in want of such a man," said the door-keeper, "because our professors of the occult sciences and our druids are very numerous." "Well, then, I am a physician," said Lug. "We are not in want of a professor of that art," said the door-keeper, "as we have an excellent one already, namely, *Diancecht*." "Well, then, I am a good cup-bearer," said Lug. "We do not want such an officer," said the the door-keeper, "because we are already well supplied with cup-bearers, namely, *Delt*, and *Drucht*, and *Daithe*, and *Taei*, and *Talom*, and *Trug*, and *Glei*, and *Glan*, and *Gleise*." (These are all female names). "Well, then," said Lug, "I am an excellent artifex" (cerd). "We are not in want of an artifex," said the door-keeper, "as we have already a famous one, namely, *Creidne* the artificer." "Well, then," said Lug, "go to the king, and ask him if he has in his court any one man who embodies in himself all these arts and professions, and if he has, I shall not remain longer, nor seek to enter Tara." The king was overjoyed to lay hold of such a wonderful person as Lug, and he was immediately admitted into the palace, and placed in the chair of the *Ollamh*, or chief professor of the arts and sciences. After the battle of *Magh Tura of the Fomorians*, he became king of the *Tuatha De Danann*, and reigned forty years, until he was slain by Mac Cuill, one of the three sons of Cermet Milbeol.

Observe: In the foregoing note *g* final in *Lug* is not aspirated, as it should be, thus *Lugh*, or *Luġ*. The reason is, in OLD Irish, up to the tenth century, *single* consonants at the close of a word were regarded as affected; whenever the full natural sound was to be given the final consonant was usually doubled. "*Lug*," therefore, in OLD Irish is same as *Lugh*; "*sab*," same as *sabh*: in *tainicc*, he came, the full sound of *c* (*k*) is heard.

The common opinion amongst Irishmen is, that the pagan Danann were some way devoted to fire-worship. The sacred fires (Bealtaine), and the history of fires in ancient Eire, being held on each of the four seasons of the year, at Uisneach, 1st of May; at Tailltén, 1st of August; at Tlactga, in Westmeath, 1st November; at Tara, 1st February—confirm this belief. But the Irish annals tell us that these fires were for purification and not for adoration; and King Cormac of Cashel, says that Bel-taine does not mean " Bel's fire," but " good fire," or propitious fire. Dr. Petrie declares, " that Irish history does not state that fire-worship was introduced into Erin ;" while Moore, the historian and national poet, and Dr. Lanigan, observe, " that fire, and the sun, the greatest of all fires, was an object, if not of worship, at least of great veneration in Ireland."—Vol. iv., p. 406.

In truth, it must be admitted that there is no clear and certain record in the national MSS. of Ireland, as far as the writer knows, showing that the ancient Irish were wont to adore the sun, or to worship fire. It is true that they held the sun and fire, as Dr. Lanigan states, " in great veneration."

After a reign of eighty years, Daghda died at Brugh, on the Boyne, from the effects of the wound received at the battle of Magh-Tura of the Fomorians; that is over one hundred and ten years previously, or, according to the Book of Lecan, and the Book of Leinster, Irish MSS., one hundred and twenty years, for Dagh-da reigned eighty years, and Lugh forty. The term Dagh-da, like the title Mayor or President, was one of office and not the name of an individual. There was one of that official title at the Battle of Magh Tura Conga, earlier still by thirty years.

Q. 7. Can the names—if official—of men of position, chiefs and kings of the Danann race, be interpreted; and, if so, does such interpretation throw any light on the character of the people ?

A. Yes: the names are Irish-Gaelic, and readily interpreted. They are undoubtedly titles of office, and convey the idea that those who held a position of honour !or emolument during the Danann dynasty, were men or women of learning and skill, of knowledge in the arts, famed for military prowess or bravery, for energy in doing the business of the state; or that they were devoted to literature, of necromancy, or the worship of the gods.

Take, for instance, the names of their kings, (1) Nuada, which means new divine-chief (nuad and dá); (2) Breas, ḃaṟṟ-ḟioṟ, superior knowledge; (3) Lugh, nerve, energy, force; ioL-ḋána, of many arts; Dagh-da—explained above; (5) Mac Coill, son of the hazel-tree; (6) Mac Ceact = Mac Iceact, son of healing art; (7) Mac Gréine—son of the sun. The names of their goddesses; (8) Brighit, goddess of poets and smiths, from *breo*, bright, and *saighit*, an arrow; (9) ḃaoḃ, goddess of war, from *bas*, or bath, death, and *bé*, a creature, a lady, &c., &c.

Take the names of their physicians and chieftains—Dianceact, god of the healing art, *i.e.* god of physic, from *Dia*, God, *ua*, of the; *iceact*, healing art. The word "ic," or "ioc," balm, is to this day common amongst the Irish-speaking classes; the word "*ioc-shlainteach*" is applied to a refreshing drink, "health-restoring," balm-healing. Delbeth, inventive power, from "ḋelḃ," to frame, ᴅec, a spark. Ealadan, eaLaḋan, science: it is the only word to this day in use to signify science, or any skilful or technical performance which men of mind can accomplish. It is applied to a piece of intricate work or mechanism, which unlettered people do not understand. Ogma, one of their chiefs, and the inventor of a "secret writing," or rather the teacher and director of the art, is a name that signifies "sacred scheme," óġ, with (g) aspirated, means *sacred, hidden*, therefore *not common;* and Mā, *a scheme, a work of mind, a clever invention*. "Ma" is a primitive Aryan term found in "man," (English), méin, *mind*, Irish; *mens*, Latin; in μᾶ of μαω, or μανθάνω, in μαθ (Greek), signifying to *learn*. The term man in English, "a creature of mind," as opposed to the brute world; its plural "men," is like the Latin *men* in *mente*. Artificers amongst the Danann are Ceird, or Goba, a smith: Hence, *Ceirdne*, the name of their chief artificer; and Gobhnenn, their chief smith.

Their leading merchant, who traded with the neighbouring isles, was called "*Mac' Lir*," son of "*Lear*," *the sea;* he was styled also Manannan, or "Manx-man:" *Mana*, means the Isle of *Mann;* its genitive case is Manann, and "*Manannan*," therefore signifies "one from Mann;" Oirib or Orbsen was his proper name, and as descended of his father "*Allod*," *i.e.* the soil or land; he was called "Mac Allóid," *son of the land*, and thus he was "*son-of-land-and-sea*." The name of Lough Corrib, in the West, will put students in mind for ever that a Danann merchant named "Oirib" lived for a time in the West of Ireland; that he carried on trade with the Nemedian and Belgian settlers in Mann, and that at length, after many battles by land and sea, he became first chief or king of that remarkable island: his name and that of Uillin, grandson of *Nuada*, the first Danann king, are welded into topographical word-boulders of ancient Irish Keltic, namely, *Loch Oirib,* and Magh Uillin—now Lough Corrib, and Magh Cullin—the latter comprises the district between the present Danesfield and the lake, midway between the towns of Oughterard and Galway. On that plain, Magh Danann, anglicised Danesfield, the two chieftains and their clans fought a bloody battle; Oirib and his party were defeated. Uillin's name survives in Magh Cullin;—in Lough Corrib the name Oirib is recorded.

The student of Irish history will bear in mind (*a*) that amongst other nations, names apparently personal were names of office, or given from some peculiar trait of character, or owing to some famous exploit performed. This was especially so amongst the Kelts of the Continent. Moses was so called because he was saved from the waters; Brennus, the name of the leader of the Gauls, was so styled because he was a Breitheamh, that is, judge of his tribe. (*b*) Proper names were not known or introduced till the eleventh century. (*c*) Keating says expressly that "Daghda" was not the personal name of "Lugh's" successor, or successors, but that *Eochaidh* was his real name—consequently, Daghda, and Oll-athair were titles of office, or names bestowed from some public cause.

Q. 8. What is the meaning of the words Tuatha De Danann, *and why were the people of this race distinguished by that title?*

A. The words are Keltic, or Irish-Gaelic, and mean tribes-of-the-god, or goddess of-skill, or *tribes of the god-like-men of-skill.*

To state the meaning of the words and to pass on would not be satisfactory to an inquiring mind: hence it is deemed proper to present here the reasons that sustain this interpretation.

1. Regarding the term *Tuatha,* the first of the three terms of which the appellation is composed—there is, speaking generally, only one opinion, that the Gaelic word *Tuatha* means *tribes.* To this present hour the term is used in Irish-speaking districts in every part of Connacht, to denote the plebeian classes as contrasted with the *aristocracy,* or with the polished members of society in towns; and, in religious works, *Tuatha* means a *laic,* as opposed to cleric. *Tuaith* (pr. *thooee*), is applied to the rural district where they dwell; and hence the "country," as opposed to "city," is called *tuaith* in Gaelic. Putting the "chief" for the people—the *leader* for the followers—*Thuath* means chief or lord; and *ban-tuathách* means

a "lady-chief," of whom amongst the Danann races there were many.

2. On the meaning of the word "*De*," there are four opinions: One, that it means (*a*) *of god* (genitive case singular); (*b*) *of gods*, (plural); that it is (*c*) for *degh, good;* that it is genitive plural of "*DA*" meaning (*d*) "god-like men." The first of these is the correct one, according to the laws of grammar; the second, that it is the *genitive plural* of "ᴅɪᴀ," is held by Nennius, the author of the tract *Historia Britonum*, written 858, A.D., in which he styles the "*Tuatha dé Danann*," *plebes* "*Deorum*." Dr. Keating seems to favour the fourth view, when he states that "Dé" is, perhaps, for "*Dée*," and the *gods* meant were the three gifted and heroic sons of *Dana*, a princess of that race; or that the *gods* were the "*druids*" as a body, priests and diviners, who, on account of their relations with the Supreme Being, were, in a secondary sense, styled "gods." The meaning of the words in *that* case would be, "*tribes of the gods of Dana*," meaning the "heroic sons" of that lady, or the "*druids*" and priests of the Danann people. Again, he states that some bards divided the nation into three classes. (1) Tuatha, that is *tribes;* (2) De, *gods;* (3) Danann, *mechanics*, or men devoted to "dana," *arts*. These meanings are forced. The fact that "De," and "Danann," are, in Irish, gen. cases, is opposed to this last opinion, that the nation was divided in that style into such classes. In old or new Gaelic writings, the term "Dia" has never been applied to designate a class or subdivision of people. "The enigmatical meaning of these words," observes O'Mahony, in his annotations on Keating, "was not understood by the bards who handed them down." p. 145. (*a*) He suggests that "Dé" is a contracted form of "*degh*," meaning *good*, or, as he thinks, *sacred*. But never yet did "*degh*" signify *sacred;* and he is unfortunate in supposing that "*degh*" (old form for *deagh*, good), qualifies "*Tuatha*," which precedes it. "Degh," or "deagh," is one of the few adjectives that, in Irish-Gaelic at least, go before the noun which they qualify. (*d*) "Da," is a primitive Aryan word, meaning a *man of knowledge*, or *of mental power*, as in "*Dagh-da*," "*Nuada*," or "*Nuadath*." "Da," in this sense, is found in the kindred Greek term δάω, the primitive of διδάσκω, to teach; in δαίς and in δαίμων, an intelligent being, a spirit. The plural of "Da" is Dae, like *lá*, a day; "*lae*," days; and *ga*, a dart; *gae*, darts, rays.

It is likely, therefore, that this fourth view of the meaning of "De," namely, the genitive plural of "Da," a god-like-man, is

ᴇ

correct, particularly when one bears in mind that the Danann chiefs were impersonations of skill and sapience. The first opinion, however, is the most striking and the most natural.

3. Danann. What is signified by the term? There are three opinions.

(a) The lady *Dana* just named, daughter of Delbeth ; or (b) the "*Danai*," from the south-east of Europe; or (c), skill, technical knowledge, wisdom. The first opinion (a) has been already rejected. Amongst this gifted race their leaders and chiefs received their titles from the people, and not the people from them, or any remarkable personage amongst them. The second (b) opinion regarding the meaning of *Danann*, which is held by Nennius, in the quotation just given, and supported by O'Mahony, is, that it means the "*Danai*," who in the Pelasgic period of Grecian history emigrated northwards, and crossed in due course the river Danube, sojourned in Dacia, moved north-west into Germany, and settled between the Elbe and the Vistula. That a Pelasgic people of that name crossed the Danube* from Thrace, and settled, at a very early period indeed, to the north of western Europe is in accord with ancient history. Herodotus names some Pelasgic tribes, and says their language was foreign (*barbaron*) to the Greek spoken at a later period by the Hellenes. Irish annalists state that the Danann who came to Eire, had been trained in the arts by these *Danai* of northern Europe, and hence the opinion that the " *Tuatha* " *tribes*, were under the guidance and provident care of the God of Danai, and therefore they received the *national* appellation of "*tribes of the God of the Danai*." O'Mahony is of opinion that the Irish colony had mixed for a time with a Greek-speaking people, or with a people who spoke a language the forms of which were adopted by the Greeks. Philology furnishes the proof.

It is this. Many terms, specially in use by the Danann race of Eire in remote ages, form the genitive case in "ann," or "enn," or its equivalent, "*and*" or "*end*," that is "*ant*" or "*ent*" for *d* and *t*, in old Gaelic were written, indifferently, to represent the same sound, and "*nn*" is only modern for "*nd*." But many nouns in Greek form the genitive case singular in the same manner (omitting os final) in *nt*. Therefore a certain sameness in the declension of nouns

---

* The *ab* in Punjab, five rivers ; Do-*ab*, two rivers, is a key to *ab*, in *Danube*, the *Danai river*, or, the *dashing* river. Ister, another Keltic name, means rapid *water*.

exists between Greek and the Gaelic language as spoken by the *Danann* race in ancient Eire. This sameness points to a time when the progenitors of the two nations, the (Greek) *Danai* and the (Gaelic) *Dananna*, spoke one primitive tongue, from which the two languages borrowed the same grammatical form of declension in *ant, ent,* or *ont,* in Greek; *and, end,* or *ond, ann, enn,* or *onn* in Gaelic.

The Gaelic nouns which form the genitive in *ann* or *and*, and which it is known the Danann spoke, are, ẽıne, Ireland; genitive ẽıneanv, Eireann; *Brita*, genitive, Britann; *Ara*, genitive, Arann; Mana (Mann), genitive, Manann; mumɑ (Munster), genitive, mumɑnn.

Alba, Scotland, genitive *Albann*, Ula (Ulster) old form, genitive *Ulann*. Names of Danann chiefs: *Elada*, Eladann; *Taillti*, (queen of Eochy, and foster-mother of Lugh), genitive, Tailltenn; *Eta*, Etann; ɢobɑ, genitive, Gobann; *Eithle*, genitive, Eithlenn, mother of Lugh; Ogma, Ogmann, Bua, Buann; and *Danann* itself is genitive case of "*Dana*." Philological sameness points to identity of cause. Therefore, the Irish Danann race had, in the early or very remote past, a lingual identity with Greek in some grammatical forms; and this shows that the races had for a time some social connection.

The last opinion (c) on the meaning of the word "Danann," is, that it is the genitive case of "Dana," meaning *skill, technical knowledge*. King Lugh is styled "Sɑb ıol-vɑ́nɑċ," "all-skilled stock;" the universal genius. The root of "dán," *an art*; "dána," *arts*; or, "dána," *skill*, is found in "*dá*," already explained. "Dán," in modern Irish is a "work of mind," therefore a poem in its present acceptation; vɑ́ntɑ, *poems, songs*. "Dán" is the "knowing god," a δαίμων, *a spirit, foresight* or *prevision*; therefore, *providence, destiny*: and in this sense it is in use to this day: as tá ɾe ann vɑ́n vɑm, "it is in destiny for me." "Dán" was a title of respect given in ancient times in England to learned or clever men, as *Don,* or *Dona*, at present in Spain, or at home. "Dána" signifies confidant, daring, one who is a child of fate. Such are the meanings of "Dán" and "Dána." In the time of "Lugh," and the Danann, the term meant, *skill, ingenuity*. Its genitive, as people at that time formed the oblique case, is "vɑnɑnn." According to this last view, the meaning of the title bestowed on this people is, "tribes of the god of genius, or skill;" or, "tribes of the god-like men of skill."

Q. 9. Were the Fomorians a distinct colony of settlers, like the Firbolg, or the Danann races?

A. No; in pre-Christian periods of Irish history they were to the ancient races, who from time to time had settled in Ireland, what the Danes, in later times—from the eighth to the eleventh century—became to the Christian inhabitants of the land. From the very earliest date the Fomorians are named in Irish annals as invaders and marauders. They attacked the followers of Partholan on several occasions, and finally caused the destruction of the entire race. In like manner, the Nemedians and Firbolg were continuously subject to their fierce incursions. The Nemedians were at one time almost annihilated, on the occasion of the great fight at Tory Island. Many of the Fomorians intermarried with the Nemedians and Belgian tribes, and subsequently with the Danann; nevertheless, as a people with a distinct dynasty, having an Ardrigh and government of their own, they never settled in Ireland.

Observe: It is well that the historical student should note that many errors arise amongst the common people, because they confound (as many writers ignorant of Irish antiquities have confounded) the Danann with the Danes, and the Fomorian. The Danann were a native Gaelic race, learned and law-loving, devoted to literary culture and skilled and practised in the art of building. The Danes and Fomorians *did not build*, but destroyed all they could; they were not native, but foreign; not devoted to the arts of civilisation, but bent on plunder and slaughter. The Fomorians date from the earliest period; the Danes, as such, only from the eighth century after Christ. The "Danes" are the Fomorians of the Christian period.*

---

* "These appear to have been rover-tribes from Norway, Sweden and Finland, who crept down the Baltic and the coast of Norway, and swarmed over the Orkneys, Shetland, and the Hebrides. They are said in our old histories and genealogies to have been of the race of Cham. They appear to have been the forerunners of the Vikings of later times, if indeed, the race and the propensities of these adventurers did not come down unbroken from the remotest times to the battle of Clontarf."—O'Curry, *Atlantis*, Vol. iii. 164.

CHAPTER VI.

FOMORIANS DEFEATED: DANANN DYNASTY CONTINUED.

Q. 1. How did it come to pass that the whole of the Fomorian Forces were arrayed against the Danann in the Battle of Northern Magh Tura?

A. The Battle was brought about in this wise : Breas, who ruled in Nuada's stead, was, as has been stated (p. 43), deposed. He yielded, of course unwillingly, to the call of the people to lay aside the robes of kingly state. After a time he took counsel with his mother, who was of the Danann race, what was best to be done in order to regain possession of the sovereignty. Both mother and son determined to retire to the court or home of his father *Elatha*, at that time one of the ruling chiefs of the Fomorian pirates, who then swarmed along the Northern Sea or German Ocean, and ruled as masters over the Hebrides to the west, and the Orkneys and the Shetland Islands to the north of Caledonia. Breas received from *Elatha*, his father, only slight encouragement. *Elatha* did not like that his son should oppose so powerful a people, and they his own relatives. Wishing, however, to have the fullest possible number of forces to fight, if it should come to that, and the largest fleet that he could put together, he recommended him to the favor of another powerful Fomorian chief, known by the name *Balor* "*of the mighty blows,*" called also *Balor* "*of the Evil Eye,*" and to *Indech*, son of De-Domnand, a Fomorian king.

It must not be forgotten that Breas during his sovereignty vastly befriended the Fomorian chiefs, and to such an extent, that the Danann lords, over whom he was king, were afraid that very soon they should be reduced to the state of clientship or serfdom to those rulers of the sea. On applying for succour to Balor and to Indech, Breas received therefore a very friendly response. The Fomorian chiefs united to strike a blow, all as one man, against the Danann dynasty, in order to secure to themselves and their posterity possession and sovereignty of " Inis Fáil."

The two chiefs, *Balor* and *Indech*, aided by *Elatha* and Breas, mustered all the men found fit to bear arms amongst the Fomorians, and gathered together all the ships lying from Scandinavia westward to the Orkneys and Hebrides, so that when the fleet set sail for Eiré, those on the headlands and hills beheld, like a high-way, a continuous line of boats and ships bridging the Northern Sea, or rather the Atlantic, from Tíri (Tiree) to Tory Island; from Fingal's Cave, in Staffa, to the headlands of Antrim, where the terminus known as that of the Giant's Causeway stands.

In a passing way, it may be well here to present special points of topography, to explain certain features of history :—In the matter in hand the "idea" of the Giant's Causeway illustrates the history of the Fomorian fleet under Balor; and the account regarding Balor's invasion receives in turn a degree of credibility from the tradition regarding the giant and his causeway. The pretty and poetic thought of a giant's highway from Staffa to Antrim had its rise, no doubt, from the vast gathering of boats and ships which on this occasion dotted the surface of the Moyle, as that ocean-stream between Malin and Mull was once called.

Balor, King of the Isles, was the giant : He was more powerful than ordinary mortals, if not in size or strength, at least by aid of art, such as glasses or reflectors, which even then were known ; by warlike weapons of a keener kind, and men of great daring and courage in his train. The burning reflectors would, no doubt, be regarded by even the Danann, who were pretty clever, as an "Evil Eye," if in the battle strong reflected light, as it is said, dazzled the fighting men. The name (*a*) Balor, means in Gaelic, "the drowning sea-god;" *bat*, drown, and *Lear*, that is Lir, sea, or sea-god. The (*b*) numerous fleet of boats and ships was the apparent highway across the waters. In process of time the voice of written and oral tradition, respecting this Fomorian passage, substituted a real road for that of boats, and a giant of fancy in place of the commanding Balor. This view was, in the minds of the unthinking, confirmed by the natural basaltic pillars which, in matchless beauty of arrangement, and in massive proportions, pave the way along the shore, and, under the waters of the sea, from Antrim coast it is supposed, right on to the opposite Scottish shore of Staffa's isle.

In company with their chiefs and men, Balor and Elatha, and Indech and Breas, landed on Tory Island and along the Donegal coast. From Tory Island they and their forces move onward by a south-eastern route, till they reach the shores of the beautiful Lough Erne. Some crossed into Leitrim by Beleek, where the waters of the lake find an outlet into the river that passes by Ballyshannon, and the spot known afterwards in history as eaſ-ᴀoba-ꞃuaꞃó (Assaroe), the waterfall of Red Hugh. There was then, as now, but not so densely peopled, by the shore of the enchanting Lake Erne, a lovely island which attracted the attention of Balor and his Fomorian Queen Kethlen. She and Balor, and their clients or followers, made the island their home as long as their forces were being prepared for the approaching battle. The record of that event is still, like a diamond in a ring, or a fish in a fossil shell, preserved to the philologist in the name of Enniskillen—a modernised form of Inis-*Kethlen*, the Island of Kethlen—Balor's Queen.

The Fomorian troops push onwards to the south, till they reach the plain lying between Lakes Arrow and Allen, the boundary of the present Barony of Tir-Errill, in the County Sligo. It was a spot admirably selected for a great engagement—a plain having lakes to the east and west—the sea not far on the north-west, and the whole immediately surrounded by high hills, rocks, and narrow defiles. Here they took their stand, and awaited the coming of the *Tuatha Dé Danann*, either to fight or to yield to the power of "the proud invader."

Q. 2. Is there any authentic record of the dress, at this time, worn by the Fomorians, or the Danann, or of the warlike weapons then in use ?

A. Yes; O'Curry states—(*Manners and Customs of the Ancient Irish*, vol. iii., p. 155)—" that all our ancient histories and romantic tales abound in references to splendid vesture and personal ornaments of gold, silver, precious stones, and fine bronze, from the first battle of *Magh Tuireadh* [fought eighteen hundred years before Christ], down to the fourteenth and fifteenth centuries," *i.e.*, at a time when Argos and Athens and Mykenæ, as cities, flourished and abounded in wealth, and for many subsequent ages.

In the battle of Northern *Magh Tuireadh*, fought between the *Tuatha Dé Danann* and the Fomorians, we are told that *Eladha*, King of the Fomorians, appeared before a Danann maiden in Connacht, dressed as follows, in the words of the Irish tract, which contains an account of the battle :—

" He had golden hair down to his shoulders. He wore a cloak braided with golden thread; a tunic interwoven with threads of gold, and a brooch of gold at his breast, emblazed with brilliant precious stones. He carried two bright spears, with fine bronze handles, in his hand, a shield of gold over his shoulder, and a gold-hilted sword, with veins of silver and paps of gold."—(*Original Text in Keltic, ib.* p. 156, vol. iii.) At parting, the Fomorian chief presented the lady with a gold ring, which he had on his middle finger.

Such was the dress of Balor, too; and of course robes of equal elegance and splendour adorned his queen, Kethlen. On the other side, it is stated the Queen of Nuadha, the Danann King, wore bracelets of gold and precious stones, and that she constantly wore rings of gold on her fingers or golden armlets on her arms, to bestow upon poets or musicians. Gold and silver pieces of coined money were not then so much in use, particularly in bestowing gifts, as were rings, armlets, bracelets, and other ornaments. Even to this day offerings of this kind are preferred to mere money value.

The warlike weapons of the Fomorians consisted of (1) a *lorica*, or breast-plate; (2) helmet on head; (3) a *manais*, or broad spear in his right hand; (4) a big, heavy, sharp sword at his girdle; (5) a firm shield at his left shoulder.

"It is stated," says O'Curry (vol. ii. p. 245, *Manners and Customs of the Ancient Irish*), "in all our ancient authorities that the Tuatha De Danann were the first to introduce pointed weapons into Erinn. Those of their predecessors, the Firbolg, were *round, broad, heavy,* sharp, but pointless. The arms of the *Tuatha Dé Danann* were, (1) a sharp-pointed, narrow spear (sleigh) for casting; (2) a *manais*, or a broad, trowel-shaped spear-head; (3) a *claidheamh*, or sword, flagger-shaped and double-edged; (4) the sling. No arrows, slings, stones, or axes are mentioned in the former Battle of Magh Tura, which was fought twenty-seven or thirty years earlier than that which the Fomorians were now prepared to fight in Tir-Errill, to the north of the Curlew Mountains, in County Sligo.*

Q. 3. How did Nuada, the Ard-righ at Tara, act on hearing of the advance of the Fomorian host?

A. On learning the news, he called what in modern times would be

---

* *Cur-lew*, or *Corr-lev*, is a phonetic form in English of the Irish Coɲɲ-ṗliaḃ, Crane-mountain. These are four hills; on the summit of one, known as "*Gearran ban*," or *white-horse*, there is a remarkable carn since the days of the Fomorian fight. O'Curry derives the name from *Corr*, a roundish, lumpy form. *Corr* is the term in common use amongst the people for *Crane*. These mountains are frequented by cranes. There is nothing special in a mountain being round or lumpy.

styled a cabinet council, consisting of Lugh and Daghda Mór, each of whom was, one day, to be Ard-righ of Eire; also Dianceacht, the Æsculapius of the Danann tribes, and Ogma. The coming of the Fomorians, and their advance southward from Lough Erne, came under their consideration. The conqueror of the Firbolg heroes was not likely now to yield to one who, like Breas, had at one time been his subject, aided though he is and sustained in the threatened struggle by Fomorian princes. Peace without honour—or war—which?—that is the question. Daghda Mór, acting as prime minister, and Lugh as commander-in-chief, or minister of war, were entrusted by the king with the preparation and management of every thing connected with the approaching battle on which, as at Marathon, the fate of two nations depended. These wise and brave commanders act with fidelity to their master and with honour to themselves. They summon in turn to their presence the heads of each department in the kingdom, whose duty or office was in any way concerned with carrying on the war with efficiency and success—namely, smiths, artificers, workmen, cup-bearers, carpenters, victuallers, sorcerers, surgeons, physicians, poets, druids, and the subordinate chiefs of the various clans. Lugh interrogated each commanding clansman, and gave him orders that, on his part, all things necessary for the great national encounter should be ready. Every department was accordingly organized most carefully, so as to make success quite certain. The ancient tract containing an account of the battle states how these two statesmen summoned to their presence chiefs of the different tribes and the " cerds," or artificers who wrought in silver and brass, and metal of all kinds. "There is not," says O'Curry, " in the whole range of our ancient literature, a more curious chapter than that which describes the questions put by Lugh to the several classes, as to the nature of the service which each was prepared to render in the battle, and the characteristic professional answer which in turn he received from each of them."—*MS. Materials of Irish History*, p. 249.

All preparations necessary for a successful battle are now made; the troops of the provincial kings have assembled at Tara under their respective commanders.

Q. 4. Where did the hostile armies meet?

A. At a place known afterwards as Kilmactraney, to the north-east of the Curlew mountain range. The spot is marked in an engraved copy of a map made (A.D. 1689) by the Down Survey. The plain of northern Magh Tura extends the whole way between Lough Arrow on the west and *Sean-Chuach* (or *Old-Cuckoo*) mountain to the east, not far, in a northerly direction, from Kilmactraney, which lies close to the line that forms the boundary between the counties of Sligo and Roscommon.

King Nuada, at the head of his troops, marched forth from *Teach-na-Righ*, at Tara, to do battle with the powerful Fomorian foe who watched from the slopes of Mount *Brah-lieve* (bneac, watch, and sliab, mountain), the advance of the Danann forces. Under Nuada the troops advance, guided by the generals— Daghda, the beacon of succour; Lugh, the intelligent and valiant; Ogma, the wise; Delbaoth (oelb, shape; and aob, fire), the warlike. On the other hand the Fomorians prepare for battle under the command of Balor, Breas, Elatha, Tethra, and Indech (*i.e.* commander-of-the-horse:—*Ech*, horse; *ind* for *inn*, *in*, or *over*).

Q. 5. In what respects do the two battles, that of Magh Tura at Cong, in Mayo, and of Kilmactraney in Sligo, differ?

A. They differ in place, in time; in hostile armies and commanders; in their respective issues; in the monuments that still remain to tell each generation those who fought and bled and conquered or died; in the narrations written in old Irish giving an account of each battle; in the varied and multiplied allusions regarding the two battles, to be seen in the Books of Leinster, Leacan, Ballymote (MSS.); in the published histories and records, such as the "Annals of the Four Masters," "Dr. Keating's Ireland," and the great number of Irish poems regarding these hostile engagements, still preserved in the Royal Irish Academy. The battles present some points that are common to the two, namely, that the Danann and their King Nuada fought on each occasion; in the first battle they fought the Firbolg and conquered; in the second also they were victors, but their King Nuada was slain; in the first battle they fought in order to acquire possessions in the island, and against the then rightful owners, the *Firbolg*; in the second, they fought against the combined power of the Fomorian invaders, and the defeated Belgæ, not to obtain new possessions, but to retain those they had acquired. In the first, the Firbolg were defeated; in the second, the Fomorians were so beaten that never again did they enjoy the same high-handed authority that they had in the past been exercising over land and sea.*

Q. 6. What has been recorded of this remarkable battle fought by the Danann against the Fomorians and their allies?

A. In the battle of Magh Tura Conga, the hostile armies were allowed one hundred and five days to prepare javelins and spears and swords of the same style and finish, so that in armour and weapons, offensive and defensive, neither of the two should have any advantage. On the present occasion the armies about to engage in deadly strife were allowed a limited, but withal a sufficient interval to have weapons of offence and defence of the same kind prepared by the smiths and artificers of the respective armies. Raths and enclosures, too, for the kings are erected by the Danann and the Fomorian. The physician Dianceacht and his sons Airmedh and Mioch, and his daughter Ochtriuil prepare healing baths made of the essences gathered chiefly in Lus-mhagh, or *herb-field*, in the present King's County. Stone circles of defence, and enclosures for support in a man-to-man struggle had been prepared, by order of Lugh and Daghda, for the Danann warriors. The latter are skilfully posted between Lough Arrow to the left, facing the right wing of the Fomorians, while their own right wing stretches onwards towards Kilmactraney.

---

* (a) The unpublished MS. that contains an account of *Magh Tura Conga*, was copied from one very old in the fifteenth century at Magh-Enné, near Ballyshannon, by Cormac O'Cuirnin, and is at present preserved in Trinity College Library, H. 2, 17. Of this a translation was made by John O'Donovan, and can be seen in the volume marked County Mayo—Letters—amongst those MSS. Tomes made for the Ordnance Survey. Another volume, marked Antiquities, contains in old Irish the original story respecting those battles, penned in the handwriting of O'Curry.

(b) Copies of the other manuscript of *Magh Tura* (or Tuireadh) na ḃ-ꝼoṁapac (of the Fomorians), giving a description of the engagement at Kilmactraney, are preserved in the British Museum.—Harleian MSS. —5280. A copy of this latter, made by a son of the late Eugene O'Curry, is now in the Library of the Catholic University, Stephen's-green, Dublin.

Sir William Wilde remarks, regarding these two manuscripts: " By very many writers, ancient and modern, these two battles and battlefields have been mixed up." It is to be hoped that the correct view suggested by Wilde, and presented fully in these pages in the narratives and topographical descriptions, will prevent further mistakes, and prove the certainty of these remote and remarkable engagements.

The morning of battle, 31st October, has dawned. The "horn-of-war," or "battle-trumpet," proclaims to the Danann the royal order to commence the dreadful struggle. The troops on each side are pale from contending emotions. They are all, however, full of hope of a successful issue; the Fomorians, on account of their numbers and the well-known bravery of their commanders, and the terror which their name and power had hitherto infused into the ranks of all opponents who had dared to encounter them by sea or land. The Tuatha De Danann are confident of success on account of victories which on a former occasion they achieved; and on account of the splendid preparation which they have made, and of the skilled and brave generals under whose command they act. As in the former battle, so in this, it is ruled that the entire army on each side, and not any select portion of it, should decide the fate and fortunes of Fomorian and Danann people.

And now the moving hosts draw nearer and nearer. Suddenly the air around is darkened with the showers of spears and darts that are cast, swift and thick by the combatants. The poets and poetesses shout the war song; invoke the hero-spirits of former warriors, and bid the men emulate the glorious deeds of their fathers, if they desire to live like them a life of immortal fame. The combatants take up the cry, and with drawn swords rush to the slaughter. The clang of shields and of crossing swords resounds through the plain. The weapons of death are fleshed deep in many a heroic heart. The earth is gory with the life-blood of the fallen. Man selects man, and hero, hero in the encounter. Among the myriad fighting men contending in that field of slaughter, observe the leaders, for around them are gathered the interests of the battle. On the Danann side are Nuada, the lady chieftain Macha, Daghda, Lugh, Ogma (son of Eladha, son of Niad), with Bruidne and Calmel; on the other are Balor, the general-in-chief of the Fomorians, and his queen, Kethlen, who, like the Queen of Scythians, takes a part in the fortunes of war and strife; Indech and Breas, and Elatha. Around these few chieftains is circled the fortune of war: Balor, named for his mighty blows baiLc-béimneaċ, singles out Nuada, the King of the Danann, the victor at the Battle of Magh-Conga. Now, in his old age, and with enfeebled frame, Nuada, with one hand able to wield the sword, stands face to face with Balor, the fierce giant of the Isles. With one blow of his terrible sword Balor lays his foe stretched on the plain. Macha, a Danann chieftainess, who rushed to the aid of the king, receives a stroke of Balor's spear, and seals her fidelity to her king by breathing her last sigh by his side. Kethlen, the Fomorian queen, wishes to signalise her presence like her brave husband, and with sure aim levels a lance or javelin at Daghda, the wisest and the bravest of all the Danann generals. Wounded by the heroic queen, he is forced to retire from the combat. Ogma, son of Eladha, is slain by Indec, the Fomorian prince. Bruidne and Calmel, two other brave Danann chieftains, are slain by a group of eight Fomorian warriors. Breas, the primary cause of the battle, is laid low by a Danann chief. And now it seems that victory is favouring the Fomorians. They are victorious all along the line. Elated with success Balor rushes on his foes. His giant sword and long spear strike terror into the ranks of the Danann warriors. He gloats over the slain. He rages like a lion in a fold. No sword of foeman can reach him. He struts like one who cannot be defeated: when lo! suddenly he falls to the earth, struck by a stone. Who has flung that fatal stone? His own grandson, the son of his daughter Eithlenn, who had for husband Cian, a Danann chief. When Lugh, with anguish, saw his Ard-righ slain, and the chieftains of the Danann host fall fast around him, then he aimed at Balor, and whirled the sling; the stone entered the eye, pierced the brain, and came out at the back of Balor's head. The battle is won. The Danann are once more victorious. The pirate power of the Fomorians is laid prostrate for centuries to come.

The fall of Balor is to them a warning for retreat. They retire from the bloody fray northward by Abhan mhór (pr. *owhen wór*), the "large river," which flows from Lough Arrow, by the modern Collooney, into the sea at Ballysadare. Pursued by the Danann, the Fomorians are slaughtered in hundreds. The waters of *Abhan mhór* and *Abhan bheag* are purpled with the life-blood of the slain. Still the survivors rush onwards to the sea with the hope of reaching their boats or ships, hard by the shore at Ballysadare. Here some of the Fomorian chiefs and the pirate warriors make their final stand, pursued by the victorious Danann. A fierce encounter ensues between the conquering chiefs, with their brave clansmen, on the one side, and the crest-fallen Fomorians on the other. Despair and dauntless courage in the face of death nerve the arm and supply fresh strength to the defeated. Victors and vanquished soon lie slaughtered on the strand. Monuments and mounds still stand, or did so until lately, to tell to each succeeding generation the tale of that day's defeat and victory. The strand at Baltra has been known iv

Irish history as *Traigh Eothaile*, from Eothail, a famous Fomorian who fell there fighting the Danann. A *tumulus* of great size was erected on the shore where he fell; and CARNS were raised to commemorate the death of the victors, who died in that fierce encounter fought on the strand at Ballysadare. Nigh three thousand Fomorians perished that day. In the quaint mode of reckoning, the number is told in the Book of Leinster (MS.), seven men, and seven times twenty men; seven hundred; seven fifties, nine hundred; twenty and forty—that is, two thousand one hundred and fifty-seven.

The victory of the Danann was complete. It can justly be compared to that which the native Irish at a later period achieved at Clontarf, where they defeated the northern seamen of the Christian period—the Danes. The Fomorians were never again able to obtain dominion or any permanent power in Ireland. As pirates many of them continued to harass the Irish coast, but, as a people forming a single united dynasty, they never acquired any directive control in the affairs of Eire.

Q. 7. Are there any monuments existing to tell the archæologist that a battle, such as that described, was fought by the Fomorians against the Danann rulers and lords of Ireland ?

A. Yes; the cromleachs, mounds and stone-circles built by Danann hands on *Tráigh Eothailé*, and *Fionn Tráigh*, or the " white strand," to the west of Ballysadare, and those found to the east in the lands from Seafield on towards the town of Sligo, or to Knocknarea, the Olympus of the county, show that the fleeing Fomorians rushed, on this occasion, for safety to their ships, moored along the shores of that harbour into which the waters of Abhan-mhòr, after many a dash and a bound over ledges of rock, stoop amid sparkling spray to kiss the rising tide, as it rushes inland from the fierce Atlantic. The natural charms of the river, with its numerous cascades, formed a barrier to the vessels of the Fomorian sailors.

Dr. Petrie declares that in August, 1837, he inspected, in all, sixty-four cahirs, circles, cromleachs, from Ballysadare to Knocknarea, and in all the lands leading to Sligo.

In the Ordnance Survey Letters, now preserved in the Royal Irish Academy Library, Dublin, Petrie gives a full description of each of these monuments. He and Dr. O'Donovan and O'Curry declare, that the cromleachs are not, as is commonly supposed, druidical altars, but monuments raised to the slain. O'Donovan bears testimony that in the year 1836, stone-circles and cromleachs, and curious caves were found by him on the battle field at Kilmactraney, and particularly in the mountain districts towards Lough Gill (or Lough Gilly, as it was called centuries ago).*

The name of *Dara*, a Fomorian druid, who in that flight was laid low by Lugh, the champion who had already slain Balor, the Goliath of the Fomorian host, is preserved to this hour in the name " *Eas-Dara*," i.e. *Dara's Waterfall*, which with the Gaelic prefix for " town " *bailé*, forms " Bailé-easa-Dara," modernised into Ballysadare. The barony to the west of the battle-field is called " Corann ;" and the mountain Cesh Corainn, near Lough Arrow, has its name from Corann, a harper of the Tuatha Dé Danann who was present at the engagement. And the " Gamh " mountains, and *Traigh Eothailé*, or " *Tràigh an Chairn*," and " *Knock na Riogh*, and other well-known names of places such as Loch Febail (Foyle), from Febal, son of Lodan, tell the antiquarian and Gaelic philologist of a race whom Irish annals represent as Tuatha Dé Danann.†

---

* In the year 1858 a great rampart was drawn by the present proprietor of the soil and of the strand, uniting an island which lies near the shore to the main land. Thus the sea has been shut out, and a large portion of the Tràigh Eothaile is now yielding abundant crops to the industrious tillers of the soil.

† The name " Gamh " (pr. *gav*), applied to those mountains, was by the unlettered understood to be *Damh*, an *ox*, and accordingly those hills are now known in English as the " Ox Mountains."

OBSERVE :—The close of the battle fought at Cong has, by most of the Irish annalists and native tale-writers, been confounded with the closing struggle that decided the fate of the Fomorians on the strand east and west of Ballysadare. See *supra* chap. iv. p. 28, where it is shewn that Eochaidh MacErc, the last of the Firbolg kings, died fighting on the shore at Lough Mask, and that his remains were interred not far from the borders of that lake. This view, presented by Sir William Wilde, rests on the authority of the manuscripts now in Trinity College, and that in the Catholic University, and is naturally the correct one. It would be a strange feat, indeed, if King Eochaidh, dying of thirst, exhausted after four days' fighting, could retreat fifty miles from Cong to Ballysadare, pursued by one hundred and fifty warriors. This strange feat never struck Irish annalists as something impossible to be done in the circumstances. Each annalist copied exactly from his predecessor, with apparent truth, asking no questions.

Dr. O'Donovan and Professor O'Curry, one of whom copied the original tract in Irish, and the other translated it, have not thought well to correct the error, the number of authorities against such a proceed-

CHAPTER VII.

THE EPONYMOUS CHARACTER OF THE DANANN CHIEFS.

Q. 1. Are not the kings, the heroes and heroines of the Firbolg and Danann race, and those of the Fomorians, regarded by some historians and by antiquarians not a few, as demigods and as goddesses?

A. Yes; the kings, heroes and heroines of the Firbolg and Danann rulers and some of the Fomorian leaders are looked on in that light by many modern historians and by antiquarians. Among the demigods are reckoned Daghda Mór, one of the great Danann kings, and his wife Mór Righan, or the Great Queen; Daghda is styled also *Oll-athair*, or the All-father, a title given by the Germans to Thór, or Donar the Thunderer, their Jupiter Tonans. The same title is also given to Odin, or Woden, Mercury, regarded by them as the impersonation of the all-powerful will of the Creator. Jupiter, i.e., Dia-pater, is a title that signifies pretty much the same as divine father, for *Ju* is only a Latin form either of the Keltic *Dia*, God, day, or of the Sanskrit *Dyaus*, the glistening Ether. The name Jupiter Tonans, is German Thor, Thunor or Donar.

Amongst the Keltic tribes the king held the position of greatfather or patriarch, and in their regard filled the place of the great

---

ing was so very great. Sir William Wilde, however, has at length suggested the correct view, or that which is natural and reasonable.

It is worthy of notice that all the cromleachs, stone-circles, mounds, knocks, or tumuli, are called by the Irish peasants Leabarò na b-pian, *beds of the Fenians*; also Leabarò na b-peap móp, *beds of the big men;* and that the towering *tumulus* which crowns Cnoc-na-Rae is styled miorcán meròb (Queen) Meave's butter-roll.

Thus the early history of Fomorian and Danann races had died away in the long roll of years; and their great deeds had perished, drowned in the stream of oral tradition amidst the unlettered and the unthinking; preserved, however, undying and imperishable in the early records of the country. The peasant people applied to the graves and mounds the names of those only who, as far as local knowledge went, were the most renowned in the early heroic ages of Irish Milesian history, when Maòb, and Fionn and Cuchullan were regarded as types of all that was noble, chivalrous and superhuman in pre-Christian times.

ruler of the world. It is not surprising, therefore, that *Daghda* who acted paternally by his people, was by them styled *Oll-athair*, or the All-father. It is a slight proof also that the Danann and Teutons had at one time mixed, or that they were taught by the same school of druidical masters. This view goes to strengthen the record of their wandering from the Pelasgic frontier, dwelling for a while north of the Danube with the progenitors of the Teutonic tribes.

Lughaidh, sovereign and sage, the Cyrus, or Cæsar of the Danann Dynasty, is ranked in the class of demigods; so is Dianceacht, the physician, who, as the god of healing, was present at the two great battles of Magh Tura Conga and Magh Tura of the Fomorians; Ogma was the patron or god of learning, whose wife was Etain; Kermaith had Ana for wife, the mother of the Keltic gods and goddesses; Niat or Neid, and sometimes written Ned, was the Belgian god of war; Eserg, his son, god of slaughter; Badhbh was the Bellona, or goddess of war; Balor, leader of the Fomorians and his queen Kethlen were real characters, yet they are regarded as more than human in the exploits ascribed to them. We have Eithle, mother of Lughaidh and daughter of Balor, with Dana and her sons, Brian, Iuchar, and Iucharba. Again there is Lear or Allod and his son Manannan, prince of merchants, known as MacLir, or MacAllóid, the son of Lear (the sea), or Allód (land): Brighid, patroness of poetry, of the fine arts, and of medicine, is regarded as a goddess, and Abhcann was the god of music.

Q. 2. Is not the record of their lives therefore, mythical, and accordingly how can it be styled history, and above all authentic history?

A. Let it be granted that those just named hold the rank of heroes or demigods amongst the Danann races, and that accordingly the narration of their exploits must necessarily include the marvellous, and appear mythical; nevertheless the record of their lives as has been presented in these pages is substantially correct. It is true that they lived and figured for a time in public life, and achieved for the people and themselves many great successes; while the minor details of their lives regarding how they were born and lived or died, or the means they adopted in gaining renown, may, let us admit, be grossly exaggerated, or perhaps pure inventions. Take a parallel case: it is certain that there was a founder of Rome, although the story of Rhea Sylvia and the she-wolf that suckled the twin princes is a myth.

It is certain that the foundations of the City of *Mykenæ* were laid by human hands—the old walls are to be seen to this day;—but who built the city is uncertain; some skilled and energetic Greek certainly first conceived the plan, and saw the foundations laid, but whether the founder was a native of Argos or not, or the fabled Perseus himself or not, no one can tell. The pretty story regarding Danaë, the mother of Perseus, daughter of Acrisius, is a pure invention, a mere myth, and the early life of her son an imperfect copy of the early history of Moses.

Take other instances in which, like ivy around the oak, myth creeps around the reality.

It is certain that letters were brought at an early period into Greece, but the story regarding Cadmus is an invention. Even the history of Charlemagne, whose life and exploits are as certainly historical as those of Napoleon I., is not without its mythical counterparts.

A historian's duty is to record those facts, for the truth of which ample data have been furnished by monuments, by numismata, comparative philology, history, by a comparison of the different races that have occupied the soil of the country; their remains, tombs, footprints, past possessions; in the names of the hills and valleys, towns and strongholds through the land: harmony of all these sources of information and even with the legends and stories regarding them for thousands of years past; lastly, in the Keltic names of many families, whose surnames are manifestly of Danann origin. Proofs like these go to support the reality of the Danann dynasty in Ireland.

Q. 3. How much of the public life of those heroes, heroines and demigods is real, and how far mythical as well as one can know?

A. To reply properly to this question, it is necessary to point out that myths are of three kinds; (*a*) beings of fancy, or creatures of the mind which have no individual or collective existence, yet presenting under a personal character some divine attribute or power of nature; (*b*) real men and women to whom actions of a superhuman kind are ascribed, and around whom as a centre the heroic deeds of a race are grouped; (*c*) Eponymous characters, heroes of a cause, leading spirits of a dynasty, champions of a race, real in their aggregate character, *or in sensu composito* as it is said, but *in sensu diviso* unreal— that is, that their history does not present personal or individual character.

In this third sense and in the second, all that has been recorded in this volume regarding the history of the Danann race is true. All the kings and chieftains, the heroes and heroines,—for ladies in those times took a leading part in the government of peoples,—were real:—Some skilled in letters like Ogma, others in medicine like Dianceacht, others famed for their bravery like Lughaidh, or noted for their fatherly foresight and care, like Daghda. These names like mayor or president, were titles of position and not necessarily personal. To this day in the Welsh language and in the Irish, Daghda (Dada) is the homely name for father. *Dada* is peculiarly Keltic. It is not in English; neither is it borrowed from Greek, nor from old or new Latin. It has been handed down from the time of Daghda Mōr who with paternal care, guided the fortunes of the Danann tribes in Ireland.

Finally, it must be remembered that a knowledge of the gods and goddesses of Aryan fame was understood by the Danann and Firbolg tribes as well as by the early Greeks, or the Pelasgi, or those of Troy, or of Asia Minor. Naturally the Danann coupled the titles of those divine beings, with the heroes of their own nation, and threw, with the name, the mantle of divinity over their kings and chiefs. The Greeks and Latins, and all the pagan nations acted just in the same manner, but such a process, although elevating mortals into supposed immortal personages, did not undo the reality of their historic life amongst their own people; neither did the fact of ascribing the actions of all to one eponymous personage—say to Daghda,—destroy the part acted by each individual who bore the eponymous name, no more than if the actions of the Napoleons were ascribed to Napoleon I., or the historic actions of all the Cæsars should be ascribed to Julius or to Augustus.

The Daghdas, the Dianceachts, the Lughs, the Belgian leaders, and the Fomorian Balor of the Evil Eye, Ler, Manannan and others were eponymous. Nevertheless, individuals amongst these tribe-men acted a public part and achieved events in the name of their tribes or clans worthy of record in the pages of historic reality.

Q. 4. Explain to the critical scholar the line of thought that directs those views.

A. The attention of the critical scholar and the philologist must be arrested here for a moment, in reading the views just put forward regarding the eponymous position which the chieftains who guided and ruled the Danann tribes, hold in Irish history.

The writer wishes to avoid two extremes, which philosophical and truthful historians as well as scholarly critics condemn, the Wolfian theory or system on the one side, on the other the method advocated by Euêmeros. The latter aimed at the extraction of historical fact from the legends of his country, and made myths historical matter by stripping them, like birds of golden plumage, of their supernatural surroundings. Euêmerism when carried to excess, as it is by the writer of the article on Mythology, inserted in the *Encyclopedia Britannica*, leads to absurdity; it may be fairly tolerated in the hands of such venerable historians as the writer of the Persian Wars—Herodotus; and of Thucydides the philosophic author of the "History of the Peloponnesian War." Amongst moderns, Professor Blackie advocates its use within certain logical bounds; whilst Rev. G. W. Cox, in his work, "Mythology of the Aryan Nations," denounces the distinguished Professor, and will not allow that any subject surrounded with a mythic mantle can be, in any sense, historical. He grants, that the legend of Roland, as told by Ariosto, is true substantially, and that Roland fell at Roncesvalles; but he states that the certainty of this event rests not on the story told by Ariosto, but on contemporary historical information.

The excavations, however, made by Schliemann at Troy and at Mykenæ, and those made within the past few years by General Cesnola at Cyprus, prove triumphantly that Professor Blackie is right; that in all those epics like the Iliad and national stories which survive for centuries there is a certain historical residuum.*

In tracing the views presented in these pages, regarding the Danann tribes and their chiefs, the writer follows the mode of proceeding recommended by that distinguished common-sense writer, Professor Blackie—while in reality he rests on foundations such as those laid by Schliemann and General Cesnola—for he furnishes the reasonings and views here given on the MS. history, and above all on the still surviving monuments of his country.

---

* The German epic, the Nibelungen Lied, is not of this class. The poem purports to be one that was actually imagined and written in the twelfth century. It is not, like the Ossianic poems and tales, a collection of fragments, written by an older hand in the second century, and presented with new features of form and language suited to the eighteenth—old, but still new. The heroes of the Nibelungen attend at Mass; and the grouping of Attila with Theodoric, as contemporaries, violates historic accuracy. Blackie shows that poems of this class, cannot, like the Iliad, retain a lasting position in the literary lore of the learned and wise.

CHAPTER VIII.

SOURCES OF HISTORICAL TRUTH REGARDING THE DANANN PEOPLE—THEY CERTAINLY BUILT THE PALACE OF AILEACH, AND PERHAPS, MOST OF THE ROUND TOWERS.

Q. 1. What are the principal sources from which proofs are drawn, attesting the reality of the Danann tribes as a people who possessed Eiré at a very early period ?

A. These are the principal sources from which proofs are furnished:—

(*a*) Monumental remains or relics of the past still standing, and pointing, as it were with historic finger, to the date of their origin. Monuments of this class are histories in stone, or in pyramidal piles. They are the best kind of record, because they present the highest and the most convincing proofs of the reality of those events, the stamp and seal of which they have, through the wreck of ages, borne unbroken to the present.

Sir William Wilde in that work from his pen, published in 1850, "The Beauties of the Boyne and Blackwater," observes (p. 215): "As a country presents more or less of ancient monuments of art or vestiges of language, even without the aid of written records, so will the antiquary or the historian possess in a greater or less degree, the data whereon to found some rational theory as to the date of its first colonisation, or the origin of its inhabitants with their religion, and their civil and social condition." Monuments, not a few still standing in this island, give evidence that a people known as Danann once were rulers of the land and its people.

(*b*) Quite a number of authentic codices or Irish manuscripts dating from the remotest period, point to the history of these Tribes and to the events achieved in their time. Those manuscript works can be seen in the Royal Irish Academy, and Trinity College, Dublin, or in the Bodleian Library, Oxford.

(*c*) Many Irish families are, to this day, known from their patronymics to be of Danann origin: as for instance names like *Niat* or Nead, Mac Neid, Mac Ellen, or Mac Eithlenn, Mac Coll, Mac Ainy Mac Leur, Mac Loid or Mac Alloid, Mac Greine, Mac Govan, Mac Kean, Mac Hugh, Luge, or Lewis, Mac Conn, or Mac Gunn, or Gunn, Mac Shethor. Many of the Mac Engus came, it is likely, from a Danann progenitor, Engus, son of the Daghda; Killein, a Danann name is formed from Keithlein, so Ellenn from Eithlcinn in the surname Mac Ellenn.

Regarding the Danann families found in Eire, Mac Firbis quotes the following as having been a well-known saying of annalists and Irish writers in his time (1580–1670).

" Every one who is fair-haired, vengeful, large; and every plunderer, every musical person, the professors of musical and entertaining performances, adepts in druidical and magical arts—they are the descendants of the *Tuatha De Danann in Eirinn*."—*Book of Genealogies.*

(*d*) Topographical names are historic boulders. Of these the historian is furnished with an abundant supply in Irish Gælic :, for instance, Lough Feabhail, now Lough Foyle; Aileach (Aily) the hill west of the Foyle, looking into Lough Swilly; Euniskillen, Easdara, or Ballysadare; and most of the remarkable mounds and hills and lakes and streams in the counties Sligo, Mayo, Galway, Limerick, Tipperary, and in Louth, such as at Taillten, and Clety and Brugh on the Boyne. Many a place in Ireland is connected with the death, or associated with the brilliant deeds, of some hero famous in days long ago amongst Danann clans.

(*e*) Certain hills in Ireland said to be under the watch and ward of mythical beings, known as faeries, were once the military sites and strongholds of Danann chieftains, held by them, even after the Milesians had gained the sovereignty of Ireland, much in the same way as the Milesian chiefs held their castles and lands subsequent to the English invasion, up to the commencement of the seventeenth century.*

---

* The leading Tuatha Dé Danann chieftains, and those who survived the terrible battle at Taillten, east of Kells, in East Meath, where all their forces were destroyed, or their final effort made at Drumlighean (now Drumleen, in the barony of Raphoe, a short distance north of Lifford town, on the river Foyle), were Bodhbh (pr. *Bowv*) Derg, son of Daghda; Manannan; Midhir; Sighmael; Finnbarr, Tadhg Mór; Ilbreac, Lir son of Lughaidh; and Derg Dian-scothach, with three others. These chieftains formed a council, and by the advice of Manannan elected the eldest son of the Daghda to be their leading chief or king, in the

(*f*) The Irish language furnishes many important points in comparative grammar, in derivation, in natural suggestiveness that indicate the period when the Danann tribes flourished in Ireland. They spoke Keltic such as is transmitted in MSS. to the present day.

(*g*) The battles already described, the mounds on the battlefields form a convincing proof to minds open to arguments of an

---

West of Ireland. For themselves they made choice of certain hills throughout the land, as strongholds for each Danann chief and his followers. These hills were by them called "*sidhe*" pronounced *shee*, signifying a "seat," or "site," akin to "*sed*" in the Latin "*sedeo*," to "sit." As the Danann regarded the Firbolg, or common people, not worthy of their distinguished companionship, while they hated at the same time the Milesian conquerors, they were pleased to live in solitary grandeur in their mansions on the hills. Their great skill added not a little to the respect which the common people entertained for those who dwelt in high places. In process of time, the term *sidh* (*shee*) came to have the same meaning that "faery" has at present—a being of another world, living unknown to men in hills or valleys, and places unfrequented by the people. The term *Bean-sidh* (Ban-shee) or lady-faery, is well known. Allusion is made to that mythical personage at present merely to point out, how it has come to pass that "*sidh*," which at first meant a "seat," now signifies "faery"; and *Bean-sidh* to signify a woman-faery, one who is supposed to look after, in some hidden and unknown way, the fate and fortune of the "old families," and to be heard crying and wailing at the approaching death of any celebrity of the Danann nobility, and latterly of anyone wealthy enough to claim such distinguished attention from the lady-spirit of the hills.

On the distribution of these national "seats" amongst the conquered Danann, Bodhbh took a hill near Portumna, close by Lough Derg—the hill retains' his name *Sidhe-Buidhbh;* Manannan retained the island of Mann, supposed to be since then "the Land of Prophecy," and "the Land of Youth" (τιρ ταιρρζιne, no τιρ nα h-οιζe); Midhir took the hill at Trim; Sighmel selected Fairymount in Roscommon, known as Sidhe Nennta; Finnbar took possession of the hill Meádh, which is known as *Sidhe Meadha*. It is now called *Knoc Meadha*, or Knoc Madhbh, near Tuam, in the county Galway. It is the Faery Hill of the West of Connacht, as Sidh Nennta or Faery Mount, is regarded in Roscommon. Tadhg Mór went to Allen in Kildare, and selected for a "*Sidh*," *Druim Dian*, the firm back. Ilbreac was appointed to defend the entrance to county Donegal, and the borders of Fermanagh, and he accordingly selected as the seat of his supreme sway over the surrounding territory, *Eas Aodha Ruaidh*, the hill north of Ballyshannon. Lir. son of Lughaidh, took the hill of Clety (*Sidh Cletigh*), near Newtown-Hamilton, county Armagh.

Amongst the Irish people for the past three thousand years, and even to this day, these hills are supposed to be the palaces of this mythical race—the Danann. As their origin is, to the body of the people, unknown, the mythical notion that surrounds the faery world is naturally associated with them.

ordinary convincing kind, and not closed against truth by prejudice or scepticism.

(*h*) In Irish manuscripts, of which there are sixty-four in the libraries at the Royal Irish Academy, or at Trinity College, Dublin, or in those of the Bodleian Library, Oxford, events quite distinct of which there cannot be any reasonable doubt, are recorded, which tell the reader, there was in former days, a race of people in Ireland known as the Danann. Events of a public kind are narrated with such circumstantial care; events that involve the life and death of thousands, the fate and fortune of nations, so that it is impossible for one to doubt that they took place, and consequently, as these events refer to the Danann people, these Tuatha or Tribes must have at one time been the ruling classes in Ireland.

(*i*) Druidism such as it existed in Ireland is in part wound up with the story of this wonderful race.

Witness, the two great battles fought at Magh Tura Conga, and Magh Tura of the Fomorians to the east of Ballysadare, in which the Druids acted an important part.

Two out of the three tragical stories of Eirinn; "the fate of the children of Lir;" "the fate of the children of Tuirenn," are founded on the supposed certainty that such a people flourished.

The fact that those stories were written regarding the Danann is not a proof that this people existed formerly, but it is a proof that the belief was common amongst the natives of Ireland at the very earliest period, that such a race had at some time previously flourished in Eire.

(*k*) These people were famed for their knowledge of the arts, and above all for their skill in architecture, as is evidenced in the buildings of Grianan Ailigh, to which a fuller allusion must be made presently. It is evidenced also in the erection of those Round Towers which manifestly are the work of their hands.

(*l*) The great periodic gatherings or fairs at Tara, and at Tailltenn in Meath, and at Carman (now Wexford), date their rise from the time of the Danann dynasty. These fairs, or national gatherings, in Ireland continued to be held for many centuries after the Christian period, that at Carman as late as the year A.D. 1023, was celebrated by Donagh MacGillapatrick.

The following is a summary, from the "Manners and Customs of the Ancient Irish," Vol. II., p. 39-49, regarding the origin of the fair and how it was held:

"Three men and one woman came, according to an ancient poem, into Erinn to bring evil upon the De Danann people by blighting the fertility of the country.

"By witchcraft and druidical spells they forced the three men from the island. Their mother Carman, left as a hostage, died of grief, and her request was that a fair and games should be celebrated in her honor wherever she should be buried, and that the fair and games should retain her name for ever, and hence Carman and the fair of Carman. The Tuatha De Danann kept up this fair as long as they occupied Erinn.

"There were seven days for sport, or racing; a week for considering and proclaiming the privileges and laws of the province for the three years to come.

"It was on the last day that the Leinstermen south of the *Gabhar* held their fair or racing, and hence it was called the steed-contest of the Ossorians. The seat of the King was on the right hand of the King of Leinster; the seat of the King of Offaly on his left; it was the same case with their wives.

"It was on the Kalends of August they assembled at it. It was held every third year. Preparations were going on for two years."

From the poem of the Fair of Carman, translated from the original Irish:

"In the Kalends of August, without fail,
They assembled in every third year,
They arranged seven well-fought races
In the seven days of the week.
Here they proclaimed in eloquent words
The privileges and laws of the province,
Every rule of over-severe law,
In every third year, they adjusted."

It was prohibited during the continuance of the fair:

"To sue, to levy, to controvert debts.
To abuse steeds in their career,
Is not allowed contending racers;
Nor elopement, nor oppression, nor arrest.
No man goes into the women's assembly,
No women into the assembly of the fair; healthy men,
No abduction is heard of,
No repudiation of husbands or wives."

O'Curry says of these stanzes, "I have translated them for the sake of the light they throw on what was called the Fair of Tara; and because they show the nature of these assemblies, and how the grave business of legislation was performed on appointed days in the midst of others set apart for pleasure or reserved for mercantile pursuits," p. 47, vol. .ii So it was at Tara, Taillten, at Cruachan. Compare with these the games of Greece.

(*m*) The harmony found to exist on matters purely historical in the vast collection of existing Irish MS. tracts, taken in relation to one another; and also in the legendary MSS. indirectly connected with historic matter.

(*n*) The fact that these proofs rest, like paintings on a wall, on a background of monumental remains, is an additional force strengthening the chain of evidence that gathers round the Danann dynasty, defending it from the attacks of those who look upon that singular people as mythical.

(*o*) Sir William Wilde, writing thirty years ago, says of the Danann Tribes:—" There are too many existing records of these fleshy inhabitants of our isle to doubt their identity, and we believe the very arts and magic assigned to them arose from their knowledge of so much chemistry as related to the art of mining and the smelting of metals."—" Beauties of the Boyne," p. 220.

And O'Curry, in the preface to the " Three most Sorrowful Tales," remarks, that the preservation of these tales is especially valuable, just at a moment like the present when every light brought to bear on this subject is of so much immediate importance. Hitherto our conclusions have been drawn from mere scattered allusions regarding the mysterious *Tuatha* Dé Danann. Again in p. 238, " Atlantis," No. vi., he says " there is much reason to believe in the actual existence of the race."

O'Donovan remarks, " letters were known not only to the Milesian colony but also to their predecessors the Tuatha Dé Danann."—*Introduction to Irish Grammar.* (*See* chap. x., infra.)

Lastly—The lives of the Danann tribes, their achievements as described in peace or war, their knowledge and practice of letters and art, are quite in keeping with the manners and habits of contemporary nations of Eastern origin.

Q. 2. I should like to hear facts: What are the facts which monuments as a ready available source of certainty supply, showing the student of history that the Danann tribes were a real, a practical, and a clever people?

A. The facts shall be put before you presently.

O'Donovan, Wilde, O'Curry, Petrie, supply facts in abundance and vindicate the reality of those famous pre-Christian inhabitants of Ireland. In the first volume of the " Annals of the Four Masters," Dr. O'Donovan tells his readers :—

" The monuments ascribed by the ancient Irish to the Tuatha Dé Danann still remain, and are principally situated in Meath, near the Boyne, as at Drogheda, Dowth, Knowth and New Grange. There are other monuments of them at Knock-Aine, and Knock-Gréine in the county of Limerick, and on the Pap Mountains, *Da Chich Danainne* (the two paps of Danann) in the south-east of the county Kerry. These monuments are of the most remote antiquity and prove that the Tuatha Dé Dananns *were a real people*, though their history is much wrapped up in fable and obscurity."

And in the only volume published of the Ordnance Survey Records, that regarding the county Londonderry, Colonel Colby, R.E., Superintendent (*Dublin, Hodges and Smith,* 1837), Dr. Petrie remarks, p. 233 : " So, in the Dinnseanchus,"—an Irish topographica. work of very high antiquity, in which is furnished a description of the royal fortress of Aileach,—" the places mentioned must have had a real, and the persons connected with them at least a traditional, existence, or its legends could have had no interest at the period of their compilation. The legends like those narrated in the Lives of the Saints do not affect the general truth or reality of the personages regarding whom they are told."

Q. 3. First fact : What is the Grianan or Palace of Aileach, and where built ?

The Grianan of Aileach is situated in the county of Donegal, about a mile from the boundary of that of Derry, between the town of Derry and Burta, on the summit of a small mountain, eight hundred and two feet high, to which it has given its name of Grianan. This mountain rises from the eastern shore of Lough Swilly, immediately south-east of the Island of Inch, from which it is separated by a channel which is passable at low water. The ascent for about a mile, from its base on the Derry side, is gradual; but within a few hundred feet of the top, it assumes a more precipitous character, and it terminates in a circular apex which commands one of the most extensive and beautifully varied panoramic prospects to be found in Ireland. A broad ancient road between two ledges of natural rock leads to the summit. The whole hill was originally inclosed by other ramparts, of which, owing to the progress of cultivation, no very distinct traces are now visible. There are three circular ramparts just now in a state of dilapidation. They are of an irregular circular outline, because they are adapted to the form of the hill which they inclose, and ascend one above the other in successive terraces. Between the third rampart, or that which is innermost, and the *cashel*, or inmost stone building, the road diminishes considerably in breadth, and diverges slightly to the right, and this approach was strengthened by a wall on each side of which the foundation stones alone remain.

The cashel, though in a more perfect state than the external ramparts, is still a mere ruin, and has, at a distance, the appearance of a dilapidated sepulchral *carn*; but, on a closer inspection, it is found to be a circular wall inclosing an area of seventy-seven feet six inches in diameter, and in its present state about six feet in height, and averaging about 13 feet in breadth. Its height was probably four times at least its present altitude. At the height of five feet from the base, on the interior face of the wall, the thickness is diminished about two feet six inches, by a terrace the ascent of which was by staircases or flights of steps, increasing in breadth as they ascend, and situated at each side of the entrance gateway. There are similar ascents to the terrace in the other parts of the wall concealed now beneath masses of fallen stones. There was originally a succession of three or four such terraces, ascending to the top or platform of the wall. On each side of the entrance gateway there are galleries within the thickness of the wall, extending in length to one-half the entire circuit, and terminating at its northern and southern points. These circuitous galleries, within the wall, have sloping sides, being three inches narrower at the top than at bottom. They are covered by large stones laid horizontally.

The circular apex of the hill contains within the outermost inclosure about five acres, one-half; within the second, four; within the third, one; and within the cashel about one-fourth of an acre.

The masonry of this great work is exactly similar to that of many other Irish *cashels* or *cahirs*. The stones, which are of the common grey schist of the district, are of polygonal forms, adjusted to fit each other and wholly uncemented. They average about two feet in length; and it is quite evident that they have been in many parts squared with the hammer but not chiseled.

Between the third and fourth walls there is a spring-well, which when discovered a few years back was covered with a large stone.—*Summarised from Dr. Petrie's Account of the Palace of Aileach.*

Q 4. Why give such minute details of this building ?

A. Because it is now the most remarkable remains of acknowledged Danann architecture in Ireland ; because this history is intended for Irish students, and it is well that Irish students should be told fully what is certain regarding this ancient palace. The ruins and treasure discovered within the past ten years at Curium and other ancient towns in Cyprus, by the American consul, General Louis Palma di Cesnola, have attracted the attention of the literary world, and proved to a certainty that a pre-historic people, unknown to Herodotus, or the earliest Greek writers, had dwelt in that island. Peoples lived in Europe and Asia whom the pen of history has never named. Written records of the remote past are imperfect and inadequate. Monuments are sure ; they are certain. This remarkable ruin, that has survived a period of three thousand and some hundred years, is therefore worthy of the student's attention. The necessity of detail is manifest, when it is borne in mind that the Grianan of Aileach was one of the most remarkable and important works of its kind ever erected by the ancient Irish—the palace of the northern Irish Kings from the earliest age of the historic tradition down to the commencement of the twelfth century : and consequently, as Petrie remarks, such careful examination of its vestiges as should help to convey a clear idea of its original form, structure and extent, would give the best evidence, now attainable, of the style of military building known to the Irish at the remotest period of their history.

Q 5. Who is supposed to have built it, and why ?

A. The origin of this Grianan Fort is given in a poem of the eleventh century on the history of the Tuatha De Danann, and particularly on the Daghda, written by Professor Flann of Monasterboice. The poem is preserved in the codices known as the

"Book of Lecan" and "Book of Ballymote," and is printed in full by Dr. Petrie in that part of the Ordnance volume which contains an account of the antiquities of Derry. The text of the published poem is that found in the "Book of Lecain" (11th century) collated with another MS. copy in Trinity College, written on vellum about the year 1560, by John O'Mulconry.

"This great cathair," says O'Curry, vol. III., p. 8, *Manners and Customs of the Ancient Irish*, " is said to have been built by the Daghda, the celebrated King of the Tuatha Dé Dananns, who planned and fought the battles of the second or northern Magh Tuircadh against the Fomorians." Niad superintended the building for the Daghda, and from him the palace received the name of Aileach Neid.*

It was by order of the Ardrigh Daghda that the fort was erected around the grave of his son Aedh (Hugh), who had been slain in a fit of jealousy by Corgenn, a Connacht chieftain from the mountain district near Cruach Patrick, who in those days was with his wife enjoying the hospitality of the supreme monarch at Tara.

The following anecdote fanciful or historical, taken from the poem of Flann of Monasterboice, and copied from others of an earlier date, shows that Irishmen in the eleventh century, and long before that period, believed that Aileach had been the work of the Tuatha Dé Danann.

"When the great Daghda was chief King of the Tuatha Dé Danann in Eire, holding his court at Tara, he on one occasion entertained at his court Corgenn, a powerful Connacht chief and his wife. During his stay at Tara, the wife was supposed by Corgenn to be on terms too familiar with Hugh, the monarch's young son. In a fit of jealousy Corgenn slew the royal prince. The Daghda, mindful of the laws of hospitality as well as of justice, did not order that his son's death should be atoned for by the life-blood of his guest. He passed sentence, however, which was equally effective, and which ended in death : namely, to carry the dead body of the prince on his back until he found a flag exactly to fit the corpse in length and breadth, and sufficiently large to form a tombstone. The Connacht chieftain had no alternative, he should comply. He took up his burden at Tara, and never stopped till he reached the western shore of Lough Foyle. Here he found the fitting flag, which he carried to

---

* Neid is genitive case of Niad.

the top of the adjacent hill, since known as *Aileach* or stone-house, buried the prince's remains; wearied, however, with labour, he dropped down dead into the same grave."—*From a historic poem in Irish by Flann of Monasterboice, a professor of Irish History; he died in the year* 1056.

Again from the ancient poem it appears plainly that not only was the outer rath or protective circle around Aileach, built of stone by the regular masons " Imcheall," that is, *circuit-builder*, and " Garbhan," *rough builder*, but that the palace and the houses within the enclosure were also built of stone, nay, even of clipped and cut stone.

All these buildings probably were circular, as the house or prison of the hostages certainly must have been, when, as the poem says, it was " closed on the top with one stone."

Q. 6. Was this a Round Tower?

A. Edifices closed after that fashion, and built high in air, must have had a tapering form, and were therefore like the ROUND TOWERS, which to-day raise " their heads sublime" all over this land. Other abodes were at this period made with a cupola roof in shape like a bee-hive, built with stones protruding inwards so as nearly "to close in at the roof." The underground buildings at New Grange, along the banks of the Boyne, and the dwellings near the town of Kirkwall in the Orkneys; the Brugh, or town of the dead, near Slane in Eastmeath, and the *Brugh*, or " old Pictish town" of Burra, a western islet of the Orkneys, are of this class, made of large stones converging towards the top, in shape like a cone, but covered outside with a thick layer of earth or turf. Dwellings of that construction were always, on the outside, for security and architectural reasons covered with clay. The " house of hostages " was not covered with earth, but high in air, and built of stone. Hence it follows, that the circular house built at Aileach must have been, not like those found in the *Brugha*, with their canopy of clay and grass, but rather like the ROUND TOWERS, which are made of large stones, circular, tapering in form, high in air, and closed with one stone.

Q. 7. Was it the Tuatha Dé Danann then who built the Round Towers?

A. The fact that the Round Towers were built is certain; uncertain, by whom, or when first erected. The former is matter of history; of opinion the latter.

The only views worth noticing regarding the time of their erection are those two, (a) that the towers were built either before the Christian period, or (b) soon after the introduction of the Christian religion into Ireland by St. Patrick.

Neither of the two views can, as an opinion, be pronounced absolutely true or certain.

It is well known that neither the Milesian race, nor the Christians of the fifth or of the sixth century, were in any remarkable way skilled in architecture. On the other hand, the Danann race were remarkable for their knowledge and practical ability in the art.

All the buildings erected by the Danann tribes are so like in style of architecture to that of the Round Towers, rotund, tapering and cyclopean, without the use of the arch, that, taking the pre-Christian theory regarding these to be true, one cannot avoid declaring that they must have been the handiwork of that gifted race.

The great proof given by Dr. Petrie of the Christian origin of these majestic piles, rests on an assertion which is not true, namely, that the pagan Irish did not know how to build, and therefore that they did not build. It is simply untrue to say that the Danann race did not build, or did not know *how* to build. Their works remain even yet. Petrie says :—

" Not the slighest evidence has ever been adduced to prove that the Irish were acquainted with the art of building with lime cement, before they received the Christian faith." *Ancient Irish Architecture*, p.34.

In reply it is stated: The masons of the Danann period did build with lime cement, see O'Curry's *Manners and Customs of the Ancient Irish;* therefore they knew how to build ; and accordingly Petrie's proof is reduced to a groundless assertion. In his opinion the Irish of that remote period did not know how to build, therefore they did not build. But, according to facts and strong evidence they did build, therefore they knew how, and hence Petrie's assertion is a mere groundless assumption.

Anthropologists and others who believe in the progressive power of man as an animal hold Petrie's views. History shows that man, in powers of intellect and will, in science, therefore, and knowledge of the arts, was, up to the coming of the Redeemer, generally speaking, retrogressive and not progressive. The presence of war was destructive of progress. Peace, as the parent of the arts, fostered architecture ; and it must be said that peace aided progress, and that nations prone to war retrograded in the arts and sciences.

MacFirbis (1580-1670) writing on this subject, the ancient buildings of Eire, says:—" We could find a countless number of the ancient edifices of Eire to name besides those above (at Tara, Aileach, Nas), and the builders who erected them and the kings and noble chiefs for whom they were built, but they would be too tedious to mention here. . . . . . .

" I have myself seen within the last sixteen years lofty lime-built castles, formed of limestone, and at this day, after they have fallen, there remains nothing of them but an earthen mound to mark their sites, nor could antiquarians even easily discover that any edifices had ever stood there. . . . . .

" Such is the stability of the old buildings that there are immense royal raths, or palaces, and forts through Eire made of hewn and polished stones, with cellars and apartments under 'ground, such as *Rath Maoilcatha* in Castleconnor, and in Bally O'Douda in Tireragh, on the banks of the Moy, near Ballina. There are nine smooth stone cellars under the walls of this rath. I have been within them." P. 223, MS. materials.—Quotation from Duald Mac Firbis.

O'Curry spent forty years at least investigating, collating, and translating Irish MSS. As an authority on this subject his word has more weight than that of Petrie, who was only an amateur at MS. lore.

But O'Curry states:—" The stone ruins at Aileach as well as several other similar stone erections in several parts of Eirenn must be referred to the Tuatha De Danann; certainly to a race prior to the Milesians." O'Curry: *Manners and Customs of the Ancient Irish*, vol. II., p. 153. The author's opinion is that the Danann built the ROUND TOWERS.

Q. 8. At what period was the Palace of Aileach first erected?

A. The time when that royal fort had been first erected was, according to the chronology followed by the Four Masters, about the eighteenth century before the Christian era (for in 1694 A.C. the foundation of the Milesian power was laid, and the reigns of Lugh and Daghda had been for nigh a century previous to that particular time).

The Round Towers, too, must have been erected at that time; a few towers like the pagan piles were, it can be admitted, built in the Christian period, but the great body of these temple towers were planned and erected in the days of Lugh and Daghda. Nevertheless, this view regarding the time of the building of the towers, now for the first time publicly asserted by the writer, is only an opinion.

G

Q. 9. Is there much historic truth gained from this conflict of opinions amongst scholars?

A. There is: men are more in earnest when they have a cause to support; and amidst the contending forces on either side, an intelligent critic can perceive the gleam of truth, like a lightning spark from a cloud, come forth from the darkness or smoke of drifting views and the storm of angry words.

In the case before us, it is certain that the Fort of Aileach presents in its ruins an example of that barbaric art, which, in Greece and in Western Europe, even in Eire, came in the wake of the splendid Egyptian style displayed even to-day in the temple at Karnac, the Pyramids, and the Monolith—Cleopatra's Needle—on the banks of the Thames. This barbaric or cyclopean art was employed, as the surviving monuments shew, by the natives of Cyprus; the immigrants to Eire; by the Pelasgi and by the Etrurians.

In Ireland, Aileach was at that period the model of other princely edifices, a countless number of which, in the language of MacFirbis, have perished, but which, certainly had had their origin during the Danann dynasty.

CHAPTER IX.

OTHER PROOFS: MANUSCRIPTS; MONUMENTARY MOUNDS; SITES SELECTED BY THE CONQUERED DANANN CHIEFS, KNOWN TO-DAY AS "FAERY HILLS," ARE FOOT-PRINTS ON THE SANDS OF THE PAST PERIOD OF DANANN POWER.

Q. 1. What is the gist of the testimony supplied by Irish manuscripts, of which a great number are still extant,[*] giving an account of the Tuatha De Danann alone?

A. That they were a real people although their kings, queens, and heroes are eponymous, and are regarded by some in the light of demi-gods; that in that age known in Grecian history as heroic, they were highly civilised, conversant with the arts such as were then

---

[*] In the Royal Irish Academy there are *sixty-four* distinct manuscripts, containing the history of these people. The same record is, however, only repeated in the leading manuscripts.

known. As signs and proofs of their civilisation they had a knowledge of letters, they had a system of laws; they had historians, we are told, who recorded events and recited them from memory ; poets like Cairpré and his mother Etana; they respected the weaker sex, and placed them in positions of trust, which, on their part, required knowledge and training to fill : for instance there were lady physicians amongst the Danann tribes, and ladies directed in battle, or sang the song of triumph. Druidism, in its two-fold influence of learning and religion, was with them a system. And as a people with some faint notion of the true God, they regarded themselves as children of destiny, of which the *Liag Fail* which they brought to Eire was the symbol. This *Liag Fail*—as commonly asserted—is to be seen to this day in Westminster Abbey.

"According to all our most ancient writings and traditions" writes O'Curry (in p. 3, vol II., *Manners and Customs of the Ancient Irish*), "the Milesians found before them (in A.C. 1694) and conquered the Tuatha De Danann colony : a people remarkable for the domestic if not the higher arts of civilised life, and enjoying a higher state of civilisation than their conquerors."

Q. 2. Are there not other buildings still to be seen which were at one time erected by the hands of the Danann ?

Yes: "cities of the dead," Knowth, New Grange, and Dowth mounds close by the banks of the Boyne.

Q. 3. Tell us all about those cities of the dead : an account of them must be very interesting, particularly as the cities of the dead, discovered some few years ago in the Island of Cyprus, have been described by the American Consul, General Cesnola, and the Necropoles of Etruria have long been known ?

A. The cities of the dead are those cyclopean tombs or *tums* erected by the Danann Kings on the northern bank of the river.

There were several royal burial grounds in Ireland in early pagan times. In Leabhar na h-Uidhre,* a work of the twelfth century,

---

* See in *Leabhar na h-Uidhre* page 60 of the photo-zincographed MS. copy, a history of ancient Irish cemetries.

compiled at Clonmacnoise, it is stated, in the record of the cemeteries there contained, that amongst the chief were Cruachan, Tailteann, Teamhair, or Tara (see Dr. Petrie, *History of Tara Hall*, p. 97), and Oenach Colmain with some others. By far the most extensive of all the Irish cemeteries was that nominated *Brugh* or *Brugh na Boinne* "the Town of the Boyne." The Dinnseanchus, a tract contained in the Book of Ballymote, and now to be seen in the Royal Irish Academy, contains an account of this city of the dead close by the Boyne.

This Brugh or town is no other than the assemblage of mounds, caves, pillar-stones, and sepulchral monuments that make up the great necropolis, which extends along the left or northern bank of the river from Slane to Netterville. To the Brugh the nobles and chiefs and kings and queens of the Tuatha De Danann went to sleep their long sleep of death; amongst those were Daghda and his queen, and their three sons, and Lugdaidh and Oe, and Ollam, and Ogma, and Etana the poetess, and Cairpré the poet, her son, and Cremthann (from Seanchus na Relic, Dr. Petrie's Round Towers p. 101). The monuments of the Boyne are the "bed" or *leaba* of the Daghda, and the two *cich*, or " paps" of Mor-Righan (Great Queen) at the place where the son of the Daghda was born. There are monuments raised to Cirr and Cuirrell, wives of Daghda; a monument to Aed Luirgnech, his son; the grave of Esclann, his brehon, and of Boinn, wife of Neckthann. These few out of a long list must suffice.

The precise situation of the Brugh is about two miles below Slane, as one goes with the flow of the stream. There the river becomes fordable, and several small islands arise mid the waters. Here upon the left or south-western bank of the river, is the place called Ros-na-righ, or the wood of the kings, and upon the opposite swelling bank of the river arise a series of art-made mounds, raths, forts, caves, circles, and pillar-stones, bearing all the evidence of ancient pagan sepulchral monuments, which formed the Irish Memphis, or city of tombs. One of these mounds is the tomb of Daghda Mor, the Danann King. This great Irish cemetery stretches out in breadth a mile from the river's bank, and in length from Knowth northwards, over a distance of three miles. In this space there are no fewer than seventeen sepulchral barrows, graves of kings, queens, and renowned heroes. Of these seventeen the three of the greatest magnitude are on the summit of the ridge which bounds this valley on the left bank, for a few are to be found at Monk Newtown beyond the brow of the hill towards Louth, making in all twenty, including Cloghelea, and the moat on which the Fortress of Drogheda now stands, known in Irish as " mound of the grave of Gobhan's wife." This latter is on the southern bank

The three greatest barrows are Knowth (in Irish Cnoḃ, nut-mound), New Grange, (original name Uaiṁ Aċaiṙ Aloai,* the cave of Aldai's field), and Dowth (in Irish Duḃaḋ, the black-mound).

KNOWTH.

Knowth is an abrupt, hemispherical mound, with rather a flattened top, rising out of the sloping hill. Enormous masses of stone, arranged in a circular manner round its base, tell that it is evidently the work of design, and from excavations made, it is known to consist of a stupendous carn of small stones covered with rich greensward occupying, in extent of surface, an acre, and rising to a height of eighty feet.

NEW GRANGE.

Like Knowth, it consists of an enormous carn or hill of small stones calculated at 180,000 tons weight, occupying the summit of one of the natural undulating slopes which on the north enclose the valley of the Boyne. It is said to cover two acres; is four hundred paces in circumference, and eighty feet higher than the adjoining natural surface.

Originally a circle of enormous detached blocks of stone, placed at distances of about ten yards from each other, stood all around.

Such is the present appearance of this stupendous relic of ancient pagan times, probably one of the oldest Keltic monuments in the world, which has elicited the wonder and called forth the admiration of all who have visited it, and which has engaged the attention of nearly every distinguished antiquary, not only of the British Isles, but of Europe generally. How many Irishmen, asks Sir William Wilde, have paid a visit to this spot, the historic ground of the Danann dynasty?

The mounds just described are hollow; that known as New Grange contains a large chamber formed by stones of enormous magnitude, and can be approached by a narrow passage which also is formed of stones of large size, placed together without mortar or cement, exciting one's astonishment how such cyclopean masonry could have been erected by people unacquainted with mechanical

---

* See Donovan's notes on *Four Masters* at A.D. 861.

New Grange is a modern name most probably given by some colonist who obtained the land on which the mound stands. Grange enters into names of places both in England and Ireland, and is generally Hibernicised Grainseach.

powers. Some of the stones belong to a class of rock not found in the neighbourhood; some are basaltic; others must have been conveyed from the Mourne Mountains.

Q. 4. Please describe the interior of those mounds or barrows?

A. Well, let us now enter the mound of New Grange by a passage that faces the river Boyne. It runs nearly north and south, and measures sixty-three feet in length; it is formed of twenty-one upright stones upon the right side, and twenty-two to the left, and is roofed with flags of immense length, resting upon the upright side-stones; in other places supported by masonry external to them. One of these is *seventeen* feet long, and *five broad*. The general height of the passage is five feet. In parts the stones are of a gigantic size, many of them eight, others ten feet high.

The passage leads to a large dome-roofed chamber. As all is perfect darkness within this cavern, it is necessary to light it up in order to form a just idea of its figure or extent. The dome is hive-shaped, nearly circular, with three offsets or recesses from it: one opposite the entrance to the north, and one on each side east and west, so that the ground plan, including the passage, accurately represents the figure of a cross.

This form of roofing evidently preceded a knowledge of the principle of the arch. It is to be found in many of our early buildings, sepulchral and pagan, and not only in this country, but in Egypt, Greece, and Asia Minor. The walls at Mykenæ, at Tirynthus, and the ruins at Curium in Cyprus are of this style.

The top of the dome of this chamber is nineteen feet six inches from the floor; from the entrance to the wall directly opposite the measure is eighteen feet; and between the extreme ends to the right and left crypts, twenty-two feet.

The third in order of these great caves is Dowth (or *Dubhad*). Its construction is like that of Knowth or New Grange which are in the same valley of the Boyne. This barrow is a mile from New Grange, seated on the higher slopes that rise from the banks of the Boyne.

SIR WILLIAM WILDE'S OPINION.

" All these sepulchres were in one district, the land of Flann son of Conang; and in all probability the Cave of Achadh Aldai, that is, the field (*Achadh*) of Aldai, the ancestor of the Tuatha De

Danann Kings, is that which is now known as New Grange. How far anterior to the Christian era its date should be placed, is matter of speculation and chronology; it may be of an age, or *de facto* is coeval, or even anterior to its brethren on the Nile." This is the opinion of a sound scholar and a great antiquarian, Sir William Wilde.

Similar *tumuli*, and containing similar remains, stretch along the borders of the Danube through both the Austrias, and extend in a north-western line into Moravia, and even Bohemia.

There are two towns of this class at Kirkwall, and in the Island of Burra in the Orkneys.*

The most noteworthy of the various forms of burial abodes, made use of in pagan periods in Ireland, is the dome-roofed stone chamber containing the remains of one or more bodies, and approached by a covered way.

When New Grange was first opened a great many years ago (about 1694), " two entire skeletons not burnt were found on the floor." The bodies were buried entire and not subjected to fire. These barrows were rifled by the Danes in the ninth century (A.D. 862, *Annals of Ulster*). (A.D. 861, Four Masters).

From the many monuments ascribed by tradition to the colony of the Tuatha De Danann, and named in ancient Irish historical tales, it is quite evident, that they were a real people.

After their subjugation by the Milesians, they withdrew to mountain fastnesses, where they built " sidhe," *i.e.* seats or keeps away from the populace. Eventually their descendants mingled with the Gael and made with them one people.

A full description has been given of one of the greatest palaces of the pagan Irish; and an account equally full of the remaining " cities of the dead," now known and standing. Students of Irish history at home and abroad, cannot but be pleased in studying those chapters, for hitherto no account of these wonderful people, or of the deeds they performed, has been supplied to the English reading public. The Round Towers, the Palace of Aileach, the barrows or Brugh of the Boyne—their style and character, so like those in Greece, Cyprus, and Asia Minor, are proof of the eastern origin of our earliest progenitors.

---

* *i. e.* Orkneys, is only a contraction for *Orc*, and *inis*: *Orc*, a Fomorian or Danann prince: and *inis* (pr. inish), island.

Q. 5. From mounds and monuments, from the *sidhe*, or *sites*, selected on the hills, as well as from the numerous reasons already presented, are the Danann races a historical reality?

A. Yes; It is impossible that effects so many, so important, and so lasting, could have existed without an adequate cause. Tradition and story, as well as monuments, point out the Danann tribes as that cause. They must, therefore, have had power at one time in Ireland.

Q. 6. Show the genealogical relation of the Danann Kings and Chiefs

A. The following is perhaps the best that can be given.

Ordai and Indai, sons of Aldai, were the twenty-first in descent from Noah, through Japhet and his son Magog. Ordai was the great grandfather of Nuada, the first King of the Tuatha De Danann. He lost an arm at the battle fought at Cong against the lawful possessors of the land—the Firbolg; Indai was grandfather of Daghda Mor.

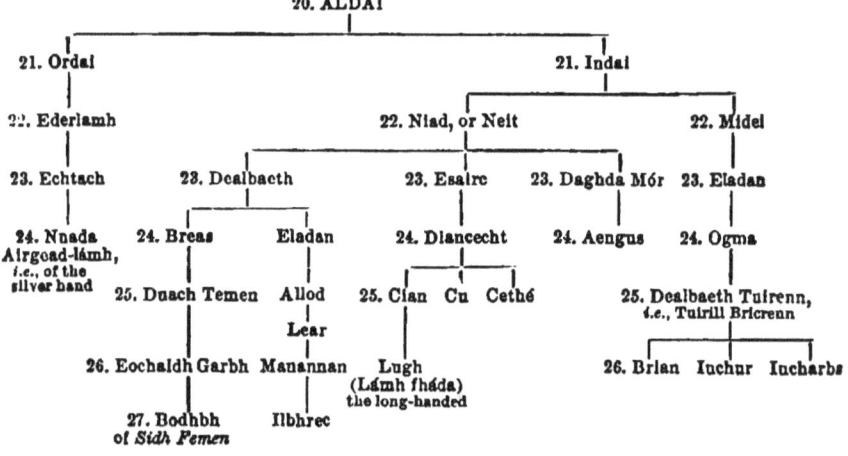

Note.—*Ai* means fire; *al*, great, prodigious: hence *Aldai*. *Ai*, fire, and for *inn*, means *in* or *on*: hence *Indai*, on fire. *Dealb*, shape, form; *ieth*, fire: *dealbaeth*, fire-like; *Dagh*, burning torch, *da* science; burning torch of science; *Ec*, horse: *Ectach*, horse owner; *Eachaidh*, master of horse. Eladan and Dianceacht, Allod (land), Ogma, and Lugh, have been explained. *Il*, all, varied; *Breac*, specked; *Tuirenn (Tur)*, tower shape.

It is compiled from the various versions of the "Book of Invasions," in the "Book of Leinster," and the "Book of Lecain," which has been lately photozincographed; and from the "Book of Ballymote" a codex to be found in the Royal Irish Academy. The table is from the pen of Eugene O'Curry. It is the nearest, perhaps, to historical truth: for, such names as Ogma, and Daghda Mor and Daelbaeth, and Eladan are certainly eponymous; and it must be said, that like the pagan deities their parentage changes according to the character they represent. The author does not present the table as one stamped with the truth of history, but as one which is in harmony with the genealogical narrations of ancient Irish writers.

CHAPTER X.
HAD THE DANANN TRIBES AND PRE-CHRISTIAN GAEL ANY KNOWLEDGE OF LETTERS? WHAT CHARACTER OR ALPHABET DID THEY USE?

Q. 1. Connected with Ireland in the early period of her pagan power, and leaning on the literary life of the Danann dynasty, are there not important questions, which, in periods just passed, have been the subject of much controversy amongst Irish and foreign savants?

A. Yes; there are three which relate, directly or indirectly, to those skilled "sons of science." These are questions which, for centuries past, have engaged the attention, and occupied the thoughts of scholars, native and foreign.

It has been often asked (*a*) were the leading sons and daughters of Eire, in the period of her pagan greatness, acquainted with letters?*
(*b*) If so, what character or alphabet letter—Aryan or Persian Cypriote or Egyptian, Phœnician, European-Keltic, Greek or Latin— did they employ in transmitting a record of events to posterity?
(*c*) Has Ogham writing come to us from pagan times, or was it in the Christian period that it was first introduced?

---

* Letters, as a term, has a two-fold meaning, one conveying the idea of literature taken generally, as: a "man of letters;" the other, special characters or signs of words.

Q. 2. Are antiquarians and Irish historians at one in their views on those interesting questions?

A. Far from it. On the very first of them, " whether the leading sons and daughters of Eire?" in the period of her pagan power, were acquainted with letters or not, there are three opinions.

First (*a*) that in pre-Christian Ireland there was no knowledge of letters; second (*b*) that even in Christian Ireland there was no acquaintance with learning, until the Danes came in their marauding masses to enlighten and civilise by the torch and sword; the third (*c*) that the leading natives of Ireland who flourished in the days of paganism, reaching back to the time when the Danann ruled in the land, possessed a knowledge of letters.

The first opinion was that of Father Bollandus, S.J. (obiit A.D. 1665), and some of his early co-labourers, Fathers Henschinius and Papebroke, who flourished (A.D. 1668) over two centuries ago. The Bollandists of the present day do not hold those views; for modern archæological researches prove that they were quite erroneous. Another Catholic Priest, a native of Scotland, Rev. Thomas Innes, M.A. (A.D. 1662–1744) defended the same opinion. Innes, however, like the Gaels of Scotland then, and even now, had not any knowledge, much less acquaintance, with the numberless manuscript works on ancient Eire and her civilisation that lay in the leading libraries at home in Trinity College, or at Rome in St. Isidore, or in Oxford, or Louvain.

The view put forward in the second opinion, was defended by Dr. Edward Ledwich (1738–1823). It is so strikingly strange and so strongly in opposition to the testimony of authentic records and the glimpses which antiquarians of all creeds and classes present, in unfolding a picture of ancient civilised life in Eire, that this phantasy of Ledwich does not deserve to be named, were it not that he has had, and even still has, followers not a few amongst the scholars and fellows of Trinity College, Dublin. These gentlemen, supposed to be well-informed, and to be men of truth, write for English and Irish periodicals. They quote Ledwich as an authority. Their views are adopted by such popular writers as James Anthony Froude, who, in a late work from his pen, states, with apparent gravity, that, in the eighth and ninth centuries, the Scandinavian invaders came to Scotia or Ireland, and that after them, in the twelfth, "came the Normans to complete the work of civilisation happily commenced by the Danes;" " a remarkable instance," as Sir

Charles Gavan Duffy expresses it, " of unconscious irony." To assert that Mr. Froude wrote seriously, as becomes a historian and a lover of truth, involves the grave charge that he perverted the known truth for party purposes, and thus published to the world untruths against millions of people who never did him any wrong. Authentic facts proclaim trumpet-tongued, that the Danes came to plunder, to slaughter, to burn sacred shrines and seats of science, to lay waste a land which, like Greece of old, was, from the fifth century to the ninth, " the nurse of science and civilisation."

The third opinion is sustained by such scholars and thinkers as Dr. John O'Donovan, Professor O'Curry, Dr. Petrie, Roderick O'Flaherty, Sir James Ware, and, at the present day, by Dr. W. K. Sullivan, and by J. T. Gilbert, author of the *History of the City of Dublin*.

O'Flaherty says, that " from the earliest period a knowledge of letters was to be found in Ireland."

Dr. O'Donovan quoting those words writes :—" In this assertion O'Flaherty is perfectly borne out by the bardic traditional history of pagan Ireland ; for, we read that letters were known not only to the Scotic or Milesian colony, but also to their predecessors the Tuatha Dé Danann."

With a knowledge of letters civilisation is always found. Irish archæology has, for the past half-century, opened up a world of facts, and stamped its discoveries with the seal of certainty.

And as for authorities, such men as Gilbert and Dr. Sullivan in the present, and O'Donovan, O'Curry and Wilde, who have left the field of life's labors, are worth all the writers who for the past eight centuries have written on Ireland's history or Irish antiquities.

Such are the authorities that support the third opinion.

The reasons on which the opinion rests are :—

(*a*) The reality of the Tuatha Dé Danann as a historic people cannot be denied. All the proofs presented, in pointing out their existence in times past, confirm with equally convincing force, that they were a literary and a civilised people, just as the sphericity and two-fold motion of the earth in its orbit is proved, by the fact that the orb of the world is shown to be a planet.

(*b*) The Danann tribes were an Aryan family ; therefore they were civilised, and probably literary, from the earliest dawn of their historic day.

(*c*) Their name *Dana*, arts, is a synonyme for skill and science and literary advancement. They had poets and poetesses ; men skilled in writing like Ogma, in the art of healing like Dianceacht; generals and leaders like Lugh and Daghda, Druids in numbers, and Brehons or judges, and priests.

(*d*) The abundant materials in Ogham writing—*two hundred and sixty books* in stone—at present in Ireland, most of which date from the pagan period, are proof positive that writing, and of course letters were known to the ancient Danann and Milesian colonies in Ireland.

Q. 3. In what character or alphabet letter did the ancient Danann and Milesian Irish transmit a record of public events? Did they make use, at that early period, of Ogham letters simply and solely, or did they employ any other form of letter?

A. The reply must be in accord with the amount of information furnished by antiquarian societies up to the present. And first as to Ogham letters.

There are no direct data or remains from pagan times extant, to show that the natives of Eiré possessed in those days any other alphabet than the Ogham. That they made use of this kind of writing is certain, from the abundant supply of books in stone just referred to, two hundred and sixty inscribed pillars. These have been discovered chiefly in Leinster and Munster, and may be regarded as proofs, to a certain extent, that literary knowledge of a special kind, including that of "letters," was an heir-loom amongst the Keltic tribes of ancient Eiré.

Of other letters, Phenician, Egyptian, or Grecian in form, or European-Keltic, or Latin, the same cannot be said. Neither history, nor archæology, nor monumental remains of any kind, since the days of the Ardrigh Leogaire, and of St. Patrick the Apostle, furnish directly reliable data. Knowledge on this head is gleaned by inference or deduction, which, though exceedingly probable, can never amount to certainty. The Ogham writing is supported, on the other hand, by direct evidence in the inscribed pillar-stones, and by indirect evidence, in the fact that the characters are in accord precisely with the style of writing known eighteen hundred years before the Christian era, at Cyprus, Lycia, Persia, India, and in the Aryan regions to the east of the Oxus and Tigris.

First, the Cypriote characters, of which there are several pages in General Cesnola's able work on *Cyprus, its Cities, Tombs, and Temples* (London : John Murray, Publisher, Albermarle-street), do not differ from the Ogham except in slight particulars. The letters of the one are precisely like the phonetic forms made use of at the present day by shorthand writers; of the other, by telegraphists.

Secondly, in the fifteenth century before the Christian era, the Hebrew people dwelt for a time along the valley that stretches by that mountain on which the two tables of the Law were given to Moses amidst thunder and lightning. During their forty years wandering, they left countless inscriptions on the rocks and ravines around that historic mountain. Hundreds on hundreds of slabs and pillar-stones are to this day found in the Valley of Sinai, bearing written records in a form of letter closely resembling the Cypriote, and partaking largely in its linear forms of the Irish-Ogham character.

Thirdly, Ogham writing bears a resemblance, though in some measure remote, to Sanskrit. Modern Sanskrit furnishes phonetic symbols that consist of a number of short strokes clustered around a stem, to express an idea which, in order to have its significancy put before the eye, requires in other languages several distinct letters. Sanskrit, in this sense, and Ogham are of the same species. The former is a highly developed form of the latter. Ancient Sanskrit partook of the linear and the current hieroglyphic character, not unlike the Sinaitic letters.

Fourthly, the cuneiform characters, arrow-headed letters, expressed the thoughts of the Chaldeans in the days of Abraham; of the Assyrians, when the famous Queen Semiramis ruled that people, and of the Persians, when Assuerus " reigned from India to Ethiopia over one hundred and twenty-seven provinces."

The cuneiform characters, at least in their lineal form, are of the same genus as the horizontal or perpendicular lines efformated in Ogham into letters.

Thus the Ogham, as a species of archaic writing, is just what Sir Henry Rawlinson, or Layard, would have expected to find in a country peopled by immigrants from the far East.

The words of Max Müller on *Freedom*, delivered at Birmingham, in 1879, are very much to the point. He says: " We call our *figures* Arabic, because we received them from the Arabs, but which the Arabs called Indian, because they received them from the Indians. This shows you how this nineteenth century of ours is under the sway of centuries long past and forgotten; how we are what we are, not by ourselves, but by those who came before us, and how the intellectual ground on which we stand is made up of the detritus of thoughts which were first thought, not in these isles, nor in Europe, but on the shores of the Oxus, the Nile, the Euphrates, and the Indus."—Vol. ii. *Selected Essays*. London: Longmans, Green & Co., 1881.

Q. 4. Can it be adopted as true that the pre-Christian Gaels, at least some centuries before the Christian era, made use of any other letter save Ogham or virgular writing?

A. Yes; it is almost certain, but still only an opinion, that they did.

(a) It is well known that linear phonetic symbols were not the only germ from which the earliest written letters or their developed combinations and matured forms arose. There was another main source, the most important of all, from which, in process of time, letters amongst the Aryan as well as the Semitic and Hamitic (or Chamitic) races sprung.

This principal fountain, from which the stream of letters flowed to all the children of men—was hieroglyphic symbols. The Chaldeans had their Hieroglyphics; so had the Egyptians and the Phenicians: three famed races descended from Cham.

Further, these picture-writings were of two kinds; (a) pictures of ideas represented by material creatures—a bull's head, a serpent, a lion, a bird; or (b) phonetic symbols assisting in expressing a word or idea. This latter form was the first crude attempt at letters or characters. In this the Egyptians excelled. The Chaldeans followed with similar improvements. The form adopted by the Egyptian priests, called from them the "*Hieratic*" letter, was taken up by the Phenicians, which they in turn improved, and from it efformated the Phenician alphabet.

That alphabet was the parent, so to speak of the Pelasgian, the Greek, the Etruscan, the Oscan, the Gallic in Europe, and in Asia of the Samaritan or ancient Hebrew, and of the Moabite letter.

"And as by our language we belong to the Aryan stratum" (says Max Müller in his *Lecture on Freedom*, 1879), " we belong, through our letters, to the *Hamitic* (or *Chamitic*). We still write English in hieroglyphics; and in spite of all the vicissitudes through which the ancient hieroglyphics have passed in their journey from Egypt to Phenicia, from Phenicia to Greece, from Greece to Italy (Oscan), and from Italy to Ireland (and England), when we write a capital F, ℱ., when we draw the top line and the smaller line through the middle of the letter, we really draw the two lines of the Cerastes the horned serpent which the ancient Egyptians used for representing the sound of *f*. The Phœnicians, who *borrowed* their letters from the Hieratic Egyptian, wrote the letter ᆛ, the Demotic Egyptian wrote it like the Greek *g* or γ. The Greeks took their letters from the Phœnicians, and wrote Ꮷ. But when they began to write from left to right they turned each letter Ӽ to *K;* so ᒣ, *Vau*, became *F*, the Greek so-called Digamma."

In the same manner the undulating line of our capital ℒ still recalls very strikingly the bent back of the crouching lion which in the later Hieroglyphic inscriptions represents the sound of L.

In our language we are Aryan, in our letters, Egyptian; in the signs I. V. VI. X., &c., on our watches, we are Babylonian.

It is plainly evident then, *à priori*, that as the Pelasgi, and the Oscans and the Kelts of Gaul had letters quite different from the lineary character, so had the Kelts of Eire, who came from the same eastern climes, particularly as the Aryans had both kinds of letter the linear and the other symbols of sound.

From the linear principle was efformated the arrow-headed writing, the Cypriote, the ancient and modern Sanskrit, the Babylonish, the Sinaitic, at least in some of its forms—the Ogham. From phonetic symbols which the priests of Egypt employed, and which again the people of Egypt used, instead of the old Hieroglyphics—were, in process of time, efformated Phœnician and all its kindred alphabets. Modern European penmanship is nothing more, as Max Müller shows, than a higher development and a skilful combination of both those primitive modes of conveying thought by written signs.

In bringing this reply to a close, let us come to Ireland of the first century of the Christian era, or some centuries previous. The Kelts of Eire had compiled a great body of laws; they had huge commentaries written regarding these laws. Not only had they books on law, but manuscripts on other subjects of science and art (*See* O'Curry's *Lectures* and his *MS. Materials*). In the opinion of the writer these works could not have been compiled in Ogham. Therefore the Kelts of Ireland must have had a form of letter like the Phœnician, the Oscan, the Etruscan, or the Gallic.

It is well-known amongst those who study and practise limning, that the art of illuminating manuscripts was carried to a high degree of perfection even before the coming of St. Patrick to Ireland. The style of art known as Keltic was peculiar to the Irish.

Having had a knowledge of it in pre-Christian times, it follows clearly, that, to practise it as they did, they must have written characters quite different from Ogham.

On this point Lady Wilde writes in an essay from her pen on the art of illuminating : " The art, as practised in Ireland, was *toto cœlo* different from the Roman. The earliest manuscripts of Greece and Rome show nothing like this distinctive Keltic art. . . . . Hence she asks, " From whence did the Irish, the acknowledged founders of Keltic art in Europe derive their ideas of ornamentation ? . . . One must travel a far way, even to the far East, before finding in the decorations of the *Hindu Temples anything approaching to the typical idea that runs through all Irish ornamentation.*"

The words of Thomas Moore on this point are very remarkable, and they aptly accord with all that has been here stated on plain lines of thought, regarding the characters made use of by the learned in Eiré anterior to the Christian period.

" It is thought," says Moore, " that the Gauls, who in the time of Cæsar made use of the Greek letters, derived from the colony of Marseilles, had possessed *originally an alphabet of their own which was then forgotten* or superseded by that of the Greeks, and that a similar fate seems to have attended the ancient alphabet of the Irish, for the letters adopted by them from St. Patrick, though differing in number, order, and power from the Roman, bear a resemblance to them in shape. St. Patrick, though unable to persuade the Irish to adopt the additional seven letters or to depart from the order, (beith, luis, nion, *b, l, n*), prevailed in inducing them to adopt the Roman character, which not long after they taught the Saxons and the Germans."— *History of Ireland*, vol. i. c. 4.

O'Curry is of opinion that it is impossible to know for certain *the nature of the writing* in which the records were kept, and history, poetry, and literature preserved among the Gaels of Eiré in the ages which preceded the coming of St. Patrick.

" Enough, however, remains to show that the pre-Christian Gaels possessed and practised a system of writing and keeping records quite different from, and independent of, both the Greek and the Roman form and characters, which gained currency in the country after the introduction of Christianity in the first part of the fifth century."—Appendix ii. p. 463 *MS. Materials.*

Thus the views which have been evolved by the process of reasoning presented above, are identical in their outcome with those which O'Curry, reasoning on the subject from the manuscript remains of the past, entertained.

TURLOUGH ROUND TOWER.
CO. MAYO.

CHAPTER XI.

OGHAM—WHAT IT WAS; MATERIAL FOR WRITING; ORIGIN OF THIS SECRET ART,—PROOFS OF PAGAN PARENTAGE, CHRISTIAN OGHAM INSCRIPTIONS, THE LETTERS, GENERAL CHARACTER OF THE DANANN RACE.

Q. 1. What does Ogham, or Ogma, mean, and why was that primitive style of writing, so called?

A. Derivation—The term appears to be composed of the Keltic roots *ogh*, and *ma*; *ogh* signifies young, primitive, hidden, pure, and in a secondary sense, virginal. The term *Oigh*, which is in use to this day, means virgin, one who has been unknown to mankind, and who represents primitive purity.

Ma, in the Aryan language, signifies to fashion, to frame, as a verb; as a noun, constructive power. In Irish it has the meaning of intelligent cause. This "*ma*" is found in *man*, *men*, Sanskrit, to think; in *man*, *men*, English, a thinking creature; in *math*, Greek, the root of *matheo* (μαθεω) I learn; in *méin*, Irish for mind or disposition; and in the Latin, *mens* and *memini*, for *menimi*, I remember.

Another opinion has it (see "Book of Ballymote," folio 167), that the term has been adopted by the old Irish chroniclers from Ogma, the Eponymous representative of poetry, of learning and knowledge generally, amongst the Danann tribes. Ogma did not invent the alphabet, but he made learning, such as it was then, the object of his special care.

Ogma, amongst the Danann races, is described as the son of "Ealadhan"—that is, "Science." Amongst the Keltic Gauls, Ogmius is named by Lucian, in his dialogues, as the god of eloquence. He was to the Gaullish tribes what Hermes was amongst the Greeks, the patron god of science, elocution, and language generally. By reason of his wisdom, he was regarded also as a universal conqueror, and therefore a kind of Hercules. He is represented as drawing men by golden chords, extending from his mouth to the ears of his hearers.

H

Lucian states that Ogmius acquired the name and character of conqueror, and was deemed brave, rather on account of his persuasive powers, than his physical prowess.

A third opinion—The term Ogma, according to Zeuss, comes from, or is kindred in meaning to, *Oidheam* (*dh* for *gh*), a tract or tablet of instruction. This may be so. The present writer, however, prefers the derivation presented in the foregoing, and is of opinion that oιoé (Irish) a professor, a teacher, not unlike οῖδε (Greek), he knows, is of the same family of words as *Oidheam* (Keltic), a tablet, while *Ogma*, as has been shown, is quite different.

Object of Ogham Writing.

As to the object of this species of writing, it was certainly secret or occult, and, by means of it, the Druids or pagan priests, and the Ollamhs, like the pagan priests amongst the Egyptians, kept secret from the uninitiated certain hidden knowledge which they pretended to possess. "It appears," says O'Curry (p. 469, Appendix ii, *Manuscript Materials*), "from all we know that the Ogham writing had often, if not at all times, a secret and complicated character, and that it required a special education to read and understand it."

An inspection of the pages of the manuscripts, known as the *Book of Ballymote, Book of Lecan, Book of Leinster, Leabhar na h-Uidhré*, shows that Ogham was secret, and that it has come down the stream of time from the earliest period.

The Irish Druids had, like their brethren in Babylon, Ninivch and Egypt, two special forms of writing, the secret and the public, or common letter: the former has been styled the Hieratic, that known to the pagan priests;—ιἑρευς;—the other Demotic, because it was taught to the people (Δημος *demos*).

The Secret Character of Ogham Writing shewn.

The following story is taken from the Book of Leinster, fol. 206. It illustrates the secret character of this species of writing, and the use made of it even in matters affecting social or political life.

Core, son of Lughaidh, king of Munster, was driven into exile by his father, about A.D. 400. Forced to fly to the court of *Feradach*, king of Scotland, he and his attendants hid in a grove near the court, and there they were soon discovered and recognised by

Gruibné, the king's poet, who had known Corc at his father's court in Munster. The poet addressed the prince, and learned his history, and while examining his shield, detected an Ogham inscription on it. " Who was it," said the poet to the prince, " that befriended you with the Ogham which is on your shield? It was not good luck he designed for you." " What does it contain ?" said the prince. " It is this," said the poet: " that if you arrive in the day-time at the court of *Feradach*, your head should be cut off before evening; and if at night-time, that your head should be cut off before morning."

Conclusions to be drawn from the foregoing—From this record it is seen that Ogham writing was inscribed (*a*) on a shield; that it was made use of in (*b*) matters of the highest moment: that (*c*) a knowledge of those letters had not been acquired even by a prince; and (*d*) that writing of this character—considering the conservative habits of the Kelts—was practised in the days anterior to the introduction of Christianity into Erin.

Q. 2. What writing material was made use of by the natives of Ireland in recording events in Ogham character ?

A. (*a*) Stone, in the most ancient times; next (*b*) wood ; (*c*) lead; (*d*) brass; (*e*) prepared skins; at a later period, (*f*) linen; and some centuries before the time of Christ, (*g*) parchment.

STONE:

Of stone pillars, engraved with Ogham characters, there have been, within the past century, from two hundred and fifty to three hundred discovered.

To write on stone was not a custom special to natives of Eire, anterior to the coming of Christ, especially in the far off period, a thousand or two thousand years before the Christian era.

In all the countries of the East, the most ancient practice was to carve records on stone.

The descendants of Seth, as Josephus testifies (*Antiquities* 1-3), wrote their astronomical discoveries on two pillars, one of stone, to withstand the water; the other of brick, to resist the force of fire.

THE MOABITE STONE.

Within the past eighteen years, namely, in the spring of 1870, at Dibon, a town in the land of Moab, east of the Dead Sea, a most wonderful discovery of one of this class of inscribed stones, carved, say, a thousand years before the Christian era, has been made, in bringing to light that which is now known as the Moabite stone. Similar discoveries, but not all of equal importance, have been made in the Valley of Sinai, where, for a time, after crossing the Red Sea, the emancipated children of Israel dwelt. The conquest of a race, and the destruction of numerous cities which once flourished in the lands of Moab and Ammon, are found recorded on this slab of basalt, four feet, less two inches, long; two feet deep; and two wide.

And similarly regarding Ogham writing, O'Curry states (Appendix to *MS. Materials*, p. 464), "that it has been employed to record historical events, and even sustained historical or romantic tales." Short histories have been recorded by such archaic but enduring means.

The form of letter on the Moabite stone is not, it is true, the secret kind, either linear or hieroglyphic, it is the current character known and practised at that period, nigh ten centuries before the coming of Christ. It was the same in form as that employed by the Phœnicians, the Moabites, and the peoples of Western Asia generally; yes, it was the character in which the Hebrew people wrote, and in which the Bible and the tables of the law were bequeathed to mankind. Those letters, or characters like them in form, introduced to Europe in those for off times, became known as the Greek, the Gallic, the Keltic, and the Roman characters.*

LETTERS OF THE MODERN HEBREW BIBLE.

* "The alphabetical characters used by the sacred writers were for the books written in Hebrew, at least those written before the Babylonian captivity (sixth century before the Christian era), not the characters found in our present Hebrew Bibles, which are in truth the Chaldaic characters, but such as are now to be found in the Samaritan Pentateuch, and *similar to the old Phœnician character*. It has been commonly supposed, that the characters used in our Hebrew Bibles now were substituted for the others immediately after the captivity, when the Ancient Hebrew ceased to be spoken by the Jews." Most Rev. Dr. Dixon's *Introduction to the Sacred Scriptures*, vol. i., p. 10; Dublin, Duffy, 7, Wellington-quay, 1852.

Another witness : —" It must be borne in mind that the present Hebrew characters are comparatively modern. It is held by the best scholars that the older forms were lost during the captivity, and were replaced by the

Other Discoveries.—There are few things amongst the myriad discoveries made within the past fifty years, more remarkable than the vast amount found in the East of inscribed stones and lettered bricks. What is better still, these Archaic symbols, whether hieroglyphic or demotic, have been at length and at last deciphered, and faithfully interpreted. The halls of the excavated palaces of Nimroud cry out in the public pronouncements of Mr. Layard, that the ancients of Niniveh wrote on stone as well as on tiles and terra cotta. Rooms have been found filled from floor to ceiling with piles of baked bricks, the disentombed archives of the Assyrian empire.

In like manner, the writings on the rock of Behistun, in the western boundary of the ancient kingdom of Media, copied and deciphered by Rawlinson, throw a blaze of reflected light back on the habits and manners of the literary world in the primeval periods of Assyrian antiquity. They form certainly, a convincing proof of the custom amongst Eastern nations of writing on stone.

THE ROSETTA STONE.

The Rosetta stone should not be passed by without some allusion. It has been the key in the hands of scholars in opening the literary treasures contained in arrow-headed and hieroglyphical writings-

---

present ones, which bear a strong resemblance to those found in the incriptions at Palmyra, and were Chaldean in their origin." *The Moabite Stone*, p. 35, by W. Pakenham Walsh, D.D., Dean of Cashel; Dublin, published by George Herbert, Grafton-street, 1878.

" The old Hebrew alphabet is represented by its Moabitic and Phoenician correlatives, but we have nearly the whole Greek alphabet, not only similar to the Phoenician in shape, but almost identical with it."[*Ibid*. p. 35,

" It is interesting to reflect that it was in characters such as these, men wrote their thoughts in the days of Achab and Elijah (Elias). Nay more, as the same system of writing prevailed all over Western Asia, it was in these (the Phoenician not the Modern Hebrew) characters that David wrote his Psalms, Solomon his Proverbs, and Samuel his histories and in letters such as these (the Phoenician and Moabite) the grandest parts of the Old Testament were originally penned." W. Pakenham Walsh, Dean of Cashel.

And Professor Rawlinson in the *Contemp. Review*, 20th August, 1870, writes :—"Further it may be over-bold to go; but a suspicion forces itself upon us, that in the characters of which the photographic traces are before us to-day, we see the forms of the letters in which *five hundred years before*, the Pentateuch itself was penned by Moses."

Rawlinson is right: Moses was trained in all the learning of the Eygptians, who, as well as the Phoenicians made use of the *demotic* letter. The Chaldaic forms did not become known to the Jews, till after their return from captivity.

The story of the early Egyptian kings is read to-day in the ruins of Memphis, Karnac, or Thebes, in the Obelisk on the Thames embankment, in the inscribed slabs of the British Museum, the Crystal Palace, and the Louvre, Paris.

THE PILLAR STONES OF IRELAND.

The two hundred and sixty inscribed pillars discovered within the past century and a-half in Munster and Leinster, do not stand in secret isolation. In the engraved character, and in the fact of making use of pillars to transmit to posterity a record of events, they are of the same family origin as the stone records which have been discovered within the present century in Media, Nineveh, Babylon, and Egypt. The stones of ancient Eiro cry out that the same manners amongst the two races (those in the East and those in the far West), were the real cause from which arose the habit of engraving on stone. The Danann chiefs in Ireland, and Job the Just in Arabia, lived about the same time amongst races of people who, though primitive, were not without skilled rulers, without knowledge and laws. Job cries out in his hour of trial: "Who will grant me that my words may be written? Who will grant me that they may be marked down in a book with an iron pen, and in a plate of lead, or else graven with an instrument in flint stone?"

The pillar stones are then another proof of the Eastern origin of the early Keltic races of Eire. The secret writing inscribed on them is traceable to the same source that gave form to the Cypriote, and the ancient Sanskrit, and the arrow-headed letters of the East.

WOODEN TABLETS.

Wood, and brass, and lead, and tablets of wax and linen came into use at a later date, but inscriptions on stone were still continued.

"As regards the material," says O'Curry, "on which the pre-Christian Gaels wrote, beside stone, we find it mentioned under four different names, *Tamh-lorga Filidh*, that is, memorial tablets of the poets; *stabhala lorga*, table staves; *taibhli filidh*, tables of the poets; and *fleasg fili*, the wand of the poet."—O'Curry, *MS. Materials*, p. 464.

With respect to the name, *Taibhli Filidh*, tablets of the poets, the ancient Gaelic tablet took, I believe, more the form of a fan than of a table, a fan, which when closed, took the shape of a staff (*lorg*), and which, indeed, actually served as such to the poet and the historian.

Conclusion.—Reasoning *a priori*, it is evident that the Danann tribes cultivated the art of writing, especially in Ogham, engraved on wood and stone. But no certain, undoubted fragments, referring especially to the Danann race, have come down to the present, surviving the wreck of the past three thousand years.

"No Ogham inscriptions have, however," says O'Donovan, "been as yet found in any of the monuments ascribed by the Irish writers to the Tuatha De Dananns, excepting the cave at the mound at New Grange, which, exhibits a few Ogham characters, and near them a decided representation of a palm branch and a series of concentric circles."—*Irish Grammar*, p. 38.

Since writing these lines the author of this work has visited New Grange,—which lies near the main road between Navan, Slane, and Drogheda. Having closely inspected the circular Ogham and the writing in form of a palm branch,—he is of opinion that the latter is the same in primitive rudeness of outline with the early written Cypriote character.

Q. 3. Is it not still a subject of controversy, whether or not, Ogham writing has had its origin in pagan or Christian times?

A. That is true. But questions of the highest certainty in history have been called into the region of doubt, by those who do not wish to credit the truth of facts which the finger of the historian points out. On the present subject tomes have been written within the past century.

Regarding the origin of Ogham writing there have been two schools of opinion, one maintaining the pagan theory, the other, the Christian.

The South Munster Society of Antiquarians, whose literary centre is Cork city, contend for the pre-Christian origin of this species of writing. The members of the Royal Irish Academy, especially those of the past fifty years, have, on the contrary, contended that Ogham was derived from the Scandinavians, and that the numerous Ogham inscriptions, which have been and are being at present recorded, belong to the Christian period.

It is a curious coincidence, that advocates for the pre-Christian progress in Ireland go in, not only for the pagan antiquity of Ogham writing, but for a marvellous development of literary life as soon as the sun of Christian knowledge shone over the island. They maintain that the pagan advance in mental activity was, as in Greece at the time when St. Paul preached the Gospel to the Athenians. a natural preparation for the reception of the seed of Christian faith. On the other hand, those who look up to Christianity as the sun of civilisation and literary life, deny that St. Patrick, his fellow-laborers, or successors had any share worth naming in the work of literary development; that it is to the Scandinav'rns the Irish owed their literary knowledge, that from them the Ogham letter first came, and that to the Danes, Irishmen are beholden for the blessings of Christian enlightenment.

The state of the question is fairly put by Dr. Graves in the following words:

"Those who maintain the affirmative, that the ancient Irish, before the Christian era, professed a primitive alphabet (Ogham), appeal to the concurrent authority of the most ancient manuscript histories, according to which an alphabet, called Ogham, was introduced into Ireland by the Tuatha Dé Danann. They refer to the oldest romances which contain frequent allusions to the Ogham, either for the purpose of conveying intelligence, or in sepulchral inscriptions or pillar-stones. Finally, they point to existing monuments of this very kind, presenting inscriptions in the Ogham character, and argue that they must be ascribed to a pagan period.

"Those, on the other hand, who dissent from these views, allege that (a) the legendary accounts of the invention of the Ogham bear all the marks of fiction; and they contend, that the nature of this alphabet, in which the vowels and consonants are separated; (b) furnishes internal evidence of its having been contrived by persons possessing some grammatical knowledge, and being acquainted with alphabets of the ordinary kind; (c) they impugn the authority of romantic tales, by questioning the antiquity of those compositions; (d) lastly, they assert that a considerable number of the existing Ogham monuments are proved by the emblems and inscriptions which they bear, to belong to Christian times."

A THIRD OPINION.

According to the view just presented, there are two opinions on this question, to which the present writer adds a third, namely, that Ogham writing dates from the earliest pagan period, but that it was afterwards practised in Christian times.

In his work on the "Aryan origin of the Gaelic Race and Language," p. 286, the author says:—"It is certain, that in the pre-Christian period, the Druids and the learned Gaels made use of a secret writing called Ogham, of which there were several kinds; and that even in the Christian period, this kind of writing was not, and is not wholly forgotten."

The only historic point that rests in doubt is, whether or not the books compiled by the Druids were written in Aryan letters resembling those used by the Phœnicians, the Greeks, or Latins, or in their own secret characters. On this point also, the writer's views are, that records were written in characters peculiar to each. The Druids wrote in Ogham those works intended for the druidical order, or for private use; while the public records like the "Seancus Mor," were written in a common, well-known, and not secret letter, be it Aryan, or Keltic, or at a latter period—Roman.

The reasons that go to confirm the foregoing view, are (a) The historic statements and archæological analogies presented already to the reader in chapter X., pages 90 to 97. It is evident that the Ogham alphabet came from the East at a primeval period.

(b) The linear form of the letters, their number, their names, their power, their affinity in form with kindred *alphabets* existing at the earliest times in Asia, point to this conclusion as certain. But recent discoveries put the truth beyond all manner of doubt.

(c) Long before the discovery of Ogham pillar-stones, nearly all Irish codices contained the fullest account of this style of writing.

(d) The legendary Irish tales, in which mention is made regarding this secret art, are of themselves by no means a proof of its origin or antiquity; neither does the authority of the tales, even if proved authentic, reach so high as the first century; they do not, therefore, constitute proof sufficient to produce certainty regarding the origin of Ogham. They confirm, however, the truthfulness of other proofs, which clearly point out the pagan origin of this secret writing.

(e) The Ogham monuments, which some antiquarians pronounce from the Christian symbols found on them, to have been engraved in Christian times, are nevertheless pagan, for, in most cases, the Christian symbols have, on inspection, been shown to be the work of a later and a ruder artist.*

AUTHORS WHO UPHOLD THE SECOND OPINION,—THE CHRISTIAN ORIGIN OF OGHAM WRITING.

* Rev. Edward Ledwich, 1738-1823, writes:—" The pretensions of the Irish to an original alphabet have been examined and rejected."

Again—" Irish literature in pagan times is ideal."—*Antiquities of Ireland*, 2nd ed., p. 349.

Edward Ledwich was a Protestant minister, LL.D., F.S.A., of London.

Q. 4. Are there features connected with the inscribed Ogham stones pointing out that they are Druidical, and were therefore Pagan, and not Christian?

A. Yes; it is well known that the Druid priests adored, turning the face to the East. The very name of front, in Irish *oir*, signifies east; the same word *iar* denotes west, and *rear*, the right hand side *deas* signifies south, and left, *tuath*, means north. The Druids facing the east, had the right side, *deas* (dexter), turned to the south, and the left, *tuath*, to the north; while the west, *iar*, was in the rear. The druid *tumuli*, or mounds, open to the east. How is it with the inscribed pillar-stones in Ogham? (*a*) Wherever the Ogham stone is found

---

and Scotland, and member of some of the most distinguished literary societies of Europe; Secretary to the Committee of Antiquities of the Royal Irish Academy. His knowledge was slight; it merely pointed out the pathway which prejudice preferred to tread; his love for truth—*nil*.

Another Irish antiquary, Thomas Wood, M.D., in his "Inquiry concerning the Primitive Inhabitants of Ireland," addressed to the members of the Royal Irish Academy, and published in Cork in 1821, writes:— "The vanity of Irish writers has induced them to affirm that the letters of their present alphabet, which are not probably older than the ninth or tenth century, were used by the bards more than a thousand years before the Christian era; but they are of Phœnician origin."—p. 198.

Rev. Thomas Innes, M.A., a Scotch priest, in his "Critical Essay on the Ancient Inhabitants of the Northern Parts of Britain or Scotland: London, 1712, writes:—"The Irish Ogham alphabet, known as the *Beith-luis-nion*, is nothing else than an invention of some Irish *seanachie*."

AUTHORS WHO SUPPORT THE FIRST OPINION,—THE PAGAN ORIGIN OF OGHAM WRITING.

On the other hand, O'Curry writes:—"The Ogham characters are still to be seen in some of our oldest books, as well as in many stone monuments, the remote antiquity of which cannot, I think, be denied. It is repeatedly spoken of in all our historical books."—*MS. Materials*, p. 464, Appendix ii.

Ogham writing is spoken of as having been employed to record historical events, and sustained historical romantic tales, long before the introduction of the Roman letter.—*Ibid.*

Sir William Wilde's "Catalogue of Antiquities of the Royal Irish Academy," pp. 134-144—"Ogham stones are found built into the walls of castles, they are not coëval with such edifices nor even with the date of the churches,—but were removed from earlier buildings."

O'Flaherty states in his *Ogygia*—"Duald MacFirbis wrote me an account of his being in possession of the Ogham tablets, of different forms to the number of one hundred and fifty, and of Craobh Ogham, *i.e.* Ogham characters." "To me," says O'Curry, "it appears that O'Flaherty must have mistaken MacFirbis, and that instead of

in situ, the inscribed face is surely turned towards the east, or north-east. If there are two lines, the first is found on the north-east and the other towards the south-east angle of the stone. If only one line of inscription is found, it fronts the eastern angle.

It must be borne in mind, that the inscription commences at the base, and is continued along the corner of the stone to the top, and over the top, at times running down along the opposite angle.

(*b*) If the stone has been moved from its vertical position, and placed horizontally, with the base towards the left hand, it then represents a page of a modern book, on which one can read the inscription from left to right, but with this difference, that the lines commence *below* and continue upwards, while the inscribed record is being read.

(*c*) The word *San*, sacred; and *leac*, or *lec*, or *liag*, a flag, is omitted: The first word of the Scripture is usually found, not in the nominative, but in the genitive case.

(*d*) The letter *p* has been found in the oldest Irish manuscripts, but there was a time in which it was not employed, *b* was made use of instead. It is curious, that in all the Ogham inscriptions, the letter has not been found, thus showing that those inscriptions were made, speaking generally, at a period anterior to the introduction of that letter.

These proofs from internal evidence are very strong and convincing—pointing to the pagan period.*

---

tablets, he ought to have understood him as meaning *alphabets*, such as are preserved in the " Book of Ballymote."

Roderick O'Flaherty (1629-1718), writes:—" Danannæ literis . . . apprime exculti tradunt *Ogygia*." And, quoting Sir James Ware's "Antiquities," chap. ii. :—" Præter characteres vulgares utebantur etiam veteres Hiberni variis occultis scribendi formulis, seu artificiis Ogum dictis, quibus secreta sua scribebant."—*Ogygia*, ed. 1685, p. 223.

Besides the common characters, the ancient Irish used various occult or artificial methods of writing called Ogham, in which they wrote their secret and mysterious affairs.

"I have," says Ware, "an old book filled with them." The letters themselves were anciently called *feadha*, *i.e.*, *woods*.

In the " Book of Ballymote " MS.:—" What is the place, and time, and person, and cause of the Ogham? The place of it, Hibernia Insula quam nos Scoti habitamus; in the time of Bres, son of Elathan; its person, Ogma, brother of Bres," &c., fol. 167 *b.*, b., to be seen at the Royal Irish Academy, Dublin.

* Baring-Gould, author of "*Origin and Development of Religious Belief*," and of " Lives of the Saints," in 12 vols., expresses his views on pre-Christian crosses in these words: " The Phallic origin attributed to the cross is destitute of evidence. I have conscientiously examined the question. If I saw that there was sufficient evidence to substantiate the

It is true, that Christian monuments in Ogham are found. Wherever one meets a monument of this class, two distinctive features connected with its Christian character attract the attention of the antiquarian: first, the cross is elaborately ornamented, and not cut rudely, or hastily scratched as in Christianised Ogham monuments; and the literary inscription commences with the words *oroit for;* or,—*oroit, for anam, etc.*, a prayer for the soul of, etc. The term *oroit* is equally written thus: $\overline{or,}$—"or," with a stroke over the two letters, the contracted form found in MSS., and on pillar stones. Finally, it is worth observing that the Ogham inscribed stones, are freestone, sandstone, claystone, limestone, or granite.

If all the inscriptions discovered up to the present were collected in one book, there would be thus obtained about from five hundred to six hundred lines of pre-Christian writing. For purposes of philology and antiquarian research, this amount would be considerable. One must bear in mind, that all Irish pagan literature had been almost entirely destroyed by St. Patrick and his committee of nine, who were appointed to revise the laws and writings of the pre-Christian Irish.

For the past half century, very little practical benefit has been obtained from this field of antiquarian research. The learning and energy of Irish *savants* have been wasted on partisan views, and the main question of the utility of these discoveries allowed to be in abeyance.

Q. 5. Explain the forms of the Ogham letters.

The best way to do so, is to present the letters engraved to the eye in the following paradigm:—

---

theory, I would adopt it without hesitation. An article on Sun-worship in a certain periodical, *assumes* the identity of the cross with the phallus. The assertions are bold and reckless, and not supported by evidence,"

. . . . . .

The speculations of the learned on the signification of the Egyptian Hieroglyphics previous to the discoveries of Champollion, are devoid of weight. The "crux ansata," that is, the cross and the circle it is said, was the sign of Venus, or Sensual Love and it is still the astronomical symbol of the planet which bears her name. Now, the *crux ansata* was not exclusively the symbol of Astarte; it was a sign of divinity simply, and was placed near every god to indicate him as being divine. It appears beside Baal as well as Astarte.

Neither can it be stated that the Indian cross is of the character alluded to.

The Indian cross is entirely and radically distinct from any form of phallic worship.

Appendix C, to Myths of the middle ages. S. Baring-Gould. Rivingtons, Waterloo-place, London. 1877.

Beth-Luis-Nion, Name special to the Ogham Alphabet						Bobel-Loth, Name of the Common Alphabet
Order	Figure	Power or Phonetic Value	Conventional Name amongst the Ancient Irish	English meaning of these Names		The second, or common Alphabet amongst the Ancient Irish; Keltic, or Old Roman, known as the Irish letter
20		i	Iohadh	Yew		1 1
19		e	Eabhadh	Aspen		e e
18		u	Ur	Heath		u u
17		o	Onn	Furze		o o
16		a	Ailm	Fir		⊿ ⊿
15						
		r	Ruis	Alder		ʀ ʀ
14						
		st, ts z	Straif	Sloe-tree		sc
13						
		ng	Ngedal	Reed		ꞑ ꝼ
12						
11		g	Gort	Ivy		ꝼ ꝼ
		m	Muin	Vine		m m
10		q	Queirt	Apple Tree		
9		c	Coll	Hazel		c c
8		t	Tinne	..		c c
7		d	Dair	Oak		ꝺ ꝺ
6		h	Huath	Hawthorn		h h
5		n	Nion	Ash ·		n n
4		s	Sail	Willow		s ꞃ
3		f	Fearn	Alder		f f
2		l	Luis	Mountain Ash		l l
1		b	Beith	Birch		b b

From this line of letters it is seen, that commencing below, or so to speak at the root, one stroke to the right represents *b*, two, *l*; three, *f*; four, *s*; five, n. Again, one stroke to the left, drawn perpendicular to the directing line, is *h*; two to the left, *d*; three *t*; four, *c*; five, *q*. Next, the strokes cross the line at an acute angle, and one of these constitutes *m*; two, *g*; three, *ng*; four, *st*, *ts*, *z*; five, *r*. Lastly, the lines are drawn across at right angles, one such stroke is *a*; two, *o*; three, *u*, the broad vowels; and *e*, *i*, slender vowels, are told off with four cross lines for *e*, and five for *i*. Thus by a series of five short strokes (*a*) to the right, and (*b*) left, at (*c*) an angle, and perpendicularly across the line, twenty alphabet letters are at once formed. The mode is very simple, and very like the process adopted on the invention of telegraphy in this country. There are four series of groups of short strokes springing like branches from a tree from one main linear stem. In these twenty, there are two double letters, and one (*q*), which has been rarely, if at all employed.

To this primitive alphabet, the following were added to represent the sounds of *p*, and of the five dipthongs :—

26	⎸	p	Peth-boc	soft B, or secondary B
25	▦	ᴀo	amhan-choll	river-hazel
24	♯	10	Ifin	gooseberry
23	⊃	u1	Uilleann	woodbine
22	⊂⊃	o1	Oir	spindle-tree
21	><	eᴀ	Eabhadh	aspen

In the order of letters, *b* holds the first place, *l* the second, *f* the third, or rather *n*, according to the manuscript authority of the Books of Ballymote and Lecan. B, L, N, were regarded as the three letters which held the leading place, and therefore, the Oghams alphabet was called beıch-Luıɼ-nıon.

Irish grammarians followed, generally speaking, the views of O'Flaherty, and have applied the term *Beath-luis-nion* to Irish alphabets without distinction; but, it is right to say, that the term is special, and denotes the Ogham alphabet, according to the highest authorities, namely, the "Book of Ballymote," and Book of Lecan," to which may be added the authority of Dr. O'Donovan.

Bobel-loth and subsequently the Roman alphabet.

As has been already shown, the Kelts of Ancient Eire were, like the Egyptians and Phœnicians, the Assyrians and Persians, in possession of a second alphabet, which was in use among persons of learning generally, and not employed for hidden or secret science. This second alphabet was called, from the names of its leading letters, *Bobel-loth.* It consists simply of the letters in old Keltic, Gaelic or Phœnician ; or, after the coming of St. Patrick, Roman—

b, l, f, r, n, h, o, t, c, q, m, s, ng, rc, p, a, o, u, e, i.

The letter *p** is not found in the " Book of Ballymote."—O'Donovan. p. 31, *Book of Ballymote*, fol. 167, R.I.A.

After the time of St. Patrick the order of the old alphabet was changed from *b, l, f,* to *a, b, c*—the number of letters however (17) is retained to this day.

Q. 6. Name a few of the unpublished Manuscripts written in Irish Gaelic that contain records regarding the De Dannan tribes.

A. There are, as has been stated, in the Royal Irish Academy alone, sixty-four tracts in MSS. relating to this wonderful people (1) A list of the Danann Kings. (2) A poem by Bochy O'Flynn, who died 984, on their history. O'Curry quotes largely in his " Manners and Customs of the Ancient Irish," from the writings of this remarkable poet. (3) An account of the Conquest of Ireland by the Danann race—Book of Lecan, fol. 278. (4) Four other tracts in the same book on the Danann people, fol. 280 *a a*, line 40. (5) An account of their battles. (6) An account of the Invasion of Ireland by the Tuatha De Danann. (7) An account of their arrival in Ireland. (8) A poem on the Tuatha de Danann in the Book of Ballymote, fol. 18, *a a.*, line 45. (9) Another poem by Eochy O'Flynn. (10) A poem on their Kings by Tanaidh O'Maolconaire. (11) Another poem by Flann Mainistreach, who in the eleventh century was chief professor of the school of St. Buite at Monasterboice. He died in A.D. 1056. He it styled by the Four Masters " Chief Professor of St. Bute's Monastery," and declared to

---

* According to the authority of the late William Williams, of Dungarvan, who deciphered most of the Ogham inscriptions, the equivalents of q, ng, or st, p, have not been found on ancient Ogham inscriptions.

have been the wise teacher of the Gaedhals in literature, history, philosophy, and poetry. Flann's poems are in the Book of Leinster. (12) A poem on the deaths of the principal Danann men and women, Book of Lecan, fol. 281. (13) A short history of the kings, chieftains, poets, artists, and remarkable women of the Tuatha De Danann, Book of Lecan, fol. 27, *b. a.*, line 30. (14) In same book (MS.) a genealogical account of their chiefs and principal women. (15) Different opinions on their origin and their history, Book of Lecan, fol. 183. (16) A poem on the Tuatha De Danann Kings of Ireland, by Giolla Caoimhghin, the most celebrated poet and historian in Ireland during the eleventh century A.D. 1072. (17) The names and the reigns of the kings. (18) The Tuatha De Danann—lovers of music, Book of Lecan, fol. 247. (19) Poems by Maolmuire of Fathan. Obiit A.D. 884, *b. b.*, line 17. The other poems and prose narrations regard all that the Tuatha De Danann did during the time they ruled Ireland, what they knew, what they achieved, what they taught, how eventually they were conquered by another race known as the Milesian.

"The pre-Christian period of Irish history presents difficulties from which," says a certain writer, "the corresponding period in the histories of other countries is free. The surrounding nations escape the difficulty by having nothing to record. The Irish historian is immersed in perplexity, on account of the mass of material ready to his hand. The early British have lost utterly all record of those centuries before which the Irish historian stands with dismay and hesitation, not through deficiency of materials, but through their excess."

CHAPTER XII.

FABLE AND FACT : MYTHOLOGY REDUCED TO A SYSTEM : THREE VIEWS : THE DANANN AN INTELLIGENT PAGAN PEOPLE : THEIR FORM OF GOVERNMENT : CLAN SYSTEM : KINGS : LAWS : RELIGION : DRUIDISM : SOCIAL HABITS, MUSIC THE "CAOIN": MARRIAGE : ARTS : PUBLIC GATHERINGS : DWELLINGS : HOW THEY LIVED.

Q. 1. In order to sift fable from fact, how is a writer to act in penning that which appears reliable and trustworthy in the history of those remote pre-Christian times ?

A. A writer must exercise a large share of critical judgment in collating records that are in part mythical, or, that relate to eponymous personages. (*a*) He must weigh well the views of other writers of the present and of the past—intelligent scholars and men of acknowledged ability, in unveiling the mythical figures which antiquity has handed down to the present generation. (*b*) He must not confine those views to the laws and customs of any one race, but look to the habits and manners of several races, and see what is common to all countries, and what is special to each, separating according to the laws of aesthetic criticism eponymous from individual character. Let us borrow an illustration from astronomy. With a powerful telescope and a good focus-glass an astronomer sees a group of stars where, to the unaided eye of the ordinary observer, only one star appears ; in a similar way a critical writer must, by enlarged views, endeavour to eliminate the mythical and eponymous from the individual character as far as can be done.

Q. 2. Alluding to mythology—what is the latest interpretation of those myths and legends recorded in the early history of almost every ancient people ?

A. Amongst the nations of mankind, it is true that a number of legends and mythic stories is found, in substance the same—though

I

varying in form, in character, in place and time—colored according to the genius of each distinctive people, to suit the prevailing views and the circumstances of the age and race.

All Myths and ancient legends may be reduced to one or the other of two principles on which, in the opinion of eminent scholars, they rest for any degree of value which furnish them with form or attractive grace.

THE WORLD'S LEGENDS AND MYTHS REDUCED TO A SYSTEM, AND EXPLAINED NATURALLY.

First View.

The first view is that proposed by the Right Honorable William E. Gladstone and his school. Its foundations are Revelation and Science.

He maintains that under corrupted forms, mythology—that of the Greeks for instance—"presents the old Theistic and Messianic traditions, that its course was from light to darkness, from purity to uncleanness. Its starting point was the idea of a Being infinite in power and in intelligence, and though perfectly good, yet good by an unchangeable internal determination of character and not by the constraint of an external law."

Second View.

The second is given by Rev. G. W. Cox, M.A. It rests on nature but does not exclude revelation. (See Mythology of the Aryan Nations, Vol. I.) "Of one fact, the importance of which can scarcely," he says, "be exaggerated, I venture to claim the discovery;—that the Epic poems of the Aryan nations are simply different versions of one and the same story, and that the story has its origin in the phenomena of the natural world, and the course of the day and year. . . . . .

"The Mythology of the Vedic and Homeric poets contains the germs of almost all the stories of Teutonic, Scandinavian, and Keltic folk-lore. This common stock of materials which supplements the evidence of language for the ultimate affinity of all the Aryan nations has been moulded into an infinite variety of shapes by the story tellers of the Greeks and Latins, of Persians, of Englishmen and Irishmen, of the ancient and modern Hindûs, of Germans, Norwegians, of Icelanders and Danes, Frenchmen and Spaniards. On this common foundation the Epic poets of those scattered and long-separated children of one primitive family have raised either their magnificent fabrics or their cumbrous structures.

" Momentous as this may be, it is one involved strictly in the facts registered by all comparative mythologists."

This view is supported by Grimm, Max Müller, and the German school of philologists and antiquarians, and in England by H. H. Wilson, Lewis, Grote, and Thirlwall.

THIRD VIEW.—THE AUTHOR'S OWN.

In the opinion of the Author who writes these lines, the objective character of pagan mythology arose from both these causes combined. Man lost sight of the Creator and deified the creature. This is St. Paul's explanation : " The invisible things of God, his wisdom, power, providence, and Divine nature, which are clearly seen from the works of creation that surround us," they did not see, but took without reasoning, influenced by passion or fancy the things created for the Creator. " They changed the glory of the incorruptible God into the likeness of the image of a corruptible man, and of birds, and of four-footed beasts, and of creeping things." (Ep. to the Romans, c. i. v. 21.)

Man had thus fallen from light to darkness ; and in this dimmed and untutored state he was unable to comprehend either abstract notions, or spiritual embodiments of power, except under concrete forms. Consequently the pagan world personified, according to Rev. Mr. Cox's theory, the powers of the sun and moon, of morning and evening, of day and night, of summer and winter, spring-time and autumn, of sunshine and storm, of light and darkness, and they peopled with beings created by fancy, land and sea, mountain and vale, fountain, stream, and lake,—the far-off stars that dash through space, or the shells that rest in the caverns of the blue deep.

The next process was to deify these fancied creatures—" to attribute the glory of the incorruptible God to the fancied image of corruptible man,—or of birds or of beasts, or creeping things."

At times pagan notions endowed the living hero, or monarch, with the fancied powers of a favorite god. The people attributed to beneficent kings, the qualities which supernatural beings should possess. In this way demi-gods, that is human beings with supposed divine qualities, were introduced into the pages of history.

Q. 3. Can the pre-eminence of the Danann races in Knowledge be accounted for on the principle propounded by Mr. Gladstone?

A. Certainly: Taking it as true that the Danann is that race of Kelts who flourished in Eire some seventeen hundred to eighteen hundred years before the coming of Christ, they were nearer than the Milesian race to the period of revealed light, and of superior natural knowledge. As ages rolled on, men as a body, had no intellectual exercise such as meditating on the invisible and supernatural world had supplied. They became less given to abstract thought, or to the exercise of mind, and in consequence they grew gross in their views, and mentally less active. If men of this class showed any knowledge of the mixed sciences, such as architecture, navigation, medicine, music, it was at best, empirical and merely imitative, copying what had been handed down from their forefathers, but never adding to, or improving their original stock of knowledge.*

Q. 4. Be those races called by the name Danann or any other,—please give some authoritative testimony that they could have been in Ireland eighteen centuries before the Christian period?

A. Geology, as far as it is a science, shows plainly that the world was, as Moses writes, created in long ages past,—" in the beginning ;"—that is, millions of years ago; so, too, the science of

---

* " The pillars of Persepolis still standing ; the remains of Ecbatana-the grand palaces of Karnac and Luxor, with the ruins of Memnomium near Thebes, the inscriptions found on the pyramids along the Nile, the Tablets of Umbria and Samnium, the excavations that have been made at the plain of Troy and the mound of Hissarlik, prove beyond all doubt, that the people of the very earliest periods had in knowledge of the arts and sciences, been far away superior to those who succeeded them, and to those who came immediately before the time when the sun of Christianity arose, spreading its light on the face of a benighted world."— *Aryan Origin of the Gaelic Race and Language.*

As a matter of fact, the more ancient the period in the pagan times, the greater the learning. Individuals arose in Cyprus, in Asia Minor, in Greece and Rome, superior to their class, such were Cyrus, Pericles, Plato, Archimedes and Cicero. These were men of thought and of great learning, but they had to go back to the ancients of past days to acquire wisdom and to drink from the fountains of early knowledge.

language points out clearly that people from the far East had, thousands of years ago, come to this far West to the "Noble" Island, as they called it, *Eir-i* ("*eir*," or "*ar*," noble, renowned, famous; and "*i*," island). "Languages are to a philologist what strata are to a geologist:" words are his fossils.

LANGUAGE, ARCHITECTURE, VERSIFICATION, LAWS, DRUIDICAL RITES; THE ART OF WRITING; POINT TO THE DANANN RACE.

Adolphe Pictet of Geneva who has written a volume on this subject shows that the Keltic race began to extend to Western Europe about two thousand years before the Christian era; that in their passage westward they found a stream of people sprung from the same blood, but no longer regarding each other as brother tribes.

All Europe—Russia excepted—was at one period, when the Pelasgi lived in Greece, filled with nations of Keltic kith and kin.

Max Müller states positively that the Kelts were, in his opinion, the first to arrive in Europe, and that their coming was about two thousand years before the Christian era. Now the very earliest migrations settled in Ireland. From external authority therefore, it is clear there were tribes or races in this island two thousand years and earlier before the Christian period.

"It is a recognised fact in science," says W. K. Sullivan, President of the Queen's College, Cork, "that from the Indus to the Atlantic Ocean, and thence across the American Continent to the shores of the Pacific, the descendants of the one primitive blue-eyed, fair-haired race divided into several branches,' and speaking dialects of what was once a common language held sway."—*Manners and Custom of the Ancient Irish*, Vol. I.

Q. 5. (a) What form of Government did the Danann tribes enjoy; (b) what form of religion did they profess?

THE CLAN SYSTEM.

A. Their government can best be described as Patriarchal. The family was the earliest standard of social government. Those who lived under one fatherly guide and governor were known as a "*clan*." The word "clan" in Gaelic signifies children or family, and the members of a tribe, or of a community, were to the chief what children in a household are to the head of the house. He was to all the members, no matter how numerous, a father or *pater*, styled in Latin "*Pater familias,*" father of the household, not family alone, but a father to all the children, servants, and clients; his ἀρχη or government, *patriarchal* like that of Job in Arabia, or Abraham in the Land of Promise. "The clan system," says Professor Blackie, "was simply a type of social Organism in which the members of society were bound together as brother to brother, under the leadership of a common father . . . . . . It was not only, not a bad system, but in respect to the moral cement which held the different classes of society together, it was the best possible system that ever has been or ever will be devised. . . . As a matter of public history and of personal experience, did this bond exist and assert itself under the clan system, by deeds of devotion and fidelity, generosity and self-sacrifice, so that as far as the true cement of the social edifice is concerned, the clan system, within its own limits, was the best possible. One defect it had; it had a tendency to weaken as the circle of its action widened, and was thus not fitted for a great kingdom. But to the clan-chief, the idea of dissociating the land from the people who lived on it, was as strange, as to a father would be the idea of disinheriting his children. The spirit of the family system taught, that the members had a right to be supported by the head of the family (*clan*) or, at all events, to be allowed to support themselves by honest labor on the part of the family inheritance. Those who are now called tenants or crofters, were then in a sense, co-proprietors."— *Inaugural Address as Chief of the Gaelic Society of Perth.*

The government then of the Danann was, tribal or patriarchal, such as the "clan" system is known to have been. The "clan" gradually grew to a tribe; and an aggregate of tribes formed a nation, and finally a number of minor nationalities constituted a kingdom under one supreme ruler,—*righ* = high man = as "Ab-'ram'" was called, "high-father." The KING-IN-CHIEF, was styled *Ard Righ*. Each *clan* had its special ruler, or *Righ* (King), whilst the chief ruler,* Ard-Righ, was king of all.

---

* "*Ri*, or *righ, ro, ra,*" in Irish and Sanskrit, mean high, elevated, chief in position or dignity, and the converse of this form, *ar*, and "*or*" and *ir* has the meaning of high, elevated, noble, grand. It is found in all the European languages. In the Hebrew, though not of the same family, "*ram*," signifies high. We have in Irish *rath*, a fort; *ard*, high; *or*, rapidity, excess; *re*, moon; *ri*, a king; *ara*, an elevated land; *rath*, increase, luck.

LAWS.

The LAWS by which they were governed were the Aryan customs that had come from the East, and which handed down from age to age eventually formed the nucleus of the BREHON LAW.

As the laws compiled by King Alfred were only collections of ancient customs, so the Brehon code, compiled, or rather expurgated in the fifth century, and published lately, is a digest of customs that were known to exist amongst the Kelts of Eire long before the time that Samuel ruled the people of God, and Saul, or David, or Solomon governed the Israelites. In this way the Brehon law throws a reflex light on the Danann period. It is certain that Seanachaidhs, Druids, poets, Ollamhs, Breitheamana, or judges and Kings, were a standing political or social institution amongst the Danann clans. The laws, therefore, by which they were governed were primitive forms of that Archaic code presented to us in those volumes published within the past ten years by order of the British Government. "Of this code," Sir Henry Sumner Maine says, "that it is an accretion of rules which have clustered round an older nucleus." And again, "The Brehon laws are in no sense a legislative construction. They are an authentic monument of a very ancient group of Aryan institutions; they are a collection of rules which have been gradually developed in a way highly favorable to the preservation of Archaic peculiarities."

These Archaic customs enable one to look back not only to the Danann times, but beyond them till one reaches the Aryan era.

The means adopted to preserve these ancient customs intact were, (a) secret writing or Ogham; (b) tradition conveyed in rhythmical numbers by the poets from one generation to another; and (c) a stern tenacity of purpose peculiar to the Keltic race in clinging to ancestral habits and customs. All legal forms and traditionary rites were clothed in verse. The law-makers of ancient Eire were obliged, as in the days of Job in Arabia, to promulgate their laws in verse.

RELIGION.

The religion of the Danann was pagan. The people did not believe in the One true and only God, who created and who directs all things. Knowledge regarding the true God had been lost. Kings and peoples adored in the open sunlight, and not shut up within temples, the god of day; they erected idols in groves, and they assembled for purificatory purposes around fountains.

THE ANCIENT IRISH DID NOT OFFER HUMAN SACRIFICES.

The manuscript records regarding these times and the Danann race, contain no reference whatever to the offering of human sacrifices. It is the opinion of Dr. O'Donovan and of O'Curry, and of the best living Irish antiquarians that neither the Danann race nor the Belgian, nor the Milesian Kelts offered human sacrifices. Although infidel, they had not sunk to the barbarous level of Asiatic or African pagans.

DRUIDISM.

Druidism did not take its rise in Gaul nor Britain, neither did it originate as an institution in Ireland. We have to travel to the far East to find the source from which it sprung. The Druids in Ireland were kindred in origin and in profession to the Magi in the East. Druidism had been an institution in ancient Eire, not only during the time of the Danann Dynasty, but long before, during the period that the Firbolg ruled, even two hundred years earlier than the coming of the Danann; and anterior to the Belgian era,—when the followers of Nemedh and those of his predecessor had lived in the "farthest island" of the West,—that is, back in the most remote period known in history that can be reached on traditional lines or by philological comparisons. *Draoi*, the Keltic for Druid, is by metathesis for *Diāear* (*i.e.*, god-man, *dia-fhear*.) *Dair, Ir.*, an oak; Gr. δρῦς—is not the root, as is generally supposed, but "Dair," an oak, is most likely called by that name on account of the "*Druid*" having selected it, as one deserving his special care. *Dru*, in Sanskrit, means a tree, and especially the king amongst trees,—the Royal oak.*

Q. 6. Tell us of their social habits and manners, and their knowledge of domestic arts ?

A. Although no rhymes written at that remote period exist, or have been recorded in our oldest manuscript authorities, still it is certain that the laws of that time were transmitted in verse. The people were therefore acquainted with the art of rhyming; and the bards, poets, Brehons and Ollamhs were skilled in versification and in the measured form of rhymthical numbers.

---

* Le chêne semble avoir été désigné ainsi comme l'arbre par excellence et le respect presque religieux dont on l'entourait chez les Celtes surtout, et les Germains, pourrait bien remonter jusqu' aux origines ariennes. *Les Origines Indo-Européennes ou les Aryas primitifs*, p. 214, par Adolphe Pictet.

Music and song came naturally in the wake of poetry, musical instruments were not then unknown.

THE CAOIN OF EASTERN ORIGIN.

The wailing of the Keltic clans over the dead was a wild weird kind of music which has been from age to age handed down even to the present day. The wild wailings are not only sad, and soul-stirring, but they are measured and tuneful, like the melodious lamentations of the prophet Jeremias, or the loud lament of the Hebrews over the dead body of Jacob, or the dirges of the Trojan matrons celebrating the funeral obsequies of Hector. The plaintive cries, heard still in the north of Mayo, are the echo of the funeral wailings described by Moses, or Homer. Even in this social habit, the Irish Kelt preserves a special trait of his Eastern origin.

The Danann possessed a knowledge of colours and of dyeing fabrics, and of painting, to a certain extent.

As a people they were skilled to a fair degree in a knowledge of letters. This has been shown fully in the foregoing chapters.

One proof more, the last that will be presented here, is the following: That the Danann must have had a literature, is shown by the fact that all the Keltic names in C sar's works are in accordance with the spelling of the Danann period.

Marriage, as an institution, was held in honour amongst them; they respected women's rights; nay they bestowed the most honorable position on woman, not only in the family, or tribe, but in the State. Ladies were allowed to study medicine, and to practise as physicians; to write poetry and to contend for the honors awarded to those most skilled in the arts; nay, they were allowed to direct armies, or at least to incite the soldiers to battle, and to assist by counsel and material aid those who were to risk their lives in the field fighting. Witness the names already recorded of the Mōr Righan, the wife of Daghda Mōr, of Tailte, of Etana, of Airmed.

From all that has come down to the present time one can say, that the Danann was skilled in architecture. He erected raths, duns, carns, caiseals, many of which are to be seen in Ireland to this day. They interred their dead in those hills of Cyclopean skill on the banks of the Boyne.

---

* See O'Curry's *Manners and Customs of the Ancient Irish*. Vols. i. and iii.

Cremation, or burning of the dead, was not unknown. Proofs from past times go to show that cremation was practised, but at rare intervals, the prevailing custom had been to bury the dead.

As far as can be gleaned from the Irish records that still remain, the Dananns had no knowledge of sculpture. They chiselled and squared stones for building purposes, but to prove that they practised sculpture no records remain. They did not build house-like graves for the dead, as did the people of ancient Etruria and Cyprus.

A Common Error.

It is certain that it is to the Danann race we owe those magnificent *raths, duns, caiseals* and the like which abound in Ireland, yet the simple peasant people and others who have acquired crude notions of Irish history at school, ascribe these works not to the Danann race but to the Danes. This error has risen from the similarity between the sounds of Danann and Dane; and from the teaching of such men as Ledwich. The Dananns had been wont to build, the Danes to destroy whatever they found built.

Q. 7. Lastly—it is well to know how they lived in public; and how in private life at home.

Public and Periodic Gatherings of the Nation.

A. The place of Carmen in Wexford, and the mounds of Tailltenn and Tara in Meath, the Brugh by the Boyne, with Cruachan, county Roscommon, are monuments that tell of the great social gatherings, which, according to the annals of the Danann period, were held each year in spring, summer, at the close of the harvest time, and at November. These gatherings did not cease fully, up to the twelfth century. On these important occasions games were celebrated, in some measure not unlike the games at Greece of old. The places became the centres of a certain kind of civilization and of national life. As at the Isthmean and Olympic games, so at these, poets recited legends, narrated stories in verse, sang songs, historians read records, brehons promulgated laws; guardians and parents proposed alliances; enmities were set aside; friendships cemented; marriages of State importance contracted and celebrated, and a healthy tone given to the social and commercial life of the whole nation

Houses in the Danann Times.

Sufficient evidence has been shown that the early Kelts were Aryans. Those who at the remotest period came to Ireland knew all that related to domestic comfort and home happiness, as far as the civilised peoples of the East had pursued such social practices.

Evidence quite ample on this point is still accessible, to show that the Dananns built their dwellings of wickerwork and plaster, formed of beaten earth or of mortar. The houses were usually oblong. There were also cylindrical edifices having a cup-shaped roof. There were usually three or more of these edifices clustered together to form a home or dwelling—a house for the men, and a house for the women apart as among the early peoples of Asia Minor, and one for the domestic servants. No evidence, written or monumental, exists to show that the houses contained an upper story. The probability is that they did not. There was an aperture for admitting light and air, and one for the emission of smoke. In that way the dwellings of the people were constructed. As a nation the Danann were skilled in the art of building with stone, and perhaps with mortar, for some traces of cement are to this hour found in the Cyclopean edifices on the banks of the Boyne.

Those authorities who affirm that there was no stone building known to the Kelts of Gaul or of Ireland till they received a knowledge of such buildings from the Romans, should bear in mind that the earliest progenitors of each people came about the same period from the same Aryan land in the far East; and that the old Etrurians who had an established monarchy—patriarchal if you will, centuries before Rome was founded,—were skilled in the art of building with stone, that thus the Kelts of Gaul had learned from them, or the knowledge of the art had come down from their Aryan forefathers. In the oblong habitation there were two doors, one opening to the east, the other to the west; and in this single room the children with the father and mother of the family dwelt. The house was by day a public parlour, where all met, and at times a refectory; a sleeping apartment by night, not unlike some of the country cabins in Ireland at the present time. The household made use of beds of rushes, or straw or heather; the wealthier classes beds of feathers, with sheets of linen and blankets of wool, and coverlets of varied form and diversity of colour.

The house or dwelling of a chief was not unusually built on a *rath*, or elevated ground, with an "*air-lis*" or area in front, and a *lios* (fort) protecting the inner buildings, while a *caiseal*, that is, a strong defence of stone surrounded the houses, the *rath*, the *air-lios*, and the "lios."

MILLS.

From the presence of the *brō*, or handmill, of which frequent mention is made, the women of each household are known to have ground the corn, oats, wheat, barley, rye, of which bread was then made in each house and baked on the hearth, either on flagstones or on frames of wood or iron. The women were like those of the eastern nations, employed at carding wool, spinning, or working at the loom; forming fabrics for family and friends; at dyeing cloth according to the variety of colour prescribed by the Keltic customs, or in attending to the wants of the household, to the care of the sick, perhaps, for many of them were skilled in the healing power of herbs and plants.

ARTS.

The mechanical arts were not neglected by the men, the tilling of the land, making implements of agriculture, as we see in the history of Lugh, who, king as he was, yet, like Peter the Great, made himself acquainted with the mechanical arts. The terms in the Gaelic language for the arts coming down from the period of the Danann power to the present time, are proofs sufficiently convincing of those statements.

CHAPTER XIII.

THE DEFEAT OF THE DANANN DYNASTY BY A COLONY OF KELTS FROM THE SOUTH OF EUROPE : CERTAINTY OF A KELTIC COLONISATION : UNCERTAINTY OF THE RECORD CONTAINED IN IRISH MANUSCRIPTS : HEROIC DEEDS OF MILESIANS RECOUNTED BY THE BARDS.

Q. 1. Was the Danann Dynasty after a continuous sway of one hundred and ninety-seven years defeated by a Colony of Kelts from the south of Europe?

A. Yes: And if no record in Irish-Gaelic were ever penned proclaiming the event, and pointing to it as a grand landmark in the ancient history of the Irish race, the footprints still visible of a conquering people speaking the same language, ruled by the same laws in origin known to have been of the same kith and kin, tell the antiquarian that a colony of Kelts, better trained, better armed, came at one time from the south of Europe, not from Britain or Gaul, landed on this island, and after some fierce fighting obtained complete possession of the land.

(a) The names of places without number on Irish soil, the language which our fathers spoke, and which some Irish natives speak still, the Brehon laws, the record of numberless battles, and of great national events, the names of hundreds of families who pride themselves on their Milesian origin, point to the coming into Ireland of a race of Kelts different entirely from the Tuatha de Danann, from the Firbolg, the Fomorians, and the older Nemedians. A student tolerably trained in the science of ethnology can to this day perceive the marked difference that exists in the facial and cranial outlines between a Milesian and a man of Belgian descent, between a Milesian and the descendants of the Danann.

(b) This leading truth receives additional confirmation from the extensive proofs furnished by Max Müller, by Latham, Prichard, and Adolphe Pictet, and the German school of Savants, namely that about seventeen hundred years before the Christian period, the south of Europe, and especially Spain, Iberia, Helvetia, Italy, Gaul, were peopled by Keltic tribes who, as a race, were always on the move westwards to lands still more remote.

Two leading lines of proof thus mark the coming of a Keltic colony to Inisfail, about the seventeenth century anterior to the Christian period, long before King Priam ruled in Troy.

The proofs which the modern German school supply and those which are furnished by writers on the Aryan origin of the Gaelic race, rest on the truths of comparative philology, topographical names, ancient law, versification, architecture, music, international archaic manners and customs.

Thus, apart altogether from the heap of Irish national records either published or yet in manuscript, which from age to age tell of the coming at one time of the Milesian heroes to Ireland, extensive proofs are at hand to show that a Keltic colony, call it by any name you wish, landed about the seventeenth century, B.C., and gained from the Danann tribes dominion of the island of destiny.

Take this great fact, as the major proposition of the historical syllogism: "It is certain that a Keltic colony from southern Europe landed in Ireland within a fixed period, and gained possession of the island." The minor proposition which is furnished by Irish annals and Irish manuscript history declaring with one voice unbroken for fifteen hundred years, that the special colony who then arrived on Irish soil and who became owners and masters of it, were the children and clan descendants of a brave chief known by the name Galamh (" gá," a javelin, and " lamh," to handle), or Miledh (a soldier), whose name Latinised is known as Milesius, is true in substance but not in form, or in the coloring,—as presented by Irish Antiquarians. Some such colony certainly came.

The chief works in the hands of Irish historians, admitted by all to be authentic, are, *The Annals of the Kingdom of Ireland, The Book of Leinster*, now published; manuscript history contained in *The Book of Ballymote*, and in *The Book of Leacon, The Book of Rights, Leabar na g-ceart*, by the King-Bishop of Cashel ; *The Duan Eireannach*, or poem of Ireland, written in the ninth century by Maolmuire, of Othian, now Fahan in Donegal, and published in 1848, for the Irish Archæological Society by Dr. James Henthorn Todd, Fellow of Trinity College, Dublin, and by the Hon. Algernon Herbert, in the volume containing the Irish version of the History of the Britons by Nennius. A short account in the body of the work by Nennuis. In each of these, and in numberless other poems and prose pieces of a later date, such as that attributed to O'Connell, Bishop of Kerry, 1704, is contained the record of the coming of the sons of Galamh or Milesius from Spain. In the history written in Irish-Gaelic by the Rev. Geoffry Keating (1570-1644) the same event is narrated, and the story of their coming and of the conquest they made is detailed most circumstantially and minutely. Dr. Keating quotes another manuscript history known in his day—but since then lost—the "*Cinn Droma Sneachta.*" This work was compiled in the early part of the fifth century from records of a still earlier date by Ernin, the son of Duach Gallach, and consequently grandson of Brian, King of Hy-Many, in the opening of the fifth century, when the apostle of the Irish came to preach the faith to our pagan ancestors.

Those Milesians were the Normans of that remote period. They were a dashing, spirited race, noble in their bearing, portly in their personal appearance, athletic, well-built, brave, fair in features, and finely framed in figure ; excelling the Danann in physical development, though not his equal in technical or mental culture. The knowledge of the Danann, like the knowledge of the Turks at the present day, or of the pagan priests of ancient Greece and Rome was fixed in a kind of moral groove, beyond which it was not permitted to pass. Naturally, knowledge so confined began to lose its force and effectiveness, and yielded at length to the fresh and active mental and physical vigor of the invading Milesians.

Q. 2. Is the history then of the Milesian colony, as told by Irish annalists, and the invasion and subsequent possession of Eire by them perfectly certain?

A. The invasion by some such Keltic colony is certain. In the question put there are two points which differ as widely one from the other as the poles of a magnet, while they actually aim at confirming the truth of the same subject.

The Milesian colonisation of Ireland is one thing, the record of it by the historians and Keltic bards is another. The colonisation may be true, and is true, while the account of it may be quite untrue. The coming of the Keltic colony to Ireland has been recorded by the native historians and bards in such a fashion, that no reasoning or intelligent student can for a moment credit the narrative; and if no other authority were found to furnish proof, then, few indeed who loved truth before family fame would give heed to the fables of ancient Irish writers regarding the story of the Milesian invasion.

When the writer of these pages was a juvenile collegiate student learning Irish history, he read again and again the account of the Milesian colonisation. He took the trouble of noting all that Dr. Keating has written regarding Fenius Farsa, that he was king of Scythia, that he purposed to found a great school or university on the plains of Shenaar; that at his own expense, he sent young men of mind and courage from the kingdom of Scythia to all the nations then known in Europe, Asia, and Africa; that they returned, every man of them, having acquired much knowledge and experience in foreign lands; that with the aid of these seventy-two sages he founded something like the present Propaganda College established some three centuries ago at Rome; that professors of the principal languages drew up outlines or elementary forms intended for the students of that school; that the leading languages taught there, if one can credit the authority of Kennfaelad, who died A.D. 677, were Hebrew, Greek and Latin. Fenius, King of Scythia, patron and head master of this famous primeval school, was son of Agenor, King of the Phenicians, for he is declared to have been brother of Cadmus and Europa of classic celebrity. Fenius left at his death, Nenual, his eldest son, heir to the throne of Scythia;—but Naul or Nel, his inheritor in knowledge, the established Chancellor of the University at Shenaar.

The account is very interesting, and the story does not lack in interest even when one has heard more of Fenius. For, we are told that the fame of the Chaldean Chancellor at Shenaar reached the ears of Pharaoh, Cingris King of Egypt, and that he was sent for by his Majesty. He came to Memphis to the palace of the Pharaohs, received a warm welcome, became famous as a teacher and a master of knowledge in directing the king; he obtained the hand of Scota, the king's daughter, in marriage, and received as a dowry a territory " *Capa-cirant*," near the Red Sea, the present Matarra; we learn that he had in his new home a son born to him, whom he called Gaodal " glas;" that the child was a contemporary of Moses, and when bitten by a serpent the babe received a complete cure from the hands of the leader of God's people ; that Niul and his numerous clients beheld the Israelites passing the Red Sea, and trained in the way of adversity Niul befriended the Hebrew race as far as lay in his power. Lastly that it is from Fenius is derived the name " Feni," as applied to the cultivated Gaelic speech, and to Military Heroes known in Ireland at the time of Fionn the son of Cumhal in the third century of the Christian period; from Scota, the Irish Nation were at a subsequent period called Scoti, and from Gaodal, Scota's son, the Egyptian prince, the people of Ireland after the Milesian invasion was styled " Gaedail," and the language which they spoke was named Gaedilge.*

---

* The name of the Lady Scota, daughter of Pharao may have been derived, if the root is Aryan, from *Scoth* (Irish-Gaelic), signifying a full-blown flower, just as Latin *Rosa*, Irish *Ros*, a rose, is a name applied to ladies. Her son's name, *Gaedal*, the supposed ancestor of the Gadeleans, and of the " Gael," may well be derived from " *Ga*" (gen. case *Gae*), a javelin, spear, dart, *da*, skilled, *ail*, prodigious, famous, renowned, mighty, or trained. Hence the name " *Gao-da-al*",means one famous for his skill in hurling his lance ; and "Gaels," mean lancers. spearmen. or warriors. The derivation of "Feni" is from " Finn," clear, intelligent, skilled, full of knowledge and capable of communicating it ; Finne, fairness, whiteness, clearness. A kindred term is found in *phain* of the Greek, *phaino*, meaning shining, beaming, bright, showing off, appearing in public. In was in this way the supposed Fenius employed his time. The Phenicians of Homer's time were " publicly known," for their skill not alone in commerce and arts, but in letters. It is no wonder they were called Pheni. *Va*, or *bha*, i.e., *fa*, Sanskrit, means to shine ; *fen*, Latin. clear, pellucid.

All this is very pleasant reading, but an intelligent student will ask the question, are the events narrated true? Boys and girls in the days of early youth believe whatever they see printed in books, and especially in historic manuals. For years the writer of these pages gave credence to all he had read in Dr. Keating's " Forus Feasa." Professors in College gave no opinion regarding Irish history.

Years rolled by. The student of 1848 became professor in 1858. Amongst other duties, the teaching of Irish history was entrusted to his control. In the College of Maynooth he had been trained to think accurately, and to take no statement put forward by historians without good authority.

The whole story succintly told in the foregoing pages regarding Fenius is entirely opposed to the truth as shown by comparative philology, by chronology, geography, facts relating to eponymous heroes of the same social period.

1. OBJECTIONS TO THE STORY REGARDING FENIUS FARSA AND HIS SON

(a) What does the history of languages teach regarding Latin? That it was not a formal language till some three hundred years after the foundation of Rome had been laid.

The early Romans and Sabines spoke, as Professor Newman shows, a mixed form of Keltic, Pelasgic and Etrurian, including under the term Keltic the Oscan and Umbrian elements. That is, Latin was not depurated into a special language until about five hundred years before the Christian era. Now, according to the story of the Shenaar school, at what time did Fenius flourish? Some two thousand four hundred years at least before the coming of Christ. There is then a mistake of nigh two thousand years in assigning Latin to have been one of the three leading languages taught by Niul, son of Fenius and the professors.

(b) The same is true of Greek, which, as a language, and in the root-words from which it has germinated is a younger offshoot of an Aryan stock than Latin.

(c) And with regard to the Hebrew tongue, the old language was written in the Samaritan or Phenician letter, and not in the Chaldaic, which is comparatively modern. (See c. x., supra.)

2. These professors could not therefore have given alphabets of languages that, at the time, had no existence, or, if they did exist, like Hebrew, had no special letter. The language spoken by the descendants of Cham or Ham in Egypt was, and is, as everybody knows,

K

toto coelo different from the Hebrew spoken by the sons of Sem; and of course it had no relation in common with the Aryan dialects. Nevertheless the writer of this story regarding Fenius Farsa and his son Niul, seems to think, that Hebrew, Greek and Latin were from the commencement the three great languages known to the learned of the world, and that Hebrew and Latin did not differ much. He knew nothing of their character, and nothing as we have shown of their origin. This opinion regarding languages prevailed at the time of St. Jerome, and from that time has been handed down in the Irish Catholic Church amongst the Canons Regular who had so many religious foundations in Ireland from the fifth century to the sixteenth. This view leads one to believe that the whole story regarding Fenius Farsa and his son Niul, and the great school at Shenaar was an invention of some Christian romancer. The introduction of Pharaoh and Moses confirms this opinion.

3. But there are other objections: (*a*) from chronology—How comes it that Niul, son of Fenius, fifth in descent from Japhet, was contemporary with Moses, who flourished say 800 years after Japhet? Keating puts this objection, but cannot well solve it. He says the predecessors of Niul on the one side lived each some hundreds of years, as did Abraham, or Seth : but, if the progenitors of Niul were so long-lived, why did not the forefathers of Moses in a climate quite as healthy, live as long as their neighbours? The objection cannot be answered. Again in topography, how was there a town called Athens, close by the Shenaar school?

4. Regarding Fenius as brother of Cadmus and King of Scythia, there are points which a critical writer must discuss. Every respectable scholar of the present day after Henry Nelson Coleridge (see his "*Introduction to the study of Greek Classic Poets*," London, John Murray, 1846) admits that there was no individual known as Cadmus. The name is eponymous. It represents a class of men who introduced a knowledge of literature into Greece. If Cadmus had no existence, he had no brother, and *e converso*, it is untrue to say that Fenius as an individual had some being of the imagination as a brother. The same reasons that show Cadmus to have been an eponymous personage prove Fenius too to have been eponymous, and therefore to have had no personal existence. The real truth is, that he existed only in the mind of the first Irish romancer, although the reality of his life has been believed in by so many thousands, even by men having some acquaintance with scholarship.

Why write so much to disprove a matter so plain? Because even now there are numbers of Irishmen who will follow the story as told by the poets and seanachaidh of the past, by Dr. Keating, and lately by many other writers, just as there are many who believe that Rome was founded by Romulus and Remus, and that they were the twin sons of Mars and Rhea Sylvia.

Lastly, regarding *Scythia* as a country or a kingdom, where was it situated? Anterior to the Pelasgic period Scythia was a name applied to the whole world, excepting Greece, Asia Minor, portions of Europe south of the Danube and of the Alps, and the north of Africa.

In the time of Herodotus, Scythia embraced all Europe to the north of the Danube; all Asia to the north of the Caspian reaching over to China and Bhering's Straits. Such a view of a special kingdom is vague. Writers in the early centuries knew comparatively nothing about geography: Diònysius, Strabo, Pliny, and Ptolocmy, masters of geography in their day, were as ignorant of the earth's surface as the poorest school-boy is at present.

It is only right therefore to conclude from the incorrect chronology, false geography, untruthful system of languages adopted, setting down as current speech languages that were not developed for thousands of years later; that the whole record regarding Fenius Farsa as king of a country called Scythia, or as patron of learning in the Chaldean district of Shenaar, is a fiction, that Fenius is a myth, and his progenitors and descendants are offspring of the imagination.

In like manner the story of Niul, son of the supposed Fenius going to the land watered by the Nile, and marrying Scota, is a pure invention of some seanachaidh who had studied the Pentateuch, and is from two sources of proof, devoid of all foundation. Derivations in harmony with the principles of etymology can be given for *Scoti*, and for *Gaodail, Gaoidelge*; and for the Fenian language and Militia.*

---

* The derivations of Scota and Gadelus or Gaodal have been already presented. Of course one does not declare that these derivations are certain, or that they will please all parties. But they are clear and natural and certainly better than those commonly furnished by Irish writers poets, or historians.

The name of *Scythia* is variously derived. If it is Greek, then it is said to come from σκοτία, darkness, of the same origin with σκια and σκοα a shade; in Irish *scath*, a shade, and *skiath, scath,* a shield which covers or protects one under its shadow. These Aryan radices Greek or Gaelic are said to give rise to the name *Scythia*, because to the Phenicians who were (foeni, or feni) bright, enlightened, the Scythians were in moral and material

Opinions of Irish Scholars.

The early history of the Gadeleans of Fenius Farsa, his son Niul and Scota, and their son has been rejected by the Most Rev. Dr. O'Brien, Bishop of Cloyne, the author of the Irish-English Dictionary. See (a) Preface to his Dictionary, also (b) remarks under the letter A.

"Nothing," says he, "could be of greater prejudice or discredit than asserting those fabulous genealogies and the stories of the travels of the supposed leaders and chiefs of their ancient colonies-such as have been rejected with just contempt by all learned nations, first invented in Ireland by bards and romancers after they had come to some knowledge both of the sacred writings and profane histories, and in Britain by Nennius and by Geoffry of Monmouth."

Again: This discovery (regarding Moses and Pharao and Scota) was reserved to our Christian bards, as their heathenish predecessors most certainly could have had no notion of the plain of Shenoaar, of Pharao, or of Moses.

Charles O'Conor of Belenagare is of the same opinion. "We find no history of the original of the Scots upon which we can with certainty depend." Nennius expresses himself much in the same fashion.

Haverty, in his History of Ireland, says:—

"There is no part of our primitive history that has been so frequently questioned or which modern writers so generally reject as fabulous, as these first accounts of the Milesian or Gadelian race; yet they are so mixed up with our authentic history, and so frequently referred to, that they cannot be passed over in silence." p. 10.

In his Dramatic History of Ireland, Standish O'Grady writes:

"There is not, perhaps, in existence a product of the human mind so extraordinary as the Irish Annals. From a time dating more than two thousand years before the birth of Christ, the stream of Milesian

---

gloom. Scythia was a country about which people in the old times knew very little. It was in darkness, it was away in the north too, far from the warm sun and the light.

Others say, *Scythians* signify *bow-men*, *archers*, from *skolios*, crooked, bent, and *Scolitoi*, contractedly *Scotoi*, bow-men. This is forced, not natural. O'Mahony derives the term "Scot," and Scoti from the Irish-Gaelic *scaoth*, a swarm, because the colonists, came as they come to-day in swarms to their new settlements.

The derivation from *scoth*, a blooming flower, is pretty. I am of opinion that O'Mahony's derivation is correct as to the origin of the term *Scoti*. They were always a vigorous race. I do not derive *Scoti* from Scythia. They are different altogether, Scythia = shadow-land, unknown land as opposed to Phœnicia, the land of light.

history flows down uninterrupted, copious and abounding between accurately defined banks, with here and there picturesque meanderings, here and there flowers lolling upon those delusive waters, but never concealed in mists, or lost in a marsh . . . To think that this mighty fabric of recorded events, so stupendous in its dimensions . . . should be after all a mirage, a delusion, a gorgeous bubble. . . .

"Early Irish history is the creation mainly of the bards. . . .

"Doubtless the legendary blends at some point with the historic narrative. The cloud and mist somewhere condense into the clear stream of indubitable fact. But how to discern under the rich and teeming myths of the bards, the course of that slender and doubtful rivulet, or beneath the piled rubbish and dust of the chroniclers, discover the tiny track which elsewhere borders into the byway of a nation's history . . . . where to fix upon any one point and say, here is the first truth. It is a task perilous and perplexing." pp. 19, 20, vol. i.

The opinion of Dr. O'Donovan on this subject is important. He states, Irish Grammar, p. 30, " Until we discover some real authority to prove by what means the Scotic or Gaelic race were able to preserve the names of all their ancestors from the time of Moses to the first century, we must regard the previous line of pedigree—thence up to Niul and to Fenius as a forgery of the Christian bards. Oral tradition at the present day does not preserve the names of ancestors with any degree of certainty beyond the sixth generation."

It must be said, however, that this was not a great difficulty, for they could have preserved the names by means of Ogham writing, and by mnemonic rhymes in which their famous deeds could have been recited.

Q. 3. In the bardic accounts of the Scoti is there any other strange episode regarding the wanderings of the Gadelians?

A. Yes: We are told that under the command of Sru they proceeded from the land of Egypt through the Red Sea, and proceeded east to the island which is called by them Tabra-fena, or " Well of Fenius," supposed to be Ceylon, and that they proceeded by a north-eastward course, which to men of the present day, having a knowledge of the earth's surface, must mean, by the Chinese Sea and

Bhering's Straits. All this is impossible, and doubly so when we are sold that they finally settled in Getulia (south of Mauritania in north-western Africa).

Another version has it, that from Egypt they returned under Heber Scot by Crete to the kingdom of their forefathers in Scythia. This was in the nineteenth century before Christ, according to the chronology of the Four Masters.

About one hundred and fifty years later another leader arose, named Bratha, father of Breogan—nineteenth in descent from Fenius, the founder of the Scythian dynasty—marshalled his followers and set sail, "ploughing the Mediterranean Sea with his fleet." He passed Crete and Sicily, and went by the pillars of Hercules to Spain, the peninsula. Here he acquired by force of arms some territory for his followers, and at his death left Breogan to rule the new nation—the Brigantes.

For the sake of clearness it is well to show the line of descent which Irish chroniclers furnish regarding the progenitors of Milesius up to the time of Noah. The following is that furnished by Cormac MacCuillenan, King-bishop of Cashel:—

FOREFATHERS OF MILESIUS OR GALAMH.

1. Noah
2. Japhet
3. Magog
4. Baath
5. Fenius Farsa
6. Niul
7. Gaedal Glas
8. Esru
9. Sru
10. Eber Scot
11. Beogamhan
12. Eogamhan
13. Tath
14. Agnon
15. Lamh Finn
16. Eber Glunfinn
17. Febric Glas
18. Nenual
19. Nuadath
20. Alloid
21. Arcadh
22. Degatha
23. Bratha
24. Breoghan
25. Bili
26. Gálamh or Milesius
27. Eber Finn; Heremon, who took possession of Ireland 17 centuries B.C.

In the foregoing tableau the real or imaginary historic characters are presented in due order, and the student will perceive clearly the supposed relation of each, as has been explained, with Galamh, the founder of the Milesian race. Fenius Farsa is the fifth after Noah; of him and his son Niul, and of Gaedal (glas) born of Scota in Egypt, enough has been written just now. Sru and Eber Scot were leaders of the Gadelians to Gaetulia. Finally, Bratha (23) led them to Spain, and Broghan became the founder there of the

Brigantes. From him, in the second generation, was descended Galamh of whom much will be said presently. There are twenty-two generations from Fenius to Eber Finn, and this number covers a period of at least seven hundred years. It must be borne in mind that according to the Annals of the Four Masters, the sons of Milesius came to Ireland before the Christian era seventeen hundred years. Add seven hundred to seventeen hundred and you are back almost to the days of Nimrod and the Tower of Babel.

Phaleg was fifth in descent from Hem; Belus, fifth from Sham, or Ham; and Fenius fifth from Japheth.

Conclusion.

To sum up (a) it is evident that the account of the Scotic colony known as Gadelian before their arrival in Spain, and Milesian afterwards, is quite mythical; that the bardic stories regarding them from the time of Fenius Farsa to the age of Milesius are pure romance.

(b) Nevertheless, the coming of a Keltic colony, their landing in Ireland and making it their own is true; but the truth of it rests for certainty on evidence supplied from extrinsic and scientific sources, and from the effects manifest to this day in the topography of the island, the names of the tribal families, the physical type of the Milesian race, the language they have spoken.

It remains to tell the exploits of Galamh as told by the bards, and to show how after his death, his sons fitted out the expedition from the north-west of Gallicia in Spain and landed in Inis Fail.

Q. 4. It is well to know the famous deeds that are by ancient Bardic writers told of Galamh, or Milesius, the founder of the leading Irish families—what are they ?

A. It is stated that he was a man of great power of body and mind; that not content with the possessions which he enjoyed in north Spain, he set sail for Scythia, the country of his forefathers; he manned thirty ships or large boats, such as were usually built at that early period, entered the Mediterranean Sea by the pillars of Hercules, and set sail north-east by the island of Sicily and Crete; sailing still to the north-east, he at length arrived in Scythia, which in the opinion of the Scotic seanachaidhs must have been north of Asia Minor, and north of the Euxine towards Colchis, or Iberia.

Arriving at the land of his progenitors he found a king named Refloir on the throne of that nation. Refloir gave a glad welcome to Galamh and to the men who accompanied him. He was soon appointed general-in-chief of the king's troops, and he received in marriage the king's daughter Seng, which in Gaelic means *slender*. Galamh being of powerful build of frame, and gifted in mind, made his presence felt; and accordingly he achieved many victories. The story of his presence at the court of Refloir is very like that told of the conqueror of Goliath at the court of Saul, King of Israel. David " who slew his tens of thousands," received Michol, Saul's daughter, in marriage ; the father-in-law grew jealous of the popularity and growing power of his son-in-law, and consequently sought to kill him. In the case of David, who was a man that believed in the God of Israel, and in a just Providence, he did not retaliate on Saul, but abstained from imbruing his hands in the blood of the king. It was not so, as the story goes, with Galamh. His father-in-law grew jealous and sought every opportunity to slay the adventurous hero of the thirty ships and the victorious general of the Scythian hosts. Galamh thought it best to try at length to escape death by putting his father-in-law to the sword. He did so, and forthwith set sail with sixty ships on the Euxine again, making his way good southward to the mouths of the river Nile. He entered and sailed up to Memphis. An embassy was fitted out by him to Pharao, King of Egypt, who in turn invited the commander of sixty ships to court; after some days created him general-in-chief of the Egyptian armies and commander of the fleet. He obtained one of the king's daughters in marriage, by name Scota,—a name remarkable because it was the same which the mother of Gaedal bore when she was given in marriage by her father to Niul, son of Fenius Farsa. The Bards contend on this point whether the descendants of Milesius were called Scoti from the name of Scota the elder, or Scota the younger. It is a silly dispute. Galamh, as the story runs, was now free to marry, for the princess Seng had died. She was the mother of two sons in Scythia, "Heber Donn" and "Arech Februadh." Scota, his second wife, bore two other sons, who were afterwards remarkable on the occasion of the Milesian invasion of Ireland, Heber Finn and Amergin—the latter became the poet and prophet of the nation. There are still extant in ancient Gaelic three short poems said to have been composed by Amergin.

It was fortunate for the fame of Galamh, that at this precise time

Pharao was fighting with the kingdom of the Ethiopians. Of course Galamh soon subdued these semi-civilised sons of Cham. He was also a man of forethought, and immediately on settling down in Egypt, he had sent twelve chosen men of his people to acquire a knowledge of the arts and sciences as they were then known in Egypt. He began to grow tired of a quiet home after seven years in the land of the Pharaos. He announced his intention to leave. He brought with him all his clan and retinue in three ships, his wife Scota and sons, and he set sail, now the third time, on the Mediterranean steering this time straight to the north. He sailed through the islands of the Archipelago, and settled for a short time near Thrace; Scota gives birth to a son "Ir" in an island near its borders, perhaps "*Samos*," *i.e.*, peaceful island, called by the bards Irené. Northward still was the cry, and after a year another son, whom he named "Colpa," or the swordsman, was born to him.

What is the strangest thing of all in this romantic story is, that the bards tell us Galamh marched onward still, till he arrived in the Northern Sea and reached Alba, that is Scotland or ancient Britain, from which, leaving Britain and France, he sailed to the west, till, steering through the Bay of Biscay, he arrived at the tower which his grandfather Breoghan had built near Corunna.

On his return, two other sons were born to him by his wife Scota, these were, Arannan and Heremon. Thus he had eight sons—Donn, and Arech Februadh, Heber Finn, Amergin, Ir, Colpa, Arannan and Heremon. Of these the most notable are Heber Finn and Heremon, from whom the leading Milesian families are descended, and Amergin the poet of the colony.

After Galamh's arrival, he found that his people were oppressed by the surrounding tribes. On these he showed his valour; he gained fifty-four victories. The children and grandchildren of Breoghan had multiplied prodigiously. They wanted larger territories; these they could not find. A famine came. A continued drought pressed on the comforts and natural wants of the people.

They formed a council. A resolve was made to acquire new homes. Accordingly Ith, uncle of Galamh, brother of his father Bili, was selected for the enterprise. A ship, with a crew of one hundred and fifty men, was fitted out for him. He had learned that there were lands to the north. He steered his course to Eire, or fate directed his ship to the land of Destiny—Inisfail. Breoghan, the father of Ith, and grandfather of Galamh, had ten sons, nine of whom were uncles of Milesius.

They were known by the names.

1. Breoga	5. Cuala	8. Nar
2. Fuad	6. Bladh	9. Ith
3. Murthemni	7. Ebleo	10. Bili, father of Galamh
4. Cuailngi		

The names of these distinguished men occur in the account of the invasion of Ireland under Heber and Heremon, and it is well, accordingly, that the student should be acquainted with them, and know how they were related to the chiefs of the expedition.

CHAPTER XIV.

MISSION FROM SPAIN TO IRELAND; ITH, HIS DEATH; PREPARATION FOR THE INVASION OF INISFAIL; THEY COME, STRANGE DETAILS; STORY OF THE MILESIAN LANDING.

Q. 1. Taking the Milesian invasion to mean historically, that at a very early period, a Keltic colony from Gallicia, in Spain, set sail for the "isle they had seen in dreams," how did Milesius' sons and his brethren of the clan Breogain prepare for so important an enterprise?

A. They sent, like the Hebrew people in their journeying under the leadership of Moses to the promised land, a party of their own people to inspect the territory of which they had intended to gain possession; to bring back an account regarding the climate whether it was hot or temperate—"the land whether it was good or bad, and the cities walled or without walls—the soil fat or barren, woody or without trees,—regarding the inhabitants, whether they were strong or weak, few in number or many."

The name of the level land, southwest of the town of Lifford, county Donegal, near the bend where the river Finn unites with the Foyle, and known even to this day to the Gaelic-speaking natives, as *Slemhna Magha Itha,* or the slippery parts of the plain of Ith,—points out the spot where Ith, son of Breoghan, and uncle to Miledh of

Spain, accompanied by Lughaidh his son, with a body of one hundred and fifty men drew up their " long " boat after a safe voyage through Biscay and Feabhal lake, now Lough Foyle. In kindred Keltic he inquires of the natives living on the banks of the river Foyle, who is it that held the sovereignty, and where did he reside? He received for answer that the sovereignty rested in the hands of the three sons of Kermad Milbeoil, son of Daghda, that they reigned each a year in turn, that just then the sovereigns were holding at Aileach Neid, a short distance to the north-west, and seen to-day in the magnificent ruins known as Grianan Aily,—a council composed of princes, druids, bards, Breitheamhas, or judges, to decide a grave question for some time in dispute regarding the amount of wealth and territory to which each of the royal brothers was by right of inheritance entitled.

Ith with one hundred of his followers soon presented himself at the palace of Aileach. He was graciously received. He told the object for which he had come, pretended stress of weather as the immediate cause of landing on the shores of their island.

The Tuatha De Danann, chieftains and people, deemed the foreigner a man of ripe intelligence as well as of princely position. The three kings unbosom their thoughts to the distinguished stranger regarding their respective hereditary rights; they ask his opinion on the question that they had come to settle. Ith with great judgment replied: That the wealth in dispute ought to be divided into three portions, that the brothers should each become owner of a single portion; that in like manner the whole island should be divided into three parts, and that each sovereign ought to be lord and master of his allotted territory. With still greater freedom he gave a kindly admonition to the contending princes, telling them to cast away the spirit of contention, to be at peace with one another, to rest satisfied each with his allotted share of wealth, of land and followers; that further, they should guard the region committed to their keeping, and govern their subjects with energy combined with wisdom, having in view the happiness of the governed as well as their own.

Recipients of the rights of hospitality Ith and his son Lughaidh, with their followers, could not have been molested. They had, however, only reached Northern Magh Itha, on their return to join their companions at the ship, when a body of one hundred and fifty warriors, under command of MacCoill, one of the sons of Kermad, attacked them. Ith defended the rear ranks of his unsuspecting band

and in the conflict received a mortal wound. By his faithful followers he was borne to the ship. On the return voyage from the Foyle to Corunna he died of his wounds. Loud and long was the wailing, amongst the clan Breogain, and deep the desire of revenge that seized the souls of Ith's brothers and nephews, and especially the sons of Galamh or Milesius. To the many motives that urged the clan Breogain to leave North Spain and acquire new territory, another strong incentive—revenge—was now superadded. They must become masters of the isle of destiny—and avenge the death of their kinsman, so treacherously slain far from home and friends. The cry is raised,—To Inisfail,—to Inisfail.

Q. 2. Tell the leading facts of the Milesian invasion as recorded by the Bards and Seanachàidh.

A. Shortly after Ith had set out on his exploring expedition—the Patriarchal Chief Miledh, sovereign of the Kelts of Gallicia, or of that portion of them known as Brigantes,—*i.e.*, the clan Breogain—died. His eight sons, Donn, Arech Februadh, Eber Fionn Amergin, Ir, Colpa, Erimhon, and Arannan, seem to have inherited his energy, his martial bravery, his dauntless intrepidity. They enter into council with their cousin Lughaidh, son of Ith, and their kinsmen; finally they resolve to set sail for Inisfail. They have been contending with many foes in the country in which they are now dwelling: The island "they had seen in dreams" was promised them by the Fates, and hence it was long known as Inis-fail, island-of-fate. It was not befitting, they said, a great and a courageous people to allow the death of so dear a friend, and so great a leader as Ith, to pass unavenged: and then the land of Eire was open to them; the people who dwelt in that country were divided in their allegiance; the subjected clans were suffering in silence; they were ready to revolt,—they wished that some courageous nation would invade the island; and positively, the climate was pleasant, not too hot, and yet not too cold. If the invasion were not attempted now it would never be undertaken with such promising omens of success. The voice of the gods above, and of heroes on earth, the natives of the island,—the spirit of their brave fathers called the children of Breogain to the enterprise.

In the spring time of the year they set sail with a fleet of thirty ships, each conveying thirty warriors, besides women and children, that is nine hundred warriors prepared for battle.

PROBABLE NUMBER OF THE INVADING FORCE.

It seems surprising that warriors so few in number, brave and valiant though they may have been,—could have been able to conquer a people undoubtedly courageous, and, at that time, numbering at least a million of souls. The account given by Nennius, a British writer (A.D. 850), presents features of a historic character which appear more in accordance with truth. He states that the Milesian expedition consisted not of thirty but of four times thirty, that is, one hundred and twenty long boats or ships, named *cuili*,—a term, according to Dr. Todd, in his Annotations on the Irish Version of Nennius,—cognate in sound and sense with the Anglo-Saxon *ceol*, a long boat,—found in the modern English term "Keel." Each of these 120 cuili carried, we are told, "thirty couple,"—that is, men fit to fight, with their wives, and doubtless, many children. They did not leave all the youthful members of their respective families behind them in the land of the "Olive and Vine." Taking this view as more in accordance with the facts as known before the Brigantes had left Gallicia,—and with the successful issues connected with their landing in Ireland—while opposed by the might of a great people,—there must have been thirty times one hundred and twenty warriors, or three thousand six hundred men in the expedition that set out for the "Emerald Isle." The student who has read these pages is already aware that amongst the Kelts, ladies of learning and high station held a very commanding position before the public. They had a voice in council; they commanded not only in the cabinet but in the field. Scota—the Queen Mother of Miledh's sons,—like Semiramis of old, or Maria Theresa in comparatively modern times, headed the invading forces.

When the Milesian fleet neared the shore of Mother Eire,—the Emerald Isle, as bards tell us, appeared,—a fitting figure of her destiny in ages to come—clothed in mist, so that her headlands and green hills,—her mountain ranges and meadow slopes, were not visible to the eye. She lay bathing in the waves of the Atlantic, like a Leviathan of the deep, undisturbed in its placid waters, while her form was shrouded from view in a mantle of mist. Soon, however, the clouds cleared off. The setting sun shone out, and scattered a shower of golden rays on the land which the children of Breogain "had seen in dreams." And now the distant hills appear to raise their heads clear and well-defined with the blue sky in the back-ground; the mountain-slopes and meadow lands assume an inviting tint of green and gold; the bright headlands glitter in the sun's reflected light; the island so long sought, arises revealed in all her beauty; the emerald bosom of dear mother Eire expands as it were, to receive her children. The sons of Miledh take the cheering prospect as a happy omen, and filled with joy at the idea of coming to land, and of obtaining a permanent and a happy home, they raise the cry: "'Tis Inisfail, 'tis Inisfail." This event, recorded by Milesian bards, Thomas Moore, our national poet, makes the theme of the following sweet song:—

I.

"They came from a land beyond the sea,
    And now o'er the western main,
Set sail, in their good ships, gallantly,
    From the sunny land of Spain.
'Oh, where's the Isle we've seen in dreams,
    Our destin'd home or grave?'
Thus sang they as, by the morning's beams,
    They swept the Atlantic wave.

II.

"And lo, where afar o'er ocean shines
    A sparkle of radiant green,
As though in that deep lay emerald mines,
    Whose light thro' the wave was seen.
''Tis Inisfail, 'tis Inisfail,'
    Rings o'er the echoing sea;
While bending to heav'n the warriors hail,
    That home of the brave and free.

III.

"Then turn'd they unto the Eastern wave,
    Where now their Day-God's eye,
A look of such sunny omen gave
    As lighted up sea and sky,
Nor frown was seen through sky or sea,
    Nor tear o'er leaf or sod,
When first on their Isle of Destiny
    Our great forefathers trod."

Q. 3. Continue the story of the Milesian landing as told by the Bards and Seanachaidh.

A. The fleet made good its way to Inber Slaingi, known at a later period as Loch Garmen or Carmen, and in modern times as Wexford. The Tuatha Dé Danann mustered their forces to oppose the invading host. On this account the sons of Miledh sailed round the island seeking for a harbour safe to land in, and free from all opposition on the part of the inhabitants. They landed at length at Inber Skeiné, the bay of wild beauty, or of fright, known in later times as the bay of Kenmare. The bards state that from Kenmare the invaders marched northward to Sliabh Mis, a mountain tract situate between Castlemaine and Tralee. In this plateau they met one of the three native queens—Banba—accompanied by a number of female attendants and her druids. Amerghin, the chief bard of the invaders, asks her,—" What is your name," " My name is Banba," she replies, "and from me the island is called Banba." From Sliabh Mis they continue their journey in a north-eastern course, till they reach Sliabh Eblind,— the modern Sliabh Felim, that raises its head high along the borders of North Limerick, looking right across the river Clare into the modern towns Newport and Castleconnell in Tipperary. On this height, they meet another royal dame, with a suitable company of ladies and their bards. Amerghin, who appears to have the privilege,—as chief bard,—of the Milesians, to divine all that was hidden or sacred, asks her name. The sovereign lady replies, that " her name is Fodla, and the island is called from her by the name Fodla." The invaders continue their route, and pass from Tipperary, till they reach the ascent so well known in ancient times, the centre, as it were, of the island, the famed hill of Uisneach situated to the north of Castletown along the line of the Midland Great Western Railway,—in the barony of Rathconrath, county Westmeath. Here they meet a third queenly personage, and Amerghin asks her name, she replies that Eri is her name, and that the island is called Eri after her. This narration regarding the interviews between the several sovereign ladies and the invaders is very poetic, and is in a sense interesting, as it presents a picture fancied or real, of the custom of the period,—reminding one of the patriarchal manners of Jacob, Esau and Laban ;—or of Abraham and Lot. From Uisneach they proceed in a body to the residence of the Ard-righ, or sovereign king at Teamhra. Here they find the three kings, the three sons of Kermad, surrounded by the nobility of the kingdom, by their bards, judges, poets, and warriors. The Milesians then proclaim their arrival and demand quiet possession of the island, and assert their claim to the sovereign power, and that if not yielded to them quietly, then it should be gained by the sword. The Tuatha Dé Danann sovereigns did not wish to resign the supreme power in so quiet a fashion,—they did not like the idea of letting so rich a guerdon as the "emerald gem of the western world" drop so readily into the lap of the adventurous stranger. So accordingly they replied in a civil sensible style, in language peculiar to the period, that the invaders had not acted like heroes and men of prowess, and in accordance with the laws of chivalry and combat amongst men of valour. They demand that they should return to their ships, at Inber Slaingi, or Inber Skeiné, and then again invite the natives to battle, and strive by martial daring to gain the mastery. The Danann chiefs further declare that they were willing to leave this matter in which were involved a question of honour and of prowess on the one side, and on the other right and supreme authority—to the judgment of the Milesian chief bard,—Amerghin. What a strange proposal when regarded according to the manners of modern times; yet, stranger still, their own bard and brother decided against the sons of Miledh and his kinsmen. His judgment is pronounced; it is, that the Milesians are bound in honour to return to the ships and challenge the sovereigns and their people, then by skill in war and by martial bravery to strive for the mastery. According to the usages then known amongst warriors and heroes the Danann claimed only what was fair.

CHAPTER XV.

A STORM : QUEEN SCOTA UNFURLS THE SACRED BANNER : BATTLES OF MIS, OF TAILTEAN, OF DRUIMLIGHEAN : DEFEAT OF THE DANANN TRIBES : HOW THE LEADERS OF THE DANANN CLANS SELECT THE "SIDHE" OR BEST SITES THROUGHOUT THE LAND : THEY FINALLY SETTLE AMONGST THE PEOPLE : STORIES RELATIVE TO THAT AGE.

Q. 1. Did the invaders retire to their ships, and with what result?

A. Yes; accordingly they made their way back to Inber Skeine east of the estuary of Kenmare, and boarding their ships they sailed out into the Atlantic a certain distance known by the measure of nine waves A wave's length meant at the time a certain determinate distance. Suddenly and before a second landing could be safely effected a storm arose. Some of the ships were during the gale, not uncommon then even as now, rushing across the Atlantic, driven south and west; others were forced to seek shelter in the islands further north on the Kerry coast. Those that sailed round Cape Clear and the Old Head of Kinsale were driven through the channel Muir Icht along the Irish Sea, till they reached the estuary at the Boyne This portion of the fleet was under the command of Heremon. Here he effected a landing—but his brother Colpa of the Sword, son of Miledh. was drowned as he strove to gain the beach. From that fatal accident to Colpa, the estuary at the mouth of the Boyne had been for long centuries later on, known as Inber Colpa—or the estuary where Colpa the Milesian warrior met a watery grave.

The galleys driven by the force of the storm north-west were under the command of Donn, brother of Arach and Februadh, and of Ir, who were accompanied by five other leaders. The ship that bore Donn and his two brothers was wrecked on the sand-hills* near Smerwick harbour, while the vessel that bore Ir was flung on the Skellig rocks,— all hands on board drowned in the waves. Thus of the eight sons of Milesius, five have already perished by the storm; five other leaders and a great number of the men fitted to meet the enemy in battle have found a watery grave.

Q. 2. Tell us of the Battle of Sliabh Mis.

A. Meantime Heber and those who manned his fleet mastered the force of the gale and landed safely at Inber Skeine or Kenmare harbour. Here it was that Skein, the wife of Amerghin, was drowned, and from her name the estuary, according to some writers, was known in the ancient Milesian writings as " Inber Skeiné." On landing the ex-queen Scota unfurled the sacred banner. The invading host now deemed it well to hasten, as they had done after their former landing, to Sliabh Mis. Here, on the third day, they encountered the Tuatha Dé Danann in great force, led on by Queen

---

* *Teach Duinn.*—This was the burial place of Donn, the eldest son of Milesius, the leader of the colony from Spain to the south coast of Ireland. He was drowned with his ship's company at the *Dumhacha*, or Sand-hills, in the west of Kerry, where all found a grave: and hence these sand-hills have ever since retained the name of *Teach Duinn*, or Donn's house; yet for all that their position has been lost in modern times. " I believe," says O'Curry, " it was in the harbour of Smerwick." O'Curry, *Atlantis*, No. 7, p. 148. London: Longmans, Brown and Green.

Eri. A hot battle ensued. It was contested much in the same manner as those which we [have already described that had been fought at southern and northern Moy Tura. The troops of the Milesians were in numbers three thousand. They were fresh and full of courage and bounding with hope, anxious to ennoble their name and make it famous for heroic deeds; and to conquer the kingdom for themselves; besides, they felt positively assured that destiny had called them to win the land for which they had sailed. Their armour, such as it was in those days, was superior to that in use by their antagonists. Scota, the ex-queen, led them to the contest. They were united and they felt resolute and certain of success. On the other hand, the Tuatha Dé Danann were not united; they were not sanguine of success; their leaders differed in council; they were jealous of those who assumed the supreme control. They had been unaccustomed to warfare. Their armour was not as well fitted for battle as that of the Milesians. They were given to the notion so common at this period and in the Homeric ages, subsequent to their time, to challenge their opponents to single combat. Each brave man selected some distinguished hero; singled him out from amidst many, and aimed at the glory of being victor. The Tuatha Dé Danann seemed to be under the impression that the Fates, as it is said, were against them, and that they could not succeed. And so it happened. They were defeated. One thousand men on their side lay stretched on the plain at the foot of Sliabh Mis. Three hundred of the victorious invaders were sacrificed in the slaughter of that terrible fight. Those individuals of name slain were—Scota, the queen mother of Miledh's sons, with Fas and two druids. Feal, the wife of Lughaidh, was drowned soon after, and from her the river known as Feale takes its name. The Milesians claiming the victory remained on the battlefield and buried their dead, placing flagstones, with Ogham inscriptions, over the spot where each hero or heroine lay in the unbroken rest of the grave.

Q. 3. Besides the fact that the record of the battle of Sliabh Mis in Kerry is still found in the annals of Ireland's story, is there any recent authentic circumstance that goes to show the truth of the bardic narrative ?

A. Yes. Within the past thirty years the very flagstones placed over the graves of the fallen heroes and heroines—those of Scota and

Fas have been discovered " between Sliabh Mis and the sea," and the Ogham inscriptions have been deciphered and explained by the late William Williams, Esq., of Dungarvan, one of the most advanced scholars in Ogham writing and antiquities known in modern times.

Q. 4. Was this battle the last fought by the Danann chiefs against the Milesians?

A. No. There were two other battles, one at Tailten (modern Teltown, near Navan in Meath), the other at Druimlighean, now Drumleen, in the barony of Raphoe, Co. Donegal. After the final defeat at Drumleen the Danann tribes never again, as a people, raised the standard of authority in Eire. Of the three battles fought on this occasion by the sons of Milesius, that at Teltown was the greatest and the most crushing. The first at Sliabh Mis was only a mere trial of strength, and the last at Drumleen was the struggling effort of a fallen foe.

After the victory obtained in the glens of Kerry, Heber Fioun the third born with his brother Amerghin, marched their forces through the country known afterwards as Limerick and King's County, crossed into Westmeath, reached Tara, and united their troops with those that had come by Drogheda and the Boyne, led by Heremon. The three Milesian brothers drew up their army to fight the foe at Teltown, the site selected by the three Danann kings—MacCoill, MacCeacht and MacGreine. The native kings and their queens, Fodhla, Banba and Eire, left Tara, and selected for a battlefield, Teltown, the place officially set apart for the martial exercises of the warriors of the nation. Each people put forth on this occasion all the ability and martial power that was at their command : the three native kings and their queens, in order that they might hold the regal sway that had been hitherto enjoyed by them ; the three Milesian brothers—in order to acquire regal power in a country not yet their own, and in which themselves and their followers were sure to perish to a man, if they should suffer defeat. The Milesians flushed with the partial victories already achieved, and desirous of establishing their dynasty, entered the struggle like men who saw they were destined to be victors. The Danann clans appeared stricken with the idea that they were doomed not to succeed : the Firbolg foe who had been to them as serfs were not devoted to the cause of the ruling powers. They fought not in favour of their masters, for in their souls they seemed glad that the Milesian invaders were gaining the ascendant. According to the manner of fighting in those days each distinguished warrior selected an opponent worthy of his lance from amidst the ranks of his foes, and conquered or died. Heber marched against MacCoill, one of the kings, and after a severe fight laid his foe stretched on the plain ; Amerghin, the poet and warrior, faced MacGreine, and after a time pierced his opponent's thigh ; and finally, Heremon, the third brother, turned on MacCeacht, the last of the kings, and laid him low in the arms of death. The three queens likewise perished ; Eire was slain by Suirghe, Fodhla by Edan, and Banba by Caicher. The kingdom of Ireland had been for centuries after that period called, and to this hour is so styled by the Irish-speaking natives, Eire, or Fodhla, or Banba.

Q. 5. What followed ?

A general route of the Danann battalions, and of the inferior chieftains by whom they were commanded, followed. The Milesians lost two of their generals in the battle, and, following up the victory in pursuit of the fleeing Tuatha Dé Danann, another chieftain, Fuadh, perished at that mountain district which since then has borne his name,—Sliabh Fuadh, near Newtown Hamilton, in the county Armagh : and yet another, Cuailgne, fell at a place called after the name of the fallen chieftain from that day to the present—Sliabh Cuailgne, or Cooley, near Carlingford, county Louth. In this wise the Danann fugitives were pursued northwards and westwards towards the palace at Aileach, till finally they made a stand at Druimlighean, but then it was only to be totally and completely beaten.

Q. 6. What plan for their own safety did the Danann survivors adopt after this ?

The surviving leaders of the Danann forces formed an assembly ; they took counsel what was best to be done. First they elected one who as king was to be obeyed by them. The choice fell upon Bodhbh Dearg, son of the Daghda. For themselves they deemed it best to offer the conquering Milesians no further resistance. It was not their wish, however, to mix with the common people of the country —the Firbolg races, whom hitherto they had treated as serfs. They adopted a middle course. They secretly acknowledged Bodhbh Dearg as their king, and made choice for themselves of the leading sites or hills throughout Ireland. In the west, and north, and east the Danann still reigned in the "high" places. These they called *sidh* or *shee*, that is, sites or commanding positions. They erected *duna*, or fortified residences, surrounding each with a *lios* and a *caiseal*. They seldom mixed with the inhabitants of the country. The lower orders regarded them as beings of great and hidden knowledge, and thus in time looked upon them as in some measure supernatural. Hence the name *sidh* (shee) in Irish Gaelic is applied to Faery—the spirit of the "hills,"—of whom people know little. In process of time their descendants dwelt like others in the plains, and formed a considerable element in the mixed races of whom Irishmen of the present day are made up. These facts are known from MacFirbis, and from those family names which are manifestly Danann, and of which mention has been already made in pages 70–71 (*supra*).*

CHAPTER XVI.
Stories and Romances regarding the early Irish Period.

For over fifteen hundred years' stories in part historical and consequently true—imaginative in part and belonging accordingly to the region of romance have been told among the people of Ireland, and have by the force of tradition been transmitted from generation to generation to the present, relative to the "*Tuatha Dé Danann Tribes*," their cleverness, their power, and their force of character as rulers.

There are four remarkable stories of this class, which for the past thousand years have been committed to writing :—They embrace the famous three Irish stories which are known so well to Irish Seanachaidhs, or story-tellers, as the τρί τρυαιξε na ϝɼeuluiɼeaċτa, *i.e.* the three sorrowful tales of story-telling, together with that famous tale known as the story relative to the Lady Curchog.

Two of the four stories refer to the period directly after the defeat of the "Tuatha Tribes," and after the almost total destruction of the

---

* This battle took place at Tailten, now called Teltown, county Meath between the three Milesian brothers and the Tuatha Dé Danaan kings, in which the latter were subdued. The mere fact only of the occurrence of this battle is given in the Book of Invasions, but in the MS. H, 4. 22, T.C.D., there are some details given. The full text, however, has not come down to us.—O'Curry, *MS. Materials*, p. 586.

Danann Dynasty; another deals with the rise of the Danann power in Eire, and brings the reader back to the great battle fought at Northern Magh Tura, when the Fomorians and their abettors were totally routed by the steady and skilled bravery of the Danann Chiefs and their warlike followers. The fourth story is of a later date, and has reference to the Milesians: it presents a picture of the manners of the times, when Conor MacNessa was Monarch of Ulster, about the first century of the Christian era.

STORIES OF THIS CLASS

furnish the reader with a *tableau vivant* of a period and of the people who lived then, in a style far more natural and exciting in its details, than the most glowing and life-like description which the ablest historian can in words convey, or with pen pourtray. It is in this sense and not as a reliable historic record that the writer presents here a summary of a few of these stories. The reader who wishes to learn more fully concerning these historic-novel tales is referred to the publications of the Gaelic Union, and the Society for the Preservation of the Irish Language; and to the works written by the late Eugene O'Curry.

STORY OF LADY CURCHOG.

Lady Curchog was daughter of Manannan, the great Danann Chief, and Druid of the Danann races. The story told of her, and that tale regarding the fate of the children of Lir, have reference in an especial manner to the events that transpired directly after the defeat of the Tuatha Dé Danann, and on the accession of Miledh's sons, Heber and Heremon to the sovereignty of Ireland. Professor O'Curry was so familiar with these tales, that he believed not only in the outlines, but in much of the details. His views on the reality of the Danann Tribes as a race, who at one time dwelt in ancient Eire, have been already quoted. "No matter," he states, "how romantic and legendary the details of this people may be found, there is as much reason to believe in the actual existence of the race as there is in the origin and existence of their collateral and contemporary races—the Firbolg and the Milesian." (*Atlantis*, No. 6, p. 382).

And respecting these two stories, one the "Tale of Woe of the Children of Lir," the other that regarding Lady Curchog, O'Curry writes: "It is to the disastrous battle at Tailtin that the tale of the children of Lir at its opening refers, but the account," he says "of the convention of the sorrowing chiefs of the

Tuatha Dé Danann is taken from another—that known relating to the Lady Curchog. This latter is found fully narrated in the Book of Fermoy, which fortunately was purchased by the late liberal-minded Dr Todd, S.F.T.C.D."

"It is not intended to claim for this tale the rank of a sober historical document, but it may be received as founded on history. However wild the fairy incidents which it is allowable to work into ancient tales of this class, the main events referred to, and the principal personages named, are always in accordance with the records and traditions of true history. In this point of view the names referred to in the tale of Curchog will be found interesting, and in a measure supporting the still wilder legend regarding the children of Lir." *Ibid.* p. 369.

"It is in this tale relative to Lady Curchog," continues O'Curry, "and now for the first time published, that the ancient legend putting orward the cause, origin, and history of the disappearance of the *Tuatha Dé Danann* from the ordinary intercourse of men, and their voluntary retirement to an invisible and supposed immortal existence in our hills, lakes, and mountains has been authoritatively placed before the world."

No doubt, the statement made by O'Curry on this subject is correct. Every scholar now-a-days feels certain, since the discoveries made in the Troad in 1874, that all the great events connected with the nine years' war, and the taking of Troy by the Greeks are true; that there was such a town as Troy, and a King Priam who ruled over it; that Grecian Kings, known as Achilles, Agamemnon, Menelaus, Ajax, and Ulysses from Greece had come to attack it, although in the poetic story in which these things are told, much is recorded regarding false deities and fanciful meetings and councils, aye, and supernatural interpositions which had no existence except in Homer's head. In the same way, there are certain features which may be deemed historic in Keltic tales, clothed though they be with much that the imagination alone has furnished, or the mind of the poet conceived.

The precise time at which the tale of "Lir's lonelydaughter" and her brothers comes in, is plainly seen from all that is narrated in the story itself, and in the tale referring to Lady Curchog.

Directly after the disastrous battle of Druim Lighean, in the present barony of Raphoe, the surviving chiefs of the Tuatha Dé Danann Dynasty deemed it their duty to hold a convention in order to see what was best to be done. They had now no king, no territory no power.

They assembled accordingly at the palace known by the name, Brugh-na-Boinne (the Big House on the Boyne) the residence of Ængus Og, situate not far from the well-known mound hard by Slane, in Meath. These were Bodbh Dearg or Bodbh the Red, Ængus Og, (young Æneas), sons of the Daghda; Ilbreac (many spotted), Lir, Midhir (the proud); Sighmall, Finnbar, Tadhg Mor, and Dearg Dianscothach: Manannan, son of Lir—called the meeting to order and presided.

The object of this gathering of the chiefs was first to select some leader or king; next how best to hold their own strongholds, against their Milesian masters. A leader, whom all alike should acknowledge and obey, they had none, and they had lost nigh all their territory. It was, therefore, their duty to select safe positions for themselves, throughout the land, and to strengthen their castles, so as to be able to bid defiance to the Milesian hosts, if at any time the latter should attack them.

Lir, and Ilbreac, and Midhir, with the two sons of the Daghda declined to take an active part in the council, for each had been under the impression, that it was himself and no other that was likely to be elected. Bodbh Dearg, however, was made choice of by the council, and he was declared to be the head or King whom all the Danann in future should obey. On learning the choice that had been made Lir grew angry; he left the assembly, repaired shortly afterwards to his *Dun* or fortified castle.

Having chosen a king they next proceeded to select secure sites (*sidh*) within which they should be able to protect themselves and their clientela from any open or secret attacks that might in time to come be made by the Milesian conquerors. As a royal home for Bodbh Dearg, a hill south of the present Portumna, near Lough Dearg on the Shannon was selected, being as nearly as could be in regard to the selection of commanding positions, the centre of Ireland. Ilbreac received his appointment to go to Ballyshannon and to take possession of the mound to the north of that ancient town, overlooking the Waterfall, known as Eas-Aoidh-Ruaidh—or the Waterfall (*eas*) of Red Hugh. Lir was to keep watch and ward on the mount, known since the late defeat as Sliabh Fuaidh, and his castle there has become known as "Sidh Finneachaidh," near the present Newtown Hamilton, county Armagh; Midhir the proud, of Bri-leith, west of the village of Ardagh, county Longford, was told to erect his *Dun*, or to fortify the house he had erected on Sidh Truim. Sighmall took possession of Sidh Neanta, in modern times, known as "Fairy Mount" in the parish of Kilgefin, county Roscommon, not far from the present village of Lough Glynn. Fionnbar was sent west to Sidh Meadha, known to-day as Cnoc Meadha, near Tuam, in the county of Galway—a lovely mound, wooded this hour to the top, and known amongst the peasantry of Connacht as Finnbar's hill—or the hill of the Galway and Mayo fairies. In connexion with all these sites there have been in after times, anecdotes and stories of an interesting kind, handed down from generation to generation amongst the simple people. Tadhg Mor, son of Nuadhat, was made Lord of *Sidhe Droma Deine*, close to the mound known at the present day as the hill of Allen, county Kildare. Dearg Dian-Scothach was constituted possessor and defender of Sidh Cleithigh, south of the Boyne bridge, near Slane.

The chieftains repaired to their allotted abodes; they fortified and rendered impregnable their homes, and helped to protect the weaker members of the Danann Tribes from oppression or from slavery.

The Story of the Children of Lir.

On returning to his mansion on the hill of Sliabh Fuaidh, Lir continued to indulge for a time in the jealous fit arising from the fact that he had not been selected to be king over the Danann tribes. Shortly after this occasion his wife died. Bodbh Dearg, in his royal residence at Portumna, heard of the sad event. As Danann king, he deemed it well to offer to Lir now—like Achilles brooding in his sulk over defeat and the late loss—the expression of his sovereign condolence; and at the desire of the other chiefs, whose opinion he had sought and received, he sent a special invitation to Lir to come to the royal castle at Loch Dearg, on the Shannon. Lir came; Bodbh offered him for wife his choice lady of three—the fairest princesses in Eire. They were, moreover, Bodbh's own foster children—namely, Aobh, Aoifé, and Ailbé, daughters of Oilell (or Oichell) Arann - that is, Oichell, chieftain of Arann, the island so well known in the bay of Galway, together with the western district comprising part of Clare and Galway counties.

Lir accepted the offer. He made choice of Aobh, the eldest of the princesses. This selection pleased Bodbh. In due time Lir returned home with his bride. The first year she bore him two babes at a birth—a daughter, Fionn-ghuala, or "Fair Shoulder," and a son, Aodh, or Hugh, that ;is, "the Blushing." Soon again, at another birth, she bore two other children—both sons—Fiachra, or "the Hunter," and Conn (hound), or "Swift Hero," and then, like Rachel the mother of Benjamin, brother of Joseph, Aobh—after great puerperal pain—died. Thus a second time was Lir left a wailing widower. A second time was he invited by the king at Portumna to come to his palace to seek consolation. He did come. The Danann Director-in-Chief pointed out to Lir that there was no use regretting the past, that he could not undo the work of death; that now he had no matron to look after the care of his house, and his dear children had no mother to look after their proper training, that the best thing he could do accordingly was to take to wife the second daughter of Oilell Arann—a princess more beautiful, if possible, than his late spouse. Lir thought that his chief reasoned very correctly. Accordingly he agreed to the proposal. The lady gave her consent; there was a new marriage and a second wedding at the royal rooms at Portumna. Lir in due time brought his new bride to the fairy home at Sidh Finneachaidh.

Things went merrily on for a time. It is not stated that his new wife became the mother of children, but it is distinctly told that the three sons and the only daughter of Aobh grew up in beauty and princely grace before the eyes of their father and their many friends. Accordingly they became the admired of all, and, in an especial manner, beloved by their father, and even by Bodbh himself, to whose home they were taken occasionally both by their father and stepmother. All their childlike grace and attractiveness, their blooming features, the love bestowed on them by their father, became to Aoifé—their aunt and stepmother—a source of jealousy, and this envious feeling increased to such a degree that Lir's wife resolved finally to slay the children with the sword. In this project she failed. Coming, however, on one occasion from Armagh to Portumna to pay, as usual, a visit to Bodbh Dearg, she caused the children to bathe in the lake which lies near the present town of Castlepollard, in County Westmeath—known in those ancient times as Loch Dairbreach (or Lake of the Oaks.) While the children were enjoying their bath, though not wholly free from fear, their stepmother, the Lady Aoifé, by her magical power changed them in an instant into swans, and condemned them to roam over the lakes and seas of Ireland during the space of nine hundred years and longer, until the time would at length arrive when the Mass-bell of Christian Ireland should awaken them from their forlorn state, and restore them to faith and freedom, and awaken human life. They were condemned to spend three hundred years on Loch Dairbreach; three hundred years on "*sruth na Maoile*," the stream of the Maoil, or Mull, the "bald" headland bounding Ceantire in Scotland, called by Thomas Moore the "Moyle;" three hundred years on the western coast of Ireland at *Iar-ros Domnann*, now Erris, in the County of Mayo, and Inis Gluaire *of Brendain* (now Inish-glory.) The nine hundred years express only an indefinite period, from the time of the defeat of the Danann tribes to the coming of the apostles of the Christian faith into Ireland. In the tale we are told that the enchantment would come to an end, and the metamorphosed swans would assume their human form when the sound of the Mass-bell should for the first time tingle in their ears in holy Ireland, and when the woman from the south and the man from the north should be united. The man was to be Lairgnen, son of Colman, son of Cobhthach, King of Connacht; and the woman Deoch, daughter of Finghin, the son of Aridh Alainn, King of Munster (sixth century of the Christian Era.) "The reader," says Thomas Moore, "must be content to learn that Fionn-ghuala, the daughter of Lir, was by some supernatural power transformed into a swan, and condemned to wander for many hundred years over certain lakes and rivers in Ireland till the coming of Christianity, when the first sound of the Mass-bell was to be the signal of her release."

Song of Fionghuala.

I.

"Silent, O Moyle, be the roar of thy water,
 Break not, ye breezes, your chain of repose,
While, murmuring mournfully, Lir's lonely daughter,
 Tells to the night-star her tale of woes.
When shall the swan, her death-note singing,
 Sleep, with wings in darkness furl'd,
When will heaven, its sweet bells ringing,
 Call my spirit from this stormy world?

---

* The whole story, with an English translation and notes, together with a copious Vocabulary in Irish Gaelic, has been published in a small volume, sold cheaply, by the firm of Gill and Son, Dublin, for the Society for the Preservation of the Irish Language.

II.

"Sadly, O Moyle, to thy winter-wave weeping,
　Fate bids me languish long ages away;
Yet, still, in her darkness doth Erin lie sleeping,
　Still doth the pure light its dawning delay.
When will that day-star, mildly springing,
　Warm our isle with peace and love?
When will heaven, its sweet bells ringing?
　Call my spirit to the fields above?"*

CHAPTER XVII.

FATE OF THE CHILDREN OF TURENN: A STORY RELATING TO THE EARLY DANANN PERIOD.

The second tale, known as "The Fate of the Children of Turenn,"—which is the third of the three sorrowful stories of ancient Eire, relates to the early record of the Danann people, about the time when Nuada Airgid-lamh (of the Silver Hand), ruled at Tara. It tells of the coming of the Fomorians,† or seafaring men, from the land of lakes and estuaries, say from the countries known to-day as Denmark, Norway, and Sweden.

These foreigners oppressed the natives of Eire, who, as the story states, were obliged to pay tax for the quern, tax for the baking-flag, for the kneading-trough, and to pay an ounce of gold every year as a poll-tax, or in default thereof the individual should suffer the loss of his nose.

Lugh of the Long Arm, a famous princely warrior, who, at a subsequent period became king, resisted this crushing impost. Hence

---

* For a full account of this tragic tale consult the little work published by Gill; or "Oidhe Cloinne Lir" in the *Atlantis*, by O'Curry; or the story as it is told by Gerald Griffin. From internal evidence, and from the language of the bards that pervades the tale, it is likely that the story was composed in the seventh or eighth century.

† *Foghmarach* is the Irish term from which "Fomorian" is taken. Its meaning is seen from its component parts, *fogh*, booty, spoil; and *mara*, gen. case of *muir*, Keltic for sea; Fogmarach therefore means one who lives by plunder or spoil collected from the sea in any way—therefore a sea pirate, or a seafarer of any kind. To this hour those who repair in summer time to the seaside for the purpose of taking baths in the waters of the Atlantic, are along the coast of Galway and Mayo called by the seaboard dwellers, Foghmaraigh.

resulted the famous battle of Northern Magh Tura, in which the foreigners were completely defeated, and peace was once more restored to the Danann tribes of ancient Eire.

It was at the period immediately *before* this battle, when preparations were being made to meet the invaders at Ballysadare, in County Sligo, that the three sons of Turenn had slain Kian, the father of Lugh. To be avenged of this foul murder, Lugh, the son, in the presence of the king and council assembled at Tara, imposed, according to law, an *eiric*, or fine, on the three sons of Turenn.

The interest of the story rests in the record and recital of the strange deeds—something like the adventures of Aladdin, or of Sinbad—which those three heroic brothers were, in the language of the narrative, obliged to perform, in order to atone for the crime which they had wantonly committed on the father of one who was destined in a few years to be the sovereign ruler of the land of Fodla. Without any definite description of the countries on the globe, to which they went, for geography was not then much known and very imperfectly cultivated, it is stated by the author of the first written version, say in the seventh century, that the sons of Turenn were doomed to proceed from the palace at Tara in Meath, to the far east beyond the Hellespont, to the unknown territory of Scythia, to countries south of the Mediterranean, not fully into the heart of Africa, or south-west of the Soudan, which even to-day is not well known to Europeans; and again to journey as far north as Iceland, performing labours incredible, not only by sea, but by land, till at length after years of travelling and fighting, and undergoing hairbreadth escapes, they return the second time to Eire, wearied and wounded, to sink into the arms of death, while their father Turenn and their beloved sister Ethnea, were looking at their dearest sons and brothers perishing, unable the while to console or relieve them. The sons having thus miserably, and after infinite fatigue and labours not unlike those of Hercules, perished, Turenn, their father, and Ethnea, their sister, threw themselves on the dead bodies, and died.

In this story regarding the children of Turenn, there are features which, divested of the veil of Keltic texture in which they have been presented, resemble very much the incidents recorded in the life of the Greek Herakleos, and Latin Hercules, or of the famed Perseus, or Theseus, proving again that the poems or stories of the Aryan nations, are simply versions in Greek, Latin, or Keltic, of one and the same primeval subject, and " that they have their origin in the phenomena of the natural world," or that, according to another, they are diversified accounts of some of the truths revealed in Sacred Scripture, or handed down by tradition from the earliest patriarchs of the human family.

That the language of the stories is ancient if we look to the time of their composition, is plain, and that the period to which they refer is remote, appears clearly from the introduction of the magic art into the incidents recorded. This fact is another link in the chain of proof connecting the early races of Ireland with those of the East from the Indus to the Tigris and Euphrates. To this hour magic is regarded as an accomplishment among the peoples east and south of the Punjaub, from Cabul to Cape Comoron. The people in these parts practice magic not precisely as something opposed to God's law, but as a species of occult science, or rather a collection of facts and hidden views, of which all people of position are expected to have acquired a knowledge. Magic is to the thinking of the people of the Eastern nations allied to the knowledge of medicine, and of those arts which persons of learning are supposed to know. On this account we find that the sons of Turenn in the story before us, were quite a match in their display of magic power with Kian, the father of Lugh ; and in the tale relative to the children of Lir, Aoifé, his wife, seems to have had, as a matter of course, a ready knowledge of magic, when at a moment's thought, she exercises the power of changing at her pleasure her step-children into swans, just with much the same skill, as if she administered medicine to them in case they had been ailing. Bodbh Dearg, the king, avenging the wickedness of Lir's wife, struck her in turn with a magical wand, and changed her into a fiend doomed to wander for ever through the air. Magic in the homes of the Danann chiefs seemingly was regarded with much the same respect that it was held in the court of Pharaoh, in Egypt, or in Babylon, or in Persepolis. Thus the habits of the ancient people of Eire, and of those living in the far east, were in the knowledge and practice of magic the same.

Those Keltic tales bring the reader back to the oldest period of Grecian story, to the ages when pagan divinities and demigods possessed seemingly some power over the forms of animate and inanimate nature, as is seen in the stories which make up Grecian mythology v.g., Zeus and Europa ; Zeus and Danae ; Zeus and Leda. The Olympian god comes to Leda in the guise of a swan ; to Danae he appears in the form of a golden shower. With the Danann or

Keltic races of Ireland, Fionn-ghuala, "Fair-shoulder," holds the same place that Leda (the swan) does amongst the ancient Greeks, or "Helen," Leda's daughter, perhaps.

"The ideas of enchantment and transformation once awakened ran riot in a crowd of stories," says Rev. G. W. Cox in his *Mythology of the Aryan Nations*, vol ii., p. 285, "which resemble in some of their features, the myths of which the tale of Psyché and Eros is a type. . . in others again the narratives of jealous wives or stepmothers found in the mythology of all the Aryan tribes. Even in mediaeval times this idea prevailed. Thus the ship and swan are both prominent in the mediaeval romance of the Knight of the Swan, in which the son of Queen Matabrune having married the beautiful Beatrice, leaves her in her mother's charge. After his departure, Beatrice gives birth to six sons and one daughter, each with a silver collar round its neck. These children the stepmother seeks to destroy. . . . . They are at length deprived of their collars, and the loss changes them into swans, all but the youngest, Helias."

This romance Baring Gould regards as a local myth. He says the name Helias is a corruption of the Keltic *Ala*, or *Eala*, or *Hala* = a swan.

Each nation branching off from the great Aryan stock, tells in those ancient tales the same story symbolizing some striking features of nature, or the altered forms of a purer revelation, so as to suit the genius of its own special race, and the ever-varying character of the times as they change in their onward descent along the vale of ages.

THIRD DANANN STORY.—THE LADY CURCHOG.

And this leads to the third romance connected with the Tuatha Dé Danann race. It is the story relative to the Lady Curchog, daughter of the great chieftain known among that versatile people as Manannan. The time to which I refer is just after the two terrible disasters endured by these people at Teltown and at Druimlighean, a mound situated in the barony of Raphoe, County Donegal, a few miles north of the present town of Lifford. The antiquity of the story is satisfactorily shown from the fact that it is contained in the Book of Fermoy.

As to the value of the narration, the opinion of O'Curry is, that the facts referred to, and the principal personages named are always found to be in accordance with the records and traditions of true history. The story, like all historic tales, consists of two parts,— one, strictly and rigidly historic in the true sense of the term, and therefore truthful and real, the other full of those incidents and playful embellishments which excite the curiosity of the reader, and deal largely with the marvellous, with the magical, and the apparently supernatural. This manner of writing was in keeping with the age in which the story was first composed, when the magical and the marvellous were not devoid of reality.

The historic portion of the tale tells how the defeated chieftains assembled at Brugh-na-Boinne; how Manannan presided at the meeting, and guided the counsels of the assembly; how he directed that the chieftains should in self defence select well secured sites for their *Duns* on the summits of hills, well known all over Eire. All this has been told in the foregoing pages. The marvellous part of the tale relates how he wished to render the nobles of Ireland invisible to their conquerors, the Milesians, to make them immortal like the gods of Olympus; and thirdly to have for them delicious food always ready and yet never entirely consumed.

To effect the first object he had a druidical charm composed known ever since under the name ꝼé ꝼıаḃ,* by reciting which a person became concealed from his adversary; next, to render mortal life undying, he established a form of feast known amongst the ancient Irish by the name, "The Smith's Banquet," or in the original phrase, Fleadh Goibhneann (*fleadh* = banquet), Goibhneann, of one named Goibhne, or Smith; for the third, Mucca Mhanannain (Manannan's pigs) to be killed, yet to be always alive for the warriors. In the "Arabian Nights Entertainment," the enchanting process, and the banqueting preparations, with kindred modes of acting, are not much unlike those named in the story of Lady Curchog.

---

* According to O'Curry the term *Fiadh*, in ancient Irish means presence. This is true, for the term is found in *Fiadhnuise*, presence or evidence. What ꝼé means, he is not able to say. It appears to the present writer to be of kindred origin with ꝼа and ꝼаoı, *under, apart, aside*, and therefore "out of the way," "hidden." ꝼа, though a preposition was originally a noun, not unlike the term "fetch," English. With this meaning, ꝼé ꝼıаıḃ, ̣as a name applied to the charm, means "concealing of the presence." And that is precisely what it was intended to effect.

It is curious, however, that the same name is applied to the Christian prayer offered to the true God by St. Patrick, on the occasion when he and his clerical companions followed by the youthful Benin, proceeded

CHAPTER XVIII.

A NEW DYNASTY; HEBER AND HEREMON; DIVISION OF IRELAND; NEW POSSESSION; A FALLING OUT; BATTLE OF GEASHILL; DEATH OF HEREMON; NAMES OF PLACES TELL TO THIS DAY OF THE MILESIAN DYNASTY.

Q. 1. What was the result of the successful battles which the conquering Milesians had gained? How and where did the conquerors settle down?

A. Heremon and Heber Finn assumed the joint sovereignty of Ireland, and divided the country between them. Heremon took as his share the northern portion of the island—making the Boyne, and the Bron, and the Shannon from Lough Ree south-westward, the boundary of his division; the southern half, from the Boyne and the Shannon to Tonn Cliodna, became the possession of Heber Finn; Amergin, the third surviving son of Milesius, poet and physician of the Spanish Brigantian race, was constituted chief bard and philosopher of the nation. His descendants were to be, in a measure, like the tribe of Levi amongst the Jews. On this point O'Curry states: "Heber Finn and Heremon divided the island into two parts between them, the former taking all the southern part from the Boyne and the Shannon to Cape Clear, and the latter taking all the parts lying to the north of these rivers."

Dr. Keating is in favour of a second view recorded by ancient Irish annalists regarding the division of the island, made by

---

from Slane towards the hill of Tara in Meath. (See the Book of Hymns, Liber Hymnorum, fol. 19—a very ancient manuscript in the Library of Trinity College, Dublin). The hymn is now very common; it was published by Dr. Petrie in his *Antiquities of Tara Hill* in 1839. It has been published by several others. (See in College Irish Grammar, Prosody, the original with modern Irish version and translation by Clarence Mangan.) Burns & Oates, London, and Gill & Son, Dublin, have published this magnificent prayer of the Irish Apostle in thousands. Father Colgan says it was called by the ancient Irish Fé Fiaoh, and by others, the Luineac Pacpuic, or the Breastplate of St. Patrick. People say oan fiaó, by my ghost or spirit.

To this day it is a common saying amongst the Irish-speaking peasantry—"to partake of Goibhnean's banquet," meaning to obtain a long lease of life.

M

Heber Finn and Heremon directly after the conquest of the Danann tribes. He is of opinion, that Heber Finn took the territory south of the Shannon, allotting to Lughaidh, son of Ith, his father's cousin german—he who had brought his father's body home to Spain from the shores of the river Foyle—the district known ever since as Corca Lughaidh.

Corca Lughaidh, or Luis' district lies at the extreme end of the present County Cork, and embraces the two baronies of West Carbery and East Carbery—extending from Bantry Bay on the west, to the old Head of Kinsale in the east. Historians have taken note of the fact that the descendants of Lughaidh—so devoted to his father—continued to hold a distinguished position, with their hereditary possessions, and an honoured name longest of all the other descendants of the race of Breoghan.

While retaining the sovereignty, Heremon gave the province of Leinster to the chieftain of the Firbolg clans, Crimhthan Sciath-Beul, for the faithful services which he and his people had rendered during the late invasion, and probably for having invited the Milesians to come and conquer the country—wresting the chief authority from so feeble and so faithless a power as had been the Danann Dynasty. To Heber, the son of Ir, he assigned a large amount of territory in Ulster; while he reserved to himself the principal patrimony of Connacht and the rest of the northern province.

Whatever arrangement may have been made at the early part of their joint reign did not continue long—only a year; and when Heremon became sole ruler of the island, he gave the Belgic or Firbolg King the sceptre of Leinster. The student will note that there were two chieftains known by the name Heber; one the brother of Heremon—Heber Finn, the other his nephew—the son of Ir, who had been drowned at the Skellig Rocks, south of Valencia off the coast of Kerry. It is true then to say, speaking generally, that natives of Munster are descended from Heber Finn; natives of Ulster and Connacht, from Heremon; at the same time, many of the Ulster clans claim descent from Heber, son of Ir. To the east and west of the Shannon are many clans of Belgic descent, or of the Danann or Nemedian tribes. To this very day, one who cares to study the facial forms of the various races can readily read in the features, in the crania, in the stature, and in the figure of the peasant inhabitants, those that are of Belgic origin, those who are Danann or Milesian.

Each of the brothers, Heber Finn and Heremon, made a selection of the surviving Milesian chiefs, who had commanded ships, or headed battalions in the field. Heremon's friends built "duns" or fortified castles. Amergin built a dun, and fortified it, at Tochur—Invir mhoir, or Abhain mhoir—now known as the Causeway at Arklow, County Wicklow. Another leader erected a dun, which became known after his name as Dun Sobharké. There was a third built in the little island of Dalkey by Sedga, one of the chieftains, and known in Irish Story as Dun Deilginnis—the fortification on the "thorny" island—contracted in process of time into the present Dalkey (*i*, or *innis* = island, *dealg*, of thorns). In the Mourne Mountains another was erected—known as *Cathair an Nair*, the town of Nar, named after one of the sons of Breoghan, and uncle to Milesius. This citadel was built under the direction of Gostenn, one of the forty captains who had set sail from northern Spain. Finally, by Suirghi, a castle, Dun Edair, was erected on the hill of Howth—a hill known at that time as Benn Edair. Heremon himself selected the banks of the Nore (Eoir) in Ossory, as the site of his royal residence at Airged Ross. The Rath called Rath-Beathaigh is now known as Rath-Beagh, County Kilkenny. On the other hand, those five chieftains who followed the fortunes of Heber, namely, Caicher, Mantan, Un, Ughi, Fulman also erected duns : Caicher built Dun-Inn in the west of Ireland ; Un, a "rath" near the town of Galway, which to this day is known as *Rahoon, i.e.*, Rath-Uin, Un's rath.

Q. 2. How long did the Milesian monarchs Heremon and Heber, as joint sovereigns, live in peace, and what was the immediate cause of their deadly strife?

A. Heremon and Heber continued not longer than one year in brotherly, or even in friendly relations. Like the founders of the kingdom that grew up on the banks of the Tiber, they were jealous each of the share of authority which the other possessed.

The ostensible reason for falling out was that Tea, wife of Heremon, was not content with all the splendid hills north of the Shannon and Boyne ; she desired to get possession of (1) Druim Clasach in Hy Mani, from Loughrea to Ballinasloe, perhaps the hill of Aughrim—*i.e.*, correctly "Eac-Druim," steed-mound ; (2) Druim Bethaigh, in Maen Magh, near Loughrea, extending to Skarif at the

Shannon; (3) Druim Finghin in Munster. It divides the Decies *within* Druim, from the Decies *without*; it extends from Castle-Lyons County Cork, to the Bay of Dungarvan.

Apparently to satisfy the wishes of his wife Tea, and to gain these hills, Heremon determined to resume fighting.

The name "Heremon," means the superior man, or the conquering man; *Her* or *Er*, high, superior, and *mon*, gen. case of *mo*, a person. "Heber" means one having possessions; *Ber* or *Bar* or *Bur*, growing, acquiring, and *aodh* (*pr.* æ), fire, reddish (man).

Q. 3. Tell all that is on record regarding the battle of Geashill, in which Heremon was victorious.

A. The brothers Heremon and Heber determined to decide by the sword which of the two should be sole sovereign, or Ardrigh. They summoned their counsellors; the wise men and the leading advisers of each chieftain gave their views, not on the merits of the case, or the probable success of the issues, but, like the young counsellors of Roboam, they gave such advice as pleased their lord and master, and that which they perceived was the view and the bent of their respective chieftains. Advisers of this class are always in force around proud and selfish commanders who are guided by passion, prejudice, and lust of power. "To arms!" was the cry raised by each party. Those invaders who only a few years before had passed through the land as conquerors, like brothers, united as one man, were now ranged in hostile camps. Heber and his four sons marched their forces to meet those of Heremon. Heremon, on the other side, with his four sons, prepared his followers to meet their foes.

The encounter came off in the barony and parish known to this day by the name Geashill, as it were the land of mighty deeds (for ڴeѻrѻ means feats imposed, and ѻιll wonderful), situate in the eastern portion of the King's County. The precise district was a place known in ancient times as bṗι-ṫѻṁ, or ox-mount (bṗί mount, and ṫѻṁ, ox), and on a "tocher," that is, a highway between two level districts—" tocher-eider-da-maigh." The " tocher," or causeway, is still, philologically speaking, traceable in the name, " Baile-an-tocher," or, in modern spelling, Ballytogher, a village in the same district; and the plains (two) are represented to-day by the baronies of Warrenstown and Cootestown, which some thousand years ago were known as *Tuaith da Maigh*, and Englished by the term "Tethmoy." The actual fighting must, therefore, have happened in the district between Geashill and Philipstown on the west, and

Edenderry on the east, on the left bank of the Boyne, near its rise in King's County.

The Esker Riada passes through what is still called Moleana (Magh Leana), between Tullamore and Durrow, about a mile to the north of the former, and through the townlands of Bracklin and Tullaghbeg.

The following note of Dr. O'Donovan is taken from the *Four Masters*:—

"This was the year (3501 A.M.) in which Heremon and Heber assumed the joint sovereignty of Ireland, and they divided it into two between them. Towards the end of the year a contest arose between Heremon and Heber on account of the three most noble Druims (or hills)—Druim Clasaigh, in the country of Maini; Druim Beith, in Maonmaigh; and Druim Finghin, in Munster. A battle was fought between them in consequence, on the banks of the 'Bri-damh,' at Tocher-idir-da-Maigh. It is it that was called the battle of Geashill." (See also ' Ogygia,' Vol. II., Chaps. 17 and 34.)

In this battle Heber and his people were slain; O'Donovan says:

"Heremon killed his brother on the borders of Bri-damh, at Geashill, in Hy Falgia (Offaly), a part of Leinster, where the brothers fought with the greatest intrepidity."

After the death of Heber, Heremon made a fresh division of the territory of Ireland. He divided it into four provinces, or kingdoms; he gave Ulster to Heber, son of Ir, his brother; Munster to the four sons of Heber Finn, his nephews; Connacht to Un, who, as has been stated, settled near Galway, at Rath-Uin; and Leinster to the Belgic Prince, Crimhthan Sciath-Beul.

Amergin fell in battle by Heremon's sword, in Bregia, in Meath.

Heremon reigned fifteen years, and died in his own palace at Rath-Beathaigh, now Rath-beagh, over the Eoir river (Nore), at Argat-Ros.

The Firbolg people and the Danann tribes, and perhaps the Nemedians, too, were a power in the land. The Belgians had a king of their own, selected and established by Heremon over the province of Leinster. They were a powerful party also in the west and north-west of Connacht. The Tuatha De Danann were in possession of the high places, and the Fomorians and Nemedians were holding commercial and social relations with the masses of the people throughout the land.

Q. 4. Are footprints of the early Milesian leaders still to be found in the names of places in Ireland?

A. Yes, and these names confirm more strongly still the historic fact that there was such a people, and that what has been recorded of them is true at least substantially.

The names Chanaan, Chus, Shem, Madai, Gomer; Alexandria, Cæsarea, Ptolemais, America, Columbia, Van Dieman's Land, are proof that at one time Chanaan, and Alexander, and Cæsar, and Columbus lived; so also the names Inver "Colpa," and Teach "Doinn," and Sliabh "Fuaid," County Armagh, and Glean "Scotin," and Grean "Faise," show that Milesian leaders, men and women like Colpa, and Donn, and Fuad, and Scotin, and Fais, lived and flourished for a time in this country. There is a long list of names of places called after Milesian heroes—Inver Skeine; Inver Colpa, Sliabh Ebhleon (in Tipperary north); Sliabh Bladhma (now Sliabh Bloom) Magh Muirtheimne, Sliabh Cuailgne, in County Louth; Sleamhna Ita, Ros Nair, in King's County; Sliabhtha Cuaileann, Rath-Uin, Loch Conn. The foregoing names suffice.

CHAPTER XIX.

THE FAMILIES DESCENDED FROM HEBER FIONN; FROM HEREMON; AND FROM IR, OR HEBER SON OF IR; THE LEADING PRINCELY MILESIAN FAMILIES OF IRELAND TRACE THEIR DESCENT FROM THOSE THREE PRINCELY HOUSES—OF HEBER FIONN, HEREMON, AND IR; LENGTH OF TIME DOES NOT DESTROY CERTAINTY OF CONNECTION; THE CHIEF MONARCHS UP TO THE TIME OF CONOR MAC NESSA; A KINGLY GOVERNMENT EXISTED IN EIRE FOR OVER TWO THOUSAND YEARS, "Eire apo, inir na Rig," NOBLE EIRE, ISLAND OF KINGS.

Q. 1. Besides the names of places—those footprints of the early Milesian landing on the soil of Ireland—are there other links that bind still more closely the living present with the remote past in connection with the colony of Kelts from Spain?

A. Yes; the names of the princely and historically noble families, ready at hand to be found in each of the four provinces—in Ulster, in Connacht, in Leinster, and Munster.

It has been already shewn that Heremon gave possessions in the two Munsters to the sons of his brother, Heber Fionn. It is natural, therefore, that the princely families descended from Heber should be found in Munster and not in Ulster or Connacht. And so it is. The MacCarthys and O'Briens trace their origin to Heber Fionn, and not to Heremon nor to Ir.

Before the time of Mogha Nuadhat (second century) the house of Heber gave twenty-eight monarchs to Ireland; but in the third century of the Christian period, the Royal house of Munster was saved from extinction by a marriage alliance between Oilial Olom, descended of Heber, and Saba, daughter of Con of the Hundred Fights, descended of the line of Heremon.

Of this marriage were born three sons, Eogan Mór, Cormac Cás, and Teige. From the first of these patriarchal princes, Eogan Mór, the MacCarthy family has descended; from the second, Cormac Cás, the O'Briens, the O'Kennedys, MacMahons, and the MacConnamaras (now written MacNamara). The O'Haras, O'Garas, the O'Carrolls of Eily also are descended from Oilial Olom through Kian, the youngest son, and are ranked amongst the princely families.

Q. 2. Name some of those living in the other provinces who claim descent, and rightly too, from Heremon, the leading conqueror of the Milesian race.

A. From Heremon are sprung the leading families of Connacht, of Ulster, and of Leinster. The O'Conor Don, and all the blood relations of that regal family; the MacDermotts, the O'Rourkes, the O'Kellys of Hy-Mani, in the county of Galway. Then there are the O'Murphys of the Hy-Briain line; O'Maddens, and those connected by blood with the progenitors of the O'Kelly family; the O'Flahertys of Iar-Connacht, the O'Malleys of the west; the O'Douds, or Douda, or Duddy of Ballina, Tirawley, and Tir-fiachra.

In Ulster we have the O'Neills, the northern and southern branches, and all who claim descent from Niall of the Nine Hostages; the O'Donnells, therefore, and the O'Kanes, the O'Gallaghers, O'Boyles, O'Doghertys, the Malachlins, MacGeoghagans MacAuleys, O'Molloys, Foxes, MacDonnells, O'Reillys, O'Fallons, O'Loughlins, O'Malones, the MacGuires, MacDowdels. In south Leinster the MacMurraghs or Kavanaghs, the O'Byrnes, O'Tooles, the Fitzpatricks of Ossory, O'Murphys of Leinster, claim descent from Heremon. There must have been, therefore, some being known by that name from whom all these families claim to be descended. He was no imaginary person from whom so many families for over three thousand years have sprung. So many could not have erred in looking up to him as their common progenitor, even as the Jews look back to Abraham as their father. The records containing the narration were public. They were kept with the greatest care, and had for object some of the highest interests of the entire nation and people. Even if one family might possibly have erred, the mistake would in time have been made right by the others The family records of each princely clan were every third year publicly revised at Tara, and collated with other well-known public records. All are agreed that those named are descended from Heremon, and not from Heber Fionn, nor from Ir, or from Ir's son, Heber. (See O'Curry's lectures.)

Q. 3. To the son of Ir, Heremon allotted possessions in Ulster; what families claim descent from him?

A. Amongst the remarkable monarchs in the long line of Ard-righs, or sovereigns of Ireland, is Ruadh-raidh (*pr.* Roory). Like Ollamh Fodla, he was descended from Ir. He flourished as supreme king of Ireland about the second century before the Christian era. From Ruadhraidh sprung in the fifth generation Conal Kearnach, a hero who lived in the days of Meav, Queen of Connacht. Conal was famed amongst the most eminent military knights of that remarkable period. He was known as being one of the "*Clan Ruadhraidh,*" *i.e.*, one of the descendants of Ardrigh *Ruadhraidh*, who were then called and known by that title, and the only surviving branch of the stock of Ir. Conal had two sons—the progenitors of princely families from Ulster. The names af these two were Irial Glunmhór (large-knee), and Laisach Lanmór (large-spear). From the former came the Dal-Aradian race of whom MacGennis *i.e.*, MacAonguis was the chief family. From the latter are descended the "O'Mores" of Laoighis or Leix in Queen's county. Now there was another remarkable personage at the period when Conal Kearnach lived, who had been king and a knight of the Red or Royal branch. He is known as Fergus MacRoigh, ex-king of Ulster. In his early years he was monarch of the province of Ulster. By the cunning of Nessa, the mother of the youthful king Conor, Fergus was deprived of his kingdom. He lived however for many years afterwards in Ulster. His name is connected with the heroic deeds of the knights of the Red or Royal branch who flourished in Emania. After the treachery of King Conor, and his treatment of Deirdre—as is told in the third tale of the Three Sorrowful Stories of ancient Eire—Fergus accompanied by a great number of military came to Connacht and offered his services to Queen Meav. This is the heroic period, so to speak, in Irish History. It corresponds with that in which Antony and Augustus flourished at Rome. Queen Meav at Cruachan, county Roscommon, bore to Fergus, three sons at one birth. These were named Kiar, Corc, and Conmac. They, too, and their descendants were known as " Clan Ruadraidh." From those three are descended —from Kiar, the O'Connor Kerry, a princely family; from Corc, the O'Connors of Corcomroe, and the O'Loghlins of Burren; from Conmac, the third son and youngest, a great number of princely families have been descended. Conmac had possessions in the west, in Conmac-ne-mara, or Conmac-by-the-sea, now known (by omitting mac) as Connemara. His descendants lived there in the barony afterwards known as Ballinahinch. Conmac had lands in the barony of Dunmore, and some of his descendants lived there. St. Jarlath, first Bishop of Tuam, was of that race. The descendants of Conmac lived also in a place known afterwards as the barony of Kilmaine. There, too, Conmac's descendants flourished in the second, third, and fourth centuries. The whole of the south of county Leitrim was possessed by the children of Conmac; and from them are descended the princely house of Reynolds, or Rannall or MacRannall, called in Irish " muıncıp' eoluıp " or the people of knowledge. Lastly Conmac's sons settled in Longford. That portion of the diocese of Ardagh, situate in county Longford was known in the early Irish Church by the name of " Conmacné," up to the ninth century. The heads of the race in that district are the O'Ferralls and the O'Quins. These are princely families descended from Ir, brother of Heremon. Conmac-ne means descendants of Conmac. *Né* in old Irish signifies people, offspring, heroes. *Né* is plural of *naidh*, or *nai*, a hero.

Q. 4. How many Ard-righs or supreme kings reigned in Eire from the time of Heremon up to the first year of the Christian era?

A. Historians differ on this particular point. They differ also in the chronology which they respectively adopt. The writers of the

"Annals" known as those "of the Four Masters," follow the chronology of the Septuagint. Although considerable difference exists, nevertheless in substance the record of the supreme kings is the same in all. One can safely say there flourished one hundred kings from Heremon inclusive to Crimhthan Naidh-Nair, in the twelfth year of whose reign Christ our Lord was born, or in the reign of Conaire the Great, according to others.

TOTAL NUMBER OF KINGS UP TO THE COMING OF ST. PATRICK.

O'Flaherty in his "Ogygia," part iii., chapter 89, writes thus of the pagan kings of Ireland:—

"We have given the heathen kings of Ireland to the number of one hundred and thirty-six (136), besides ten others whom some writers insert in the catalogue of Irish kings, though they did not attain to the monarchy of the island. . . ."

How THEY WERE DESCENDED.

But the 136 were absolutely kings, of whom nine were of Firbolgic descent; and nine, Danann. Heremon and his posterity as kings amounted to sixty of the remaining one hundred and eighteen. Of these sixty, thirty-seven were lineally descended from him down to Niall; seven others left no issue. There were eight kings from Leinster; three from Ulster, one named Colla Uais of the Orgillians; one from Connacht, 'Dathy. Twenty-nine of the posterity of Heber Fionn (Munster); twenty-four of the line of Ir (Ulster): Macha, a queen in her own right; three of the family of Lughad, the son of Ith; and one elevated from the ranks of the plebeians, Carbry Cinn-chait.

How THEY REIGNED.

Some of these kings reigned in turn one year each. For instance, the three sons of Heremon who succeeded to the throne on their father's death, assumed the power of Ardrigh, each in turn for one year. This system was very defective.

How THEY DIED.

Of these 136, one hundred perished by the sword; seventeen died a natural death; six were taken away by plague; three were killed by lightning; and ten departed this life, called away by accidents of different kinds. One set himself up like Jeroboam to establish idolatry in the island, Tighearnmas; one died in the most excruciating tortures; another was crucified: another expired without any visible cause or mark; one was drowned; another burned to death; one died of grief; another was killed by his horse; another was choked by the bone of a fish; and finally, another was poisoned. The ancient annals are particularly accurate in recording the leading events connected with the history of each of these Ardrighs.

Q. 5. How many of these were in any degree remarkable above the ordinary run of supreme pagan kings up to the Christian period ?

A. Not more than a dozen. Each supreme monarch lived like a prince just as his predecessor had done at Tara; or in the palace of Emania during the period that it flourished, or in the northern palace of Aileach near Derry. It is pitiable to read the records how the ancient Irish kings, like the kings of the Heptarchy in England, or the emperors of Rome, perished—one hundred of them by the sword. Those remarkable above the rest are (1) Tighearnmas; (2), Enna Airgetheach; (3), Ollamh Fodhla; (4), Siorna; (5), Kimbaeth, who first built the palace of Emania; (6), Hugony Mór; (7), Labhraidh (or Lowry) Loingseach; (8), Ruadhraidh Mór, descended from Ir; (9), Eochaidh Feidleach (Meav was his daughter); (10), Fergus MacRoigh; (11), Conor Mac Nessa; (12), Conaire Mór.

Tighearnmas is a name that implies power, command, or sovereignty, from *Tighearna*, Lord, and *mos*, manner. He lived, it is said, eighty years, in the second century after the death of Heremon. Discoveries in gold were made in Wicklow, and vessels in gold were fashioned during his time.

He was victorious in battle against all his enemies. He conquered the Firbolg people who arose against him. He chastised the Fomorians or pirates who had attacked the sea-board. He overcame all the enemies of his sovereign power.

He it was who formally introduced idol worship. It is not known whether or not the ancient Irish regarded the sun itself as a god, or merely the symbol of a god-like power, and therefore whether they gave supreme adoration to the sun, like the Persian fire-worshippers, or merely respected it as a sign of divine agency which sustains all things. It is stated that there were no idols in Eire up to the days of Tighearnmas. At all events, it is certain, as far as can be known, that there were no human sacrifices ever offered in Eire.

Tighearnmas lost his life at a sacrifice offered in the plains of Magh-sleacht (field of worship) in Breffni, in the County Cavan, to his idol, Crom Cruach. (The meaning of *Crom* is bent, crooked; and *Cruach*, a "lumpy figure," a term applied to this day to a mountain, or to a stack, or corn-rick.)

The first Sunday in August is to this day called by the peasant people "Domhnach Crom Duibh"—the Sunday of Black Crom—probably because at that season the idol received special honors from the pagan progenitors of the Irish people. (See Life of St. Patrick by Canon O'Hanlon.)

(2). Enna Airgetheach, that is Enna the silverman. He it was who ordered the making of silver spears.

(3). Ollamh Fodla is named here in third place. His real name was *Eachaidh*, a common name amongst the Irish kings, and like *Marcus*, from Marc, a horse, signifies "horseman;" from *each* or *eoch*, a horse. He was called Ollamh on account of his learning, and *Fodla* which is an ancient name of Ireland—that is, he was, at the time, "the learned man of Ireland." It was he who built at Tara the great hall for the learned men of that period. The hall was known by the name Mur Ollamhan or the "stone-house of the Ollamhs." He it was who instituted the triennial parliament at Tara. The meetings were held at Samhain time, that is, "the close of good weather." Now, the name of November in Irish Gaelic is Mina Samhna. Samhain is derived from *Samh*, pleasant, fine, and *fuin*, end—that is end of good weather. Ollamh Fodhla appointed rulers and governors over districts and towns. He is one of the most renowned amongst the ancient monarchs of Eire.

(4). Sirna—Another Irish Ardrigh is said to have lived one hundred and fifty years, one hundred of which he ruled prosperously as chief king. *Sir* in Gaelic means continuous, or always, and *nai*, a hero.

(5). We come now to Kimbaeth, of whom Tighearnach, Abbot of Clonmacnoise in the eleventh century (1088 A.D.) writes, "that all the records of the Scots up to the time of Kimbaeth are uncertain." It is to be noted that Tighearnach does not state that the coming of the Milesians to Ireland, or any of the events of a public kind, connected with the race is uncertain, but the records were, in his opinion, uncertain, or not as certain before that period as they were at a subsequent period.

King Kimbaeth was the first who dwelt in the palace of Emania which he had built and embellished.

(6). The next on the list of remarkable *Ard-righthé* or chief kings is Hugony Mór, or the Great, called by that title on account of the deeds ascribed to him, namely, that he gained sway by his military prowess over much of Western Europe; that he commanded his fleets, such as they were in those days, and led them through the Mediterranean, that he made successful incursions into the islands and effected a landing in Sicily. He was great in the numerous progeny of whom he was parent and progenitor. He had twenty-two sons and three daughters. He determined to make each independent and to lower the power of the sub-kings. Accordingly, he divided each of the five provinces into five parts, or the whole island into twenty-five portions—assigning one for each of his children. He thus satisfied their desire for power and the exaction of dues usually paid to chieftains. He prevailed on the subordinate kings, and on the people, to swear by the sun and moon and by the elements, that they would never disturb any of his posterity in this settled sovereignty, which, he thought, he had now firmly established. This arrangement continued for three centuries. The monarch himself was slain after a reign of forty years.

(7). His great grandson, Labhraidh Loingseach, was another remarkable sovereign. To avoid being murdered in his tender years, he was, when a child, sent to his relatives in Gallia or France. When he grew to be a man he was invited home. He returned by the largest boat that could then be made. Hence he was called by the name "Loingseach," or the "Shipman," *long* means ship in Gaelic. "Maen" was his real name. The term "Labraidh," means "speaks," or "talks,"—and he was styled so because he talked either like a foreigner, or like a seaman.

(8). Ruadhraidh Mor, or Rory the Great, from *ruadh*, red, and *righ*, king,—was a remarkable Ardrigh. Like all monarchs styled *great* in those days, he fought many battles in Ireland and out of it, and won them. It is stated by some writers, that Ruadhraidh aided the African King Masinissa in his wars against the Romans. He is remarkable for the length of years he reigned as sovereign—seventy years according to some authorities. This Ardrigh is especially remarkable in his descent and in his posterity. He was descended not from the line of Heber or Heremon, but from Ir,—and the leading saints and sovereigns of Ireland in the Christian period have been of the line of Ruadhraidh. His descendants were known by the name *clanna Ruadhraidh*, or the children of Rory. This sovereign had four sons of whom three reigned as kings; his son

Ross was the father of Fergus at one time King of Ulster; Cas, father of Factna the wise, whose son was the famed Conor Mac Nessa, King of Ulster at the time of Christ; Conga, a third son was father of Conall Kearnach; these men and their cousin Cuchulainn were the leading heroes of the Red Branch Knights who flourished about the opening of the first century of the Christian period—say in the days of Julius Caesar and Pompey.

(9). Eochaidh Feidleach father of the renowned Queen Meav, restored the pentarchy.

(10). Fergus Mac Roigh, was so called, from his mother's name Roigh. His father was Ross, son of the Ardrigh Ruadhraidh. Fergus was King of Ulster; he made love to Nessa the widow of his deceased cousin Factna, and she consented to become his wife, on condition that he should permit Conor, her son, to sit beside him on the judgment seat of his kingdom for one year. The superior manner of Conor, like another Absolom, and the plotting and seductive bearing of his mother, Nessa, gained the affections of the people. After a time the people wished to dethrone Fergus and to make Conor Mac Nessa, king. Fergus quietly resigned in favour of his stepson. The great Irish story known as *Deirdré*, the third of Three Sorrowful Tales of story-telling among the Gael, relates to this period. King Conor Mac Nessa, and ex-King Fergus Mac Roigh, with their cousins the sons of Uisneach and their followers are the leading characters in this dramatic story.

The *Táin-bó-Cuailgné* in Irish, or the Tain-quest by Sir Samuel Ferguson or, Lady Ferguson's *Ireland before the Conquest*, should be read in order to get an insight to the manners and customs of this period, and to learn the achievements of the heroes who lived and fought for duty, for reward or glory. The manners of the people of the time, and the spirit that animated the knights and military heroes are not unlike those of the Homeric period—when Agamemnon King of Men, Achilles and Ulysses flourished. See the *Foray of Queen Meav* by Aubrey de Vere, and other legends of Ireland's heroic age—amongst those legends that known as " the Sons of Uisneach," is worth the student's perusal.

The best and fullest version of all yet published regarding the Sons of Uisneach and the Irish Deirdré is the neat volume from the pen of Dr. Robert Dwyer Joyce, M.D., M.R.I.A. Dublin: M. H. Gill and Son, O'Connell-street upper, 1877.

Q. 6. For the sake of clearness and distinctness mark the era that elapsed from the time of the Kings Fergus Mac Roigh and Conor Mac Nessa to the death of Dathi, the last of the Pagan monarchs.

A. For students it is best to divide that term of years into three periods. The first is known amongst antiquaries and Irish literary men as the Heroic period, sometimes called the "golden age" of Irish story—the second is known practically as the Fenian period; the third may be termed the Christian dawn, or the marauding period,

This division has not hitherto been formally made; nevertheless there should be a line drawn between the two periods first and second named above. Sir Samuel Ferguson hints at this division in his introductory note to the poem "The healing of Conall Carnach," when he says alluding to the story of Deidré, "the best part of *Irish heroic tradition* connects itself with the reign and period of Conor Mac Nessa, preceding, by nearly three centuries, the epoch of Cormac Mac Art and the Fenian or Irish romances." The line cannot well be drawn pointing out the exact year that separates the first period from the second, but Conor Mac Nessa may be regarded as the central figure around which may be grouped all the events connected with the first period—say from the reign of Ruadhraidh to the days of Conn of the Hundred Fights, A.D. 145. This includes the historic exploits of Conor himself; the story of ex-king Fergus Mac Roigh; the tale of Deidré, and the part taken by the sons of Uisneach; the flight of Fergus and his followers to Connacht; the exploits of Queen Meav, her character as a historic personage, and her subsequent mythical existence; the events connected with the palace of Emania, or Navan near Armagh; the five orders of Knighthood then flourishing in Ireland—namely :—

(*a*). Niagh Nasc,—or Knights of the Golden Collar.
(*b*). Curraidh na Craoibhé ruaidhe, or Knights of the Red Branch or, as O'Curry thinks, Knights of the Royal Branch.
(*c*). Clanna Deagha,—the Munster Knights,
(*d*). Clanna Baoisgne,—Leinster Knights,
(*e*). Clanna Morna,—Connacht or Belgian Knights.

The "Fenian" period, on the other hand, includes from the reign of Conn (A.D. 145) or of his grandson Cormac Mac Art, up to the year A.D. 350. And from A.D. 350, up to the death of Dathi may be called the "Christian dawn," for Ireland, a period when the Kings of Eire made it the study of their lives to make incursions into Alba, and into Britain, into Armoric Gaul and even, like Dathi, to cross rivers and mountain ranges till they reached the Alps. It was during those years that the Picts and the Scots dashed into Britain and drove the native inhabitants from the south of Alba, and from the territory north of the Humber southwards. It was then the natives called on the Roman authority for help—and the Irish soldiers—the "Scoti," were brave enough [to meet the Roman legions face to face in the field of battle. This time may well be called the marauding period. The heroes of the Fenian period are quite distinct in time, in character, in place and in exploits, from those who flourished at an earlier date. Such are Fionn Mac Cumhaill the leader of the Fenian hosts, son-in-law of the monarch Cormac, Diarmaid, Graine, daughter of the reigning monarch, Cailte Mac Ronain, Oisin, Oscar; and then the place around which these heroes figure is usually the hill of Tara—or, Fionn's residence at the hill of Allen near Kildare. The heroes of the "golden" period—time of Conor Mac Nessa—are connected with the palace at Emania, or with Cruachan. It is true that the spirit of Knighthood had continued from the first age up to the time of Treunmor, of Cumhal, of King Cormac and his son-in-law Fionn, when it it attained its fullest development. Garaidh Mac Morna was at this time chief of the Fiann of Connacht.

A fair sized volume could readily be compiled on each of those two periods, the heroic or golden, and the Fenian period, properly so-called. Another volume to explain the events fully, should present the Scoti and the neighbouring nations, with the kings and their followers who invaded Alba and Britain and the kingdoms of Western Europe in the fourth century of the Christian era.

CHAPTER XX.

IRELAND'S ROYAL BACKBONE: HER LINE OF KINGS REACHES NIGH THREE THOUSAND YEARS. THE NATURE AND CHARACTER OF THE BREHON LAWS, BEST TEST AND PROOF OF THE SOCIAL STATE AND MANNERS OF THE IRISH IN THE FAR PAST; THE CLAN SYSTEM— THE RIGHTS OF THE CLAN AND OF THE CHIEF :— ELECTIVE POWER, TANISTRY; GAVEL KIND; MORAL AND PHYSICAL CHARACTERISTICS OF THE IRISH PEOPLE.

Q. 1. A certain writer on Irish History styles a continuous line of monarchs "the spinal column of a Nation;" using this metaphor, he boldly states "the History of Ireland is invertebrate," *i.e.*, it has no such regal backbone—be good enough to say is there any truth in that statement.

A. The detailed record already presented in the preceding pages supplies the answer—that there is no truth in the statement; nor even the shadow of a foundation for such an expression of opinion.

It is enough for one to go back to the second race of immigrants who had landed in this country before the coming of the Milesians from the south of Europe. These were the Belgæ or Firbolgs, as they are called in our national annals. They ruled in this land before the arrival of another Keltic shoal of immigrants known as Tuatha Dé Danann. Each people spoke a tongue known as Keltic; each were ruled by primitive laws, kindred to those known amongst the early Latin and Greek races. These people had a government directed by kingly power and authority;—they had rulers and an Ardrigh, or supreme king who was monarch of all.

Dr. Petrie, in his history of Tara Hill, tells us that the "Firbolg was the first who erected a palace at Tara, and divided the island into five provinces, that each province had its own king, and that the Ardrigh or supreme monarch ruled the whole island."

N

Reckoning a regal succession in Pagan or Christian Ireland, it is the Ardrigh or monarch who alone, is taken into account, and not the kings of subordinate power or position. Now those two Keltic races just named had laws and a civilized state of society and a regular established policy carried out with efficiency and success, considering the early period in which those dynasties flourished. They had a parliament too; they recognised religious rites; they had military orders even then, or early model combinations that subsequently produced the military systems so famous in Ireland in later Pagan times; they had Ollamhs, that is doctors learned in science and art; they had Druids, and at a later time Brehons or Judges and Bards, Chroniclers and professional story writers, or Scanachaidhs.

Next the Milesian immigrants succeeded the Belgæ and the Danann races; and of the Milesian line alone, there flourished, according to O'Flaherty, one hundred and thirty-six (136) monarchs in Ireland before the people came under the influence of Christianity.

One dynasty possessed regal power in Ireland for three thousand years, up to the time when Henry II. landed in this country. That was rather a large backbone! The last elected Ardrigh of Ireland was Monarch Roderick O'Conor—who finally retired from the turmoil of a troubled life, and found place in the seclusion of religious retirement at Cong in Connacht.

Taking the Belgian and the Danann lines of chief monarchs along with those of the Milesian race, from Heremon to Roderick O'Conor—what a lengthy array of monarchs presents itself, forming "a spinal column" and a "royal backbone" such as no other nation can boast of. In fact no country west of China, has had another such spinal column—extending through three dynasties along a period of years calculated by thousands. If the history of a nation is, as some state, the biography of her kings, Ireland even in pagan periods has had a sufficiently full history in the record—if nothing else—of those famous monarchs, who hold an honoured name in the ancient annals of our people.

The statement, therefore, that Ireland had no royal backbone; and that she was not a nation before the conquest, is a gratuitous assertion, devoid of even a shadow of truth, and quite opposed to the facts of history.

Q. 2. Give some idea of what the Brehon laws are—that body of laws under which in ages past, the natives of Christian as well as Pagan Ireland were governed.

A. The name Brehon in Irish-Gaelic means a judge—one who decides or pronounces on a case according to an established code of customs or of law. It is formed from the Keltic term *beir*, to bear, to carry, to bring forth, like the Latin and Greek *fero*. The mind grasps as it were the bearings of the question to be adjudicated and efformates the correct decision and pronounces it, or puts it forth. Hence the name " Brehon " phonetic form of *Breitheamhan*, genitive case of *Breitheamh*, a judge : genitives ending in *an* come to us from the time when the Belgæ were a power in Eire.

" There are " says Maine (Lecture II. p. 32) " some strong and even startling points of correspondence between the functions of the Druids in the pagan time as described by Cæsar, and the office of the ' Brehon ' as suggested by the law tracts (of ancient Ireland). The extensive literature of law just disinterred testifies to the authority of the Brehons in all legal matters, and raises a strong presumption that they were universal referees in disputes." What then were the functions of the Druids ? Cæsar says that the Druids were supreme judges in all public and private disputes; and that all questions of homicide, of inheritance and of boundary were referred to them for decision. The Druids presided over schools of learning to which the Keltic Irish flocked eagerly for instruction, remaining in them sometimes for twenty years at a time. The pupils in these schools learned an enormous quantity of verses which were never committed to writing. By this means the memory was strengthened. At their head there was a chief Druid, whose place at his death was filled by election, and the succession occasionally gave rise to violent contests of arms. (De Bello Gallico, VI. 13. 14).

The schools of literature and law were numerous in ancient Ireland, and Professor O'Curry states that the course was over twelve years. All literature, including law seems to have been then identified with poetry. All the instructions given, all records and events, precepts of law, counsel imparted, like King Cormack's advice to a Prince, were all delivered in verse and committed in rhyme to memory. The Brehon was the teacher and director in those schools. He was to the Irish at a later date, what the Druid was to the Keltic Gauls in Cæsar's time.

As to the origin of the Brehon Laws : they were in the earliest form a collection of the primary principles of moral right and wrong, existing amongst a number of families or a community. They were like the laws of the Twelve Tables; or like the Hindu laws of the present time.

The law of England has come in part from the Roman law and from the law of the Catholic Church and from Statute law. The Roman law was founded on the laws of the Twelve Tables. These Roman archaic laws came from Eastern lands. The Brehon law, and the Roman law, and therefore the law of England, were in their earliest forms the same in the far past. They were the outcome, so to speak, of the law of nature. From the same early germs have grown—each assuming a different form and shape—the corpus of Roman Law, and of English Law. The Brehon Law is to day just what it was fourteen hundred years ago. The books of law present the primitive texts, with the comments of Irish Brehons and sages. We quote the following from the pages of *The Aryan Origin*, strengthened by the views of Sir Henry Sumner Maine, and the view of the writer of the preface to Vol. III. of the Brehon Laws, now published.

The Brehon Law, like the rich vases and works of art that lay buried in the tombs of Etruria, had not only been sealed up in the Irish language, unseen by the eye of any scholar outside Ireland, but had been for a period lost. Now, at length, they have been discovered, and are open to the view of the whole literary world.

Thus, the present generation of inquirers are brought back, at a bound, to the time when they can behold the social and civil state of Ireland in the fifth century, and even at a period much more remote.

" Up to the early dawn of civilisation, the very causes," says Sir H. Sumner Maine " which have denied a modern history to the Brehon law, have given it a special interest of its own, in our day, through the arrest of its development." It is this arrest of the development of the Brehon laws in the past, that causes the translation and publication to be so much prized at present. Like the Round Towers, like the family features of the Japhetic race, like the laws of linguistic science, the Brehon Law comes in and forms an arc, in the circle of newly-discovered truths, that point up to the primitive Aryan period, full of knowledge, of action, of cyclopean power and grandeur.

It is in no way surprising that the Brehon code should appear archaic to moderns. The text now presented to the public—with translations by O'Donovan and O'Curry—has been a literary fossil for over a thousand years.

This fossil condition of Ireland's ancient law, morally speaking, is owing to four causes—the insular position of Ireland, its freedom from Imperial Rome, the antagonism of Britain and of British Law, the love of the Keltic race to preserve traditional usages.

Value of the Law

"The value which the ancient laws of Ireland—the Brehon Laws—will possess when they are completely published and interpreted, may," says Maine, "be illustrated in this way. Let it be remembered that the Roman Law which, next to the Christian religion, is the most plentiful source of the rules governing actual conduct throughout Western Europe, is descended from a small body of Aryan customs, reduced to writing in the fifth century, before Christ and known as the Twelve Tables of Rome.

"Let it be further recollected that the Roman Law was at first expanded and developed, not at all, or very slightly by legislation, but by a process which we may perceive still in operation in various communities—the juridical interpretation of authoritative texts by successive generations of learned men. Now the largest collection of Irish legal rules which has come down to us, professes to be an ancient code, with an appendage of later glosses and commentaries. This ancient Irish code corresponds historically to the Twelve Tables, and to many similar bodies of written rules which appear in the early history of Aryan societies."

That a kernel, or some kernels of written law existed is highly probable; and it is also probable that the whole of the Brehon Laws consists of them, and of accumulations formed upon them. The Brehon Laws are in no sense a legislative construction; and thus they are not only an authentic monument of a very ancient group of Aryan institutions: they are also a collection of rules which have been gradually developed in a way highly favorable to the preservation of archaic peculiarities.

The Brehon Law had been expanded by the juridical interpretation of authoritative texts, just like the laws of the Hebrew race, or like the code of the Spartan State. The Roman Law became transformed and modified by legislation, to suit the altered times, the varied new forms of society, the changes connected with growing States and with diverse races.

"Two causes (says Maine) have done most to obscure the oldest institutions of the portion of the human race to which we belong.

One, the formation throughout the west of strong centralised governments; the other has been the influence, direct and indirect, of the Roman Empire, drawing with it an activity in legislation unknown to the parts of the world which were never subjected to it. Ireland had never been exposed to these influences—she never formed a part of the Roman empire; she had a central government, but never a strong one, capable of exercising—like Rome of old, or England at present—a special centralising, legislative power."

"Under these circumstances, it is not wonderful that the Brehon Law, growing together without legislation upon an original body of Aryan customs, and formed beyond the limit of that cloud of Roman juridical ideas which for many centuries overspread the whole continent, and even at its extremity, extended to England, should present some very strong analogies to another set of derivative Aryan usages, the Hindu law, which was similarly developed" (Maine).

The laws of Europe, divested of their legislative and judicial accessory forms, and reduced to first principles, are found to be identical—one with the primitive Aryan. "Wherever (says Maine) we have a body of Aryan customs, either anterior to, or slightly affected by, the Roman empire, it will be found to exhibit some strong points of resemblance to the institutions which are the basis of the Brehon law."

To conclude, the Brehon Law is not what the Parliament of Kilkenny or Edmund Spenser, or Sir John Davies pronounced it to be—either "wicked" or "damnable" "repugnant to God's laws and man's," or "lewd" or "unreasonable." On the contrary, it has been shown to be, and scholars versed in law declare that it is, just, and in accord with the natural law, and with the written law, which is from God. It comes to us from the Aryan period. It is twin sister, in legal parentage, of the code known as the "Laws of the Twelve Tables." It is therefore kindred in its institution to European law, and especially to the laws of England. The Eastern or Hindu law and itself flow from the same source, and have been in time enlarged and extended quite in the same fashion.

Irishmen governed, in days that are gone, by such a code, must have, like other nations grown up, children of honour and truth, with a strong aptitude for religion. The men must have been, as they were, truthful, brave, chivalrous and noble; the women, free, honored, devoted; learning was fostered and respected; the arts and sciences cultivated; works of civilisation and material progress patronised.

The good resulting from such a code, was manifold, not alone in social life, and in the political, but in the religious and the literary.

It was admirably suited to the times and the people.

The best way to become acquainted intimately with the social life and manners of the early Milesian races is to read, or rather study the volumes of the Brehon law now published.

Q. 3. Explain the " Clan " System amongst the Gaels; and the customs known as Tanistry and Gavel Kind.

A. The " Clan " System which existed in Ireland up to a late period and flourished in the Highlands of Scotland, presents nothing more than the idea of the family system, enlarging its bounds as widely as one chooses, or grouping different families together, all under one *Keann* or head, *i.e.*, King. The term *Clan* means children in the Gaelic tongue, and *Keann* signifies head or chief. It is the patriarchal system. which is fully illustrated in the life of Abraham; or it is like the family system kept up to this day by the Slavs in the Eastern confines of the empire of Austria—say in Croatia or Servia.

In a small tract known as *A Plea for the Evicted Tenants of Mayo*, written by the present writer, and published by Browne and Nolan, Nassau-street, Dublin, 1883—the following view of the clan system is presented:—

THE " CLAN " SYSTEM.

" The peasants of Ireland still cling to the idea that every Government ought to be paternal in regard to its subjects. It is now some two hundred and seventy years since the Brehon laws ceased to have any legal directive force in Ireland. The "clan" system, as it was called, had prevailed up to the "flight of the Earls." These laws— or the first principles of them—have come down from the very infancy of human society. The family, it is well known, was the earliest standard of social government. Those who lived under one fatherly guide and governor were known as a "clan," which in Irish Gaelic signifies children or family. The members of the tribe were to the chief what the children of a household are to the head of the house. To all the members, no matter how numerous, the chief was a "father" or "pater," and his $αρχη$ government " patriarchal." It is worth keeping in memory that wherever the "clan" system prevailed, as it did invariably amongst the Kelts—the clan Chief, in times past, could no more entertain the idea of dissociating the land from the people who lived on it, than a father could entertain the notion of dispossessing his children. The chieftain in past times was regarded by the Gaels as head of the clan—that is chief father Such was the form of government amongst the Gaels in Ireland. To this hour the traditionary notion abides in the minds of the masses, that the ruling administration ought to be fatherly.

OTHER PEOPLES' VIEW—THE GOVERNING POWER AS FATHERLY.

"The Keltic race is not singular in its views of early primitive sovereign authority. In the East, throughout Hindustan, from Pekin to Stamboul, the inhabitants look up to the "King" as to a great father, and the Queen, or Empress, as a great mother. Kingdoms have been altered, and the forms of government changed, but the essentials of good government have never changed, and cannot change. The patriarchal spirit influenced the Emperors Augustus and Trajan, as well as it did Romulus or the early kings of Alba-Longa. We find that Assuerus, who reigned from India to Ethiopia over one hundred and twenty-seven provinces, was as fatherly as ever had been Astyages, the grandfather of Cyrus the Elder—the founder of the Persian Empire."

How exceeding like the " clan " system amongst the Gaels is the system of " house-communions " amongst the Slavs, the following quotation from a note in vol. III. of the Brehon Law plainly shows:—

"The system of house-communion stated succinctly is as follows: The land in the countries and among the classes in which it prevailed did not belong to individuals, but was held as a sort of trust in perpetual entail for the benefit of house-communions. A house-communion consisted of a number of individuals united by an actual, or occasionally a fictitious tie of cousanguinity. All the children of members of the house-communion were *ipso facto* co-partners in the property of what we may call the family corporation. Membership in a house-communion descended only through the male line. Unmarried women belonged to the house-communions of their fathers, and widows to those of their late husbands. An adopted member took the surname of the house-communion—(in Ireland the name of the clan) into which he was adopted."—Quoted from the *Fortnightly Review*. No. LXIV. pp. 372, 373.

The head of each house-communion had no right to sell or do away with, or give up any part of the property of the house-communion, without consulting the members of the communion. In like manner no chieftain amongst the Gaels had any right to resign or appropriate the property of the clan of which he was head. He held the lands for the whole tribe and not for himself.

TANISTRY.

The chief of a clan, was at first in ruling, patriarchal. The interests of the community demanded that the head of the clan should be a man of sound sense and of a healthy frame, capable to guide and to defend those under his charge. When the days of patriarchal government amongst the Hebrews had passed away, and when God's chosen leaders, were, as in the case of the prophet Samuel set aside, then the people were allowed to elect leaders, such as Saul and David. So it was amongst the Gaels. After a time the " Leadership " became elective. No one with any corporal or mental blemish was eligible to the position of chief of a " clan." Tanistry then means simply the election by the voice, or the votes of the people composing the clan, of one worthy to rule and lead the family community. The term *tán* signifies land, wealth, and *táin* booty, power, wealth; *táinté* in the plural has that meaning—as " is fearr an sláinté na an táinté " an Irish adage, meaning that " health (sláinté) is better than wealth (táinté.)" *Táin*, then is applied to one having wealth and dignity; and *tánaiste* is the name given to one elected to the position of lord or dynast, or ruler of a clan ; it is also applied to the presumptive or apparent heir to a chieftain or prince.

GAVEL-KIND.

What does it mean ? The term *Gabh* in Gaelic means, to hold, to seize, to get possession of, the infinitive form is *Gabhail* or *Gavel*. Hence *Gabhaltas* is the term in use to this hour amongst the people to express a *hold-ing* " of land." *Kinn*, a clan under the same head,—was written in former times *Kind*, nd for nn. The compound term " Gavel-kind," means then, the possession of the " clan," as opposed to individual rights. The land belonged to the whole community and not to any special family. Hence on the death of any particular householder, his portion of the common property did not descend by entail to his eldest son, or to any of his children, but became the property of the entire clan. It was the Gabhaltas of the Kinné,* and not of a special family. When a land-

---

* *Kinné* is gen. case of *Kinn* a Sept—*Kinn* is a Sept, under one *Keann*, or head.

owning member of an Irish Sept died, its chief made a re-distribution of all the lands of the Sept. He did not divide the estate of the dead man among the children, but used it to increase the allotments of the various house-holders of which the Sept was made up.

Q, 4. There is one other question, a very practical one : first, what are the moral and physical characteristics of the Irish as a people, comparing the three different races, the Firbolg, the Tuatha Dé Danann and the Milesians with one another, and next contrasting Irishmen as a body, those descended from early and later settlers, with Englishmen, Scotchmen, Flemings and Frenchmen?

A. The question consists of two parts, the first refers to the three great races of which Irishmen, in the pre-Christian period were composed, namely, the Firbolg race, the Tuatha Dé Danann, and the Milesian race. We must bear in mind that the first people were brought into subjection by the second, and the latter in turn were conquered by the Milesians. It is clear that all along the Belgian-Irish were more or less held down as a conquered race, not alone by their conquerors, the Tuatha Dé Danann, but by the Milesians who conquered both. It is true that the Belgian body of Irish in the time of Heremon arose to the social rank of having a ruler of their own race appointed King of Leinster, and that they were the recipients of favours from the Milesian dynasty, still the spirit of subjection special to a subdued people grew up within them, and shaped their lives.

In the far past the Grecian heroic poet sang that

"Jove decreed that whatever day
Makes man a slave takes half his worth away."

In this manner the Firbolg clans became when contrasted with the Danann tribes, less noble in their bearing, less enlightened in their training, and like the Hebrews amongst the Egyptians, they were in the eyes of their conquerors, mere hewers of wood, and drawers of water; they were consequently amongst their Keltic brethren held in disesteem, at least in those days anterior to the Christian religion in Ireland.

On the other hand the Tuatha Dé Danann in Eire, who had themselves been conquered by their Milesian superiors, arose to a certain extent, above the waters of slavery; they kept together more, held councils amongst themselves, assisted each other; and like the Jews in the dispersion, they followed some calling or business which made their neighbours look up to them as a clever people ; for, they were either merchants, or music masters, or medicine-men, or mediums of occult science—the black art, and in some way they made a show of knowledge high above that which their Belgian neighbours did not even pretend to possess. Thus nature and circumstances combined to draw a marked distinction between two of the greatest races known in pre-Christian Ireland. The Milesians were the conquerors —they were the lords of the land, the sovereigns of the whole island and rulers of the provinces; they were the aristocracy, they were learned in law, in general knowledge and in religious rites. Physically they were endowed with a commanding appearance, symmetric in form, fair-haired, able-bodied, tall, like Saul amongst his brethren, fit to command and to take the mastery.

This distinction between the three leading races of Irish Kelts before the Christian period has been noticed from the earliest date and put into verse and transmitted from generation to generation to the present. Duald MacFirbis, the last of the great genealogists of Eire has published it (A.D. 1650-1656) in his writings, and O'Curry presents it to his readers in lecture, x., p. 223.

" Here, too, is the distinction which the profound historians draw between the three different races which are in Erinn—that is, between the descendants of (1) the *Firbolgs, Fir-Domhnanns* and *Gailiuns* (as one), and (2) the *Tuatha Dé Danann* and (3) the *Milesians.*

"Every one who is white [of skin], brown [of hair], bold, honourable, daring, prosperous, bountiful in the bestowal of property, wealth and rings, and who is not afraid of battle or combat; they are the descendants of the sons of Milesius in Erinn.

" Every one who is fair-haired, vengeful, large ; and every plunderer ; every musical person ; the professors of musical and entertaining performances; who are adepts in all Druidical and magical arts ;'they are the descendants of the Tuatha Dé Danann in Erinn.

" Every one who is black-haired, who is a tatler, guileful, tale-telling. noisy, contemptible ; every wretched, mean, strolling, unsteady, harsh and inhospitable person ; every slave, every mean thief, every churl, every one who loves not to listen to music and entertainment, the dis turbers of every council, and every assembly, and the promoters of discord among people, these are the descendants of the *Firbolgs*, of the *Gailiuns*, of the *Liogairne*, and of the *Fir-Domhnanns* in Erinn. But, however, the descendants of the *Firbolgs* are the most numerous of all these. "

" This" (the foregoing), says MacFirbis, " is taken from an old book." He does not go in for anthropology ; he does not think it possible to identify a race by their present facial appearance. It is not surprising that a writer at that period, A.D. 1650, should think and say so. Truly it is difficult, but to a person who has made the doctrine of races a study, it is not quite so difficult. At the present time the races of Irishmen are much more mixed than they had been even in the days of Oliver Cromwell. Other races have come to Ireland since then, and like the Anglo-Normans of the twelfth century and later, and the Welsh of the thirteenth and fourteenth, their descendants are to-day more Irish than the Irish themselves.

Commenting on the words of MacFirbis, the characteristics of the races are to be taken only in the moral acceptation of the terms. It does not follow that every undignified individual Irishman was of the Belgian race ; or that every man of high moral tone was a Milesian. The statement was, at best, true only in a limited sense. It is true to this day, that the Milesian Irish are taller and more symmetric than those of Belgian descent. The present writer in travelling through Flanders was forcibly reminded of the almost perfect likeness between the Flemings and some of the peasant people of north east Mayo, and of parts of Counties Galway and Clare.

The second part of the question contrasting Irishmen as a body with English and Scotch, with Flemings and French is one that naturally arises from the foregoing, as the present people have to a great extent been descended from those races already described. .

It is now well known that the early inhabitants of England, of Wales, of Devonshire and Cornwall are a Keltic race, like the Irish. The Saxons even are, like the Irish, Aryan in their early origin The Scots, are merely a branch of the Milesian Irish who went over, settled in, and gave a name to Argyle (ꜰɪʀ-ɢᴀᴇʟ); and their race with the Picts spread through Alba. Thus the early inhabitants of Britain, north and south, and of all the islands are the same in race and origin with the Irish. Nevertheless in periods now past, and even lately Irishmen have been caricatured and held up to scorn, as no people under heaven have been, pointed to as creatures not connected with the human family; ay! at this very day for the amusement of the British public are presented in the pages of *Punch* cartoons of Connacht peasants, that bespeak the type of the baboon, or that of the " missing link." Is this fair, is it honorable, is it truthful; nay, rather is it not a libel, a gross libel on Irishmen, a scandal to Christendom, " a conspiracy against truth?" Even at home in the capital of Ireland was published some years ago in the *The Dublin University Magazine*, a libellous description of some of the peasantry of Mayo or of county Sligo, representing them as dwarfish, pot-bellied, wry-featured abortions, more like brutes than men. It was written regarding a few, as a specimen evidently of a class, connected with the aboriginal type of the pagan period Irishman. The person who penned that libellous word-picture thought himself Irish, and fancied himself a scholar, but he was certainly a degenerate son of Eire, and in reality his knowledge was only the tinsel of fancy. He was not an honest man for he sold himself to be the instrument of a party, and sacrificed historic truth at the shrine of bigotry begotten of hate and party spirit.

The Irish people of to-day are all one—whether descended from Belgian, Danann or Milesian ancestors, or whether the blood that flows through one's veins came down from the Fomorian pirates, or Danish plunderers, or the Anglo-Normans or Welshmen,—or German soldiers. We are all one nation, born in the same mother-land, just as Americans are one nation, though her sons to-day are born of parents of different and varied nationalities. As Irishmen, what opinion do Englishmen and Frenchmen of learning and knowledge entertain of us? Let us hear: go back to the thirteenth century. What does Giraldus Cambrensis say regarding the physical qualities of Irishmen? " All animals of Ireland were smaller than those of other lands,—man alone retaining all his majesty. Nature alone has moulded the Irish: she has given them countenances of most exquisite colour, and bodies of great beauty, symmetry, height and strength."

Barnaby Rich (1610) writes: " the Irish appear to every man's eye to be of good proportion, of comely stature and of able body."

The poet Spenser writes:

" I have heard some great warriors say, that in all the services which they had seen abroad in foreign countries, they never saw a more comely man than the Irishman, nor that cometh on more bravely in his charge. . . . They (Irishmen) are very valiant and hardy, for the most part great endurers of cold, labour, hunger and all hardness, very active and strong of hand, very swift of foot, very vigilant and circumspect in their enterprises, very present in perils, very great scorners of death."

In the life of Sir Walter Raleigh by Sir John Pope Hennessy (London, Kegan Paul, Trench and Co. 1883) it is stated that the bodies of those slaughtered in November, 1580 in cold blood by order of the Queen's Deputy, Lord Grey de Wilton, at Smerwick, were stripped and laid out on the sands. Most of those slain were Irish. Lord Grey writes regarding them that " they were as gallant goodly personages as ever were beheld."

Sir John Davies writes: " the bodies (of the Irish) are endued with extraordinary abilities of nature."

In the seventeenth century, two companions of the Nuncio Rinuccini observed that the men of Ireland were good-looking, of extraordinary strength, swift runners, able to bear patiently and with alacrity any hardship and were all given to arms. The women are of surpassing height and exceeding beauty and with comeliness combine matchless modesty and piety by which their native attractions are enhanced. They have large families and their children are very handsome, of great stature and muscular strength; the majority of them have fair or yellow hair and white and ruddy complexion.

Swift represents the close of the seventeenth and early part of the eighteenth century. He writes: "I do assert from several experiments I have made in travelling over both Kingdoms, I have found the poor cottagers here who could speak our language to have a much better natural taste for good sense, humour, and raillery, than ever I observed among people of the like sort in England. . . . . I have known crowds of English coming about an Irishman in a country town, and wondering to see him look much better than themselves." Swift's *Works*, vol. VIII., vol. XII. p. 257.

Arthur Young made his tour through Ireland in the last quarter of the eighteenth century. He writes : " When I see the people of a country, with well-formed vigorous bodies, and their cottages swarming with children, when I see their men athletic, and their women beautiful, I know not how to believe them subsisting on unwholesome food : . . . . . Every unprejudiced traveller who visits them, will be as much pleased with their cheerfulness, as obliged by their hospitality, and will find them a brave, polite and liberal people."

We have in the nineteenth century the testimony of Dr. Brownson when he states, "the race is remarkable for its manly and female beauty, and unmatched strength. This may be explained by their freedom from vice, and from the purity of their women."

Dr. George Petrie descended of Scotch parents, praises the Irish people for their primitive simplicity, ingenuous manners, singular hospitality and honesty. "They are," he says "brave, hardy and industrious, enterprising, thoughtfully intelligent, innocent. They are healthy, comely and prepossessing, of fine intellect and delicate sensibility."

"The race" says De Lasteyrie "possesses every charm, grace, elegance, beauty and misfortune." Another Frenchman Count d'Avèze observes that "The women of Galway have oval faces, hooked noses, and blue eyes. The colour of their hair is brown, and their skin is singularly white. The smallness of their hands and feet rivals that of the ladies of Andalusia. The men have handsome and strongly marked features with bright intelligent eyes, their build is generally athletic and slender and their bearing is noble. Artists will find in this remote corner the purest specimens of the original race of this island. . . . . To conclude, the beauty of the peasant women of Connacht is one of the greatest surprises that a traveller in Ireland will meet with."[*]

From measurements made in colleges, where youths from England, Scotland, Belgium and Ireland, are on equal footing and in the same relations, it has been found that the Irishman is uppermost in the scale of stature and in physical strength and muscular power.

The conclusion from all that has been here shewn, is that, contrasting Irishmen as a body, those descended from early and later settlers—with Englishmen, Scotchmen, Flemings and Frenchmen, the Irishman is uppermost in height, in strength, in symmetry, in muscular power, and in those moral and physical features of which a well-developed manly form is at once the expression and the type.

---

[*] Consult on this subject an able article in the *Month*, March, 1887, written by Rev. Edmund Hogan, S.J.

CHAPTER XXI.

THE QUESTION OF THE ROUND TOWERS OF IRELAND; THREE LEADING OPINIONS REGARDING THEM,—THE CHRISTIAN THEORY AS IT IS CALLED, ADVOCATED BY DR. PETRIE AND HIS FOLLOWERS; THE PAGAN THEORY; A THIRD OPINION, THAT MANY OF THE TOWERS WERE ERECTED IN THE CHRISTIAN PERIOD, THAT OTHERS HAD COME DOWN FROM PAGAN TIMES—BUT IN ALL, THE FIGURE AND FORM OF THE EDIFICES, AND THE PURPOSES FOR WHICH THEY WERE FIRST ERECTED WERE OF PRE-CHRISTIAN ORIGIN AND GROWTH. REASONS FOR THE DIFFERENT OPINIONS, THE CONTROVERSY NOT YET CLOSED; THE TOWERS DESCRIBED; THEIR PROBABLE NUMBER; THEIR DURABILITY.

Q. 1. The controversy regarding the Round Towers has been renewed within the past year, 1886 :—what phase of this interesting subject is at present before the literary public?

A. Within the past year a brochure, has been published in Belfast " On the Round Towers in Ireland, their Origin and Uses."

The pamphlet is a summary of the matter—(omitting the quotations)—contained in the large volume from the pen of Dr. Petrie—it is issued in its present form at a cheap price for the benefit of the masses. It brings the controversy up to the present.

The writer of the brochure is a great admirer of Dr. Petrie, and throughout he follows his leader's views in all their fulness,—namely that the Round Towers are of Christian origin, that they were built within the period that passed from the year A.D. 432 when St. Patrick came to preach the Christian faith in Ireland, up to the thirteenth century, when the Anglo-Normans came to make a home for themselves within the shores of Eire. The object intended in their erection was to serve as appendages to ecclesiastical establishments as belfries, as monastic castles, as homes of safety in the hour of danger or of surprise, as towers of defence for ministers of religion, as safes for vessels and vestments used at the holy altar. This opinion which appears so natural, was put forward by Dr. Petrie—himself a Protestant—and has been ably defended by him in a large vol. of 450 pages, imperial octavo, entitled: " The Ecclesiastical Architecture of Ireland, anterior to the Anglo-Norman Invasion comprising an Essay on the origin and uses of the Round Towers of Ireland." Dublin: Hodges & Smith, 1845.

The opinion of Petrie is at present held commonly by all the ecclesiastics in Ireland who have read his work: it is the view of a great many scholars who have, in a passing way, paid any attention to the subject.

There was an idea entertained at one time by some savants, but not now, that the Round Towers *had been erected by the Danes.* A strange opinion certainly,—for the unconverted Danes were always destroyers of every edifice they could seize which had been erected by Christian hands.

This notion arose from a vulgar tradition which gave the name Dane for that of Danann, who were the real builders.

The second theory regarding the Round Towers is that they are of pagan origin. The advocates of this opinion are General Vallancey, Mrs. Beauford, Dr. O'Conor, Moore, D'Alton, Windele, O'Brien Keane, and others amongst whom may be classed Giraldus Cambrensis.

The third is one put forward by the writer of these pages, some twelve years ago, when he penned the work known as *The Aryan Origin of the Gaelic Race and Language:* " That the Round Towers were first built in the early pagan period by those of the Aryan race who had settled in this island of destiny (say, the Firbolg or the Tuatha Dé Danann or both), but that after the Gospel had been preached in Ireland St. Patrick turned the Round Towers, as he did the pagan fountains to the service of Christian rites and hallowed them by Christian practices and religious associations." In those words he expressed his views. To these he now adds that which had been always in his thoughts, that some at least of the towers must have been built in Christian times, but copied and improved from specimens of pre-Christian Irish Keltic architecture.

There are two Round Towers in Scotland, one at Abernethy, at Brechin the other. No one can deny that these towers were " built in imitation of the Round Towers of Ireland," as Sir Walter Scott writes, "and under the direction of Irish Monks who brought Christianity into Scotland." In like manner no one can deny that the tower of Hythe in Kent (England), or that at Peel in the Isle of Man had been erected in imitation of the Towers in Ireland, by Irish Missionaries, who went as was usual in numbers to Britain; or by some English ecclesiastics who had been for a time in Ireland. No one could deny that the Round Tower in memory to the Liberator O'Connell in Glasnevin has been erected in modern times.

Q. 2. Be good enough to give the arguments which Dr. Petrie furnishes in favour of his own opinion known as the "Christian" theory, and which the Author of the brochure just published recapitulates.

A. The arguments made use of by Dr. Petrie may be classed as positive and negative. They are (see *Aryan Origin* p. 360.) (1) That the towers are never found unconnected, as a rule with ancient Ecclesiastical foundations. (2) That the uses to which the Round Towers are known by a uniform and concurrent tradition of the country to have been applied—a tradition corroborated by written testimony and authentic evidence—accord precisely with the Christian and ecclesiastical character of those ancient buildings. (3) That Christian emblems are observable on several of those cylindrical edifices. (4) That they are of the same style of architecture as that found in well-known Irish Ecclesiastical buildings of the early Christian period; or, as Dr. Petrie states, that the Architectural style of the towers exhibits no feature or peculiarity not equally found in the original churches with which they are locally connected, where such remain. And (5) that in some few records of an early date, it is actually stated that bell-houses had been erected at a certain period of the Christian era. This last is one of the strongest.

The negative arguments are; (1) That the reasons assigned by General Vallancey for the pagan theory are futile and that they prove nothing. (2) That the arguments furnished by Dr. Lanigan, Mr. D'Alton, Thomas Moore, Mr. Windele, can be reduced (he says) to the same category with those put forward by Vallancey, and hence can be refuted by the same process of reasoning as Vallancey's have been. (3) That supposing the towers had been built in pagan times, no one can tell either the precise period, or the special purpose for which they were erected. (4) That no mention is made by any writer in any of the early authentic records that the towers had been built in pagan times. (5) That the pagan Kelts did not know how to build.

Take the first argument of a positive kind, namely that the Round Towers are, as a rule, found close by, or within the precincts of those ruins which all confess to be the remains of Ecclesiastical buildings, and therefore that they had been made use of and erected by the growing Christian Church of Ireland. Next, the Round Towers were made use of by the early Christians of Ireland for the service of religion, for the safe-keeping of vestments, altar plate, as citadels of safety, and of defence for priests and religious in troublous times. Some of them had been belfries perhaps,—indeed the specimens of bells then in use were rather small for such towers. They served as signal turrets to light and direct pilgrims to the sacred shrines. We grant the argument which taken as a whole is one of Dr. Petrie's strongest. But what then? Does it prove that the towers were built by Christian hands? By no means. The argument proves equally in favour of the opinion of the writer, that St. Patrick selected the site of the Round Tower or near it, as a suitable place on which to erect a church, just as he made choice of the localities where the Druids had their sacred fountains. The Apostle with a kind of worldly wisdom and good common sense selected the places most frequented and held in [greatest veneration for some cause or other by the pagan teachers. In that case, the adopted monumental tower would be as much an Ecclesiastical house, as if the Christians had erected it for church purposes. So much for arguments first and second.

But it is said the tower was called (1) *Cloig-teach*; and *Coilgeach*, reed, which according to Dr. O'Brien is by metathesis for *Cloig-teach* that is " bell-house," just as *epscop* is turned into *caspoc* bishop; or *apstol*, apostle, into *easpol:*—It is called *Clochteach*, that is "stone-house." The towers are also called *gail*, pillar stones,—and so they were; they are styled *Clogad* from *clog*, a bell, and *ed*, dress, that is a cover for bells; we answer,—they were so called, and rightly for they served purposes expressed by those names. (3) Christian emblems are carved on some of the towers. That only proves that the towers were turned to Christian uses. That fact proves as much in favour of our thesis as for that of Dr. Petrie. (4) That they are of the same style of architecture as that found in well known Irish Ecclesiastical buildings.—granted that the proposition is true of some of the Round Towers. It must be admitted that some of the Round Towers were built,— or at least re-constructed in the Christian period. In Clon-mac-noise, the writer examined one of the towers some years ago, and to him it appeared that the building of the tower was dove-tailed into that of the church or monastic building. There was manifestly a distinction between the two, both in the manner, and the matter of the work to suggest that the Round Tower was anterior to the Church. (5) That in some few records of an early date, it is actually stated that Round Towers had been erected within the early Christian period. This also may be granted. All these arguments may be true, and granted that they are true, still it is equally certain that the first models and the idea and taste connected with such structures had come from the pagan period as shall be shown in reply to the coming question.

Regarding the negative arguments of Petrie in support of his theory it is well to state that the refutation of false or useless arguments does not prove in every instance, that the opinion is erroneous, or the thesis false; it does not prove that another view offered in its stead is correct. The theory may be right, like the theory of eclipses of the sun and moon, although the person who undertakes to explain the subject, does not understand its bearings fully.

(1) It does not follow as a logical sequence because General Vallancey brought worthless arguments in favour of his theory, that it was not for all that, correct. The only right conclusion to be drawn from the refutation of General Vallancey's arguments is, that they were of no avail in proving the particular thesis.

Dr. Lanigan says, he sees no reason to deny that the Round Towers existed before Christianity, and that their style proves them very ancient. Now that is true; and Dr. Lanigan is as much entitled to hold that opinion as Dr. Petrie is to hold his own views.

Dr. Charles O'Conor is of opinion that the Round Towers have come to us from pagan times " that they are from time immemorial." Certainly Dr. O'Conor was as conversant with Irish antiquities as Dr. Petrie,—perhaps more so ; he wrote much and studied much on things Irish, relating to pre-Christian times. In any case his opinion is as trustworthy as that of Dr. Petrie. Thomas Moore states :—

"To be able to invest, even with plausibility, so inconsistent a notion as that, in times (6th century and 7th) when the churches were framed rudely of wood, there could be found either the ambition or the skill to supply them with adjuncts of such elaborate workmanship is, in itself, no ordinary feat of ingenuity." Dr. Petrie simply puts his own opinions against those of Moore, Windele, D'Alton, and Dr. Lanigan; such a proceeding is no refutation of the opinions of those learned men, and of others who believe that they had good reasons on which to ground their views. (3) The third negative argument is of no importance no one can tell the precise period (in the pagan time) when they were built. Therefore, they were not built then. There are many who cannot tell the precise date of their birth. Does it follow that they were never born? (4) No mention is made by any early writer that the Round Towers were built in pagan times, therefore, &c. The reply is —no *direct* mention is made of those special Towers now known to us, but direct mention is made that Towers were *de facto* built; this fact indirectly shows that others too, may have been built. (5) Finally Dr. Petrie denies that the pagan Kelts knew how to build such structures, and therefore they did not build them.

It is simply untrue to state that the ancient Tuatha Dé Danann did not know how; for, as a matter of fact, they built several as we shall show in reply to question (3).

Q. 3. What are the arguments that go to support the opinion, that many of the Round Towers were erected in the pagan period, and that the figure and form of these cylindrical piles, and the custom of making such memorials had come from an Irish Keltic source, and were not either ecclesiastical as such, nor derived from any foreign source?

A. In proposing the first argument, the writer refers to his work, *The Aryan Origin* in which he treats at page 333, of the early art of Keltic Illumination of manuscript writing. Books written and embellished by the art of the limner are found in all parts of the civilized world. There are various styles of limning. Amongst those there is one known as distinct from all others, and regarded as the best, the grandest, and most ancient of all— namely, the Keltic or Irish. " The Book of Kells " written in this style by the fingers of St. Columba about the year, A.D. 540, is the wonder of the artists of the world.

The argument then is, the Book of Kells has been written by St. Columba, or by him and his Irish monks. The work is no myth or fancy. It is to be seen and read, if one please, in Trinity College, Dublin. The writer has seen it, handled it, read some of its pages.

How did St. Columba learn the art of illuminating to such a pitch of perfection? Who taught him? St. Patrick, or St. Patrick's disciples those of the same school to whom he had taught the Roman letters? No: Why? Because St. Patrick himself did not know; neither did any of his disciples of the Roman school of learning know the art themselves. There was nothing like the Keltic art known in Rome. That is certain. How then did St. Columba learn? By inventing it? No. It is not given to man to invent an art, and become perfect in it in a day.—How then?—the only answer to the question is, that the art had been taught him by the Irish masters, and that they had learned the art of writing, and of illuminating from other masters who went before them in Ireland, who were acquainted, not only with letters; but with the art of painting, and of mixing colours. This view is confirmed by the opinion of Lady Wilde, and of O'Curry.

In this manner the argument regarding the Round Towers can be put. It is admitted by Dr. Petrie and by nearly all his followers that Round Towers were built in the fifth century; they admit that certainly Towers were erected in the sixth century, and in the seventh. Very well, who taught the Irish ecclesiastics to plan such edifices, or the builders—the *Gubain Saora* of the time—to erect them? Was it St. Patrick or those whom he had instructed in Roman art? No,—on the contrary we are time after time told in the early records that he planned *Domhnachs* or churches, and basilicas having four walls, square like, that is, in form like a parallelogram. He taught as he had seen and had learned. Who then taught the Irish house-builders to erect circular towers? Was it an invention cogitated at the moment, and brought to perfection at once? That could not be, or had the Irish builders or architects seen anything like the Round Towers in England, or France, or Spain, or Italy? Nothing like them had been seen in those countries. Neither Rome had taught them, nor the example of the builders throughout Europe, neither was the style an invention cogitated at the time; what then? It follows that it had been handed down from the forefathers of the Irish race for ages previously, and in addition that the new builders copied from those edifices they had with their eyes beheld in their native island. The very houses in which they dwelt were circular, the *raths*, so numerous in the land for nearly two thousand years since the days of the Belgic power, and the coming of the Tuatha Dé Danann, were circular; the *Caisils* and *Cathairs* made of stone were circular or rotund; the Tumuli or Tombs erected over the departed nobles were rotund, the hillocks erected over the champions of their race were rotund. The Towers commemorative of battles were round, and why should not the Keltic idea and the Keltic art be seized and improved, if needed, by Irish artists.

But it is too great a stretch for one at the present day to believe that men deemed ignorant at that far-off period, could have erected such piles. One can safely say in reply, it was not too much for men skilled as manifestly those were, who taught the arts of limning, of colouring and of drawing. Who says they were unskilled? Those who have not studied their history, or who cared not to study it; and those who take a notion regarding anthropology, and fix a view in their minds, and take it as a certainty, that man in ancient times was growing from the state of barbarism to that of civilized society. Men of this class are poor judges of the early civilization of the Irish Kelt, pagan or Christian.

The conclusion then to be drawn from this first argument is that the figure and form of the Round Towers, and the custom of erecting them came to the early Irish from the pagan period—and that some at least of the towers were built by pagan hands, improved and adopted by the early Christians. Second argument, Dr. Petrie admits the towers were called *gail* or pillar stones; and such they were in pagan times. Towers were built by the Tuatha Dé Danann—first after the battle of "Magh Tura Conga," or Moy Tura of Cong, fought between the Belgæ and the invading forces of the Tuatha Dé Danann (see pages 22 to 36 of this history supra) next after the battle of "Magh Tura of the Fomorians" fought twenty-seven years later between the Tuatha Dé Danann and the Fomorians their invaders, the pirate robbers, known by that name. Magh Tura means "plain of towers."

The second battle was fought in Tir-Errill the south eastern barony of the county Sligo. The final struggle took place on the strand south west of Ballysadare. To this day, or up to a few years ago, monuments of the battle were to be found north of Loch Arrow and hard by Keish Curran. It is enough for the argument that these memorial erections deserved, and were called by the name of *Tura*, or towers. Every tower, as such, in the olden time amongst the Kelts was rotund. It is silly therefore to state—"Oh! they are not stated to have been round"—well, when one names a circle he does not say it is "round," for the very term conveys the idea of rotundity when one says "egg" he does not say it is "oval" for the idea of egg expresses the shape,—so with the ancient Irish in naming the tower or *Tur*. There is a village near Lough Mask, known to this day as *Tuirin*, or the village of the little towers, called by that name on account of the number of towers, *Tuir*, erected to the memory of those heroes, who fought with and against Eachy, King of the Firbolg, who on the fourth day of the fight, while fainting with thirst ran towards Lough Mask. He was slain near the shore by the phalanx of Danann heroes who went after him in pursuit. He was defended by one hundred of his own forces. The bodies of those heroes on both sides were there interred and *Tuirin*, or little towers erected over them as a memorial of the last day's fight in that terrible battle.

Similarly "Tory" Island is so called on account of the early *Tor* or tower erected there. To deny that there was such a tower in this island is puerile; or to say the island was called "Tory" because it was like a tower,—that is playing with the question.

Again in page 155 of his Essay on *The History and Antiquities of Tara Hill*, Dr. Petrie admits there was a (round) Tower on Tara. He says, " that *Cathair Crofinn*, was called in Ancient Irish Poems by the name 'Cúp cpeun Ceaṁpaċ,' the strong *Tower* of Temur, an appellation constantly applied to a *circular stone fort*."

From all this we draw the inference that the pillar towers were known as memorials of battles and great events, or, were strong-holds and erected for that purpose—such were the towers just named. The name *gail* applied to them points to this view.

3. The erection of the palace of Aileach in which there is a round tower. The fact proves two things, that the early Keltic Irish knew what Round Towers were, and knew how to build them, although Dr. Petrie states that the Pagan Kelts did not know how to build, and therefore they could not have erected them.

"I must observe," says O'Curry, *Manners and Customs of the Ancient Irish*, vol. ii., "that the ancient name of Aileach was certainly *Aileach Neid;* and the investigations of antiquaries (including the cautious Dr. Petrie) have led to the same conclusion to which we should come by following the ancient MS. authorities,—that the *stone* ruins at Aileach as well as several other similar stone erections in several parts of *Eirrinn* must be referred to the *Tuatha Dé Dananu*, if not to the Firbolg; certainly to a race prior to the Milesians. The Milesians always used *wooden* buildings in preference to the *stone* used by their predecessors; we can easily understand why they should emphasize such an erection under the name of *Aileach*. The word *Aileach* in fact signifies *stone building*, since *ail* is a stone, or cliff, and *ach* the common adjective termination:—so *aileac* means building made of stone."

" The next great building in point of antiquity and historical reminiscence is the great *Cathair* of *Aileach (*in the County Derry) so well described by Dr. Petrie in the Ordnance memoir of the parish of Templemore. This great *Cathair* is said to have been built by the *Daghda,* the celebrated King of the *Tuatha Dê Danann,* who planned and fought the battle of the Second or Northern Magh Tura against the Fomorians." *Aryan Origin,* p. 387.

Duald MacFirbis in his *Book of Genealogies* writes :—

" The place, time, author, and cause of writing this book are—the place, the College of St. Nicholas, in Galway ; the time, the time of the religious war between the Catholics of Ireland, and the heretics of Ireland, Scotland and England, particularly in the year 1653 ; the person or author, Dubhaltach, the son of Giolla Isa Mor MacFirbisigh, historian, &c., &c.; the cause of writing the book is, to increase the glory of God, and for the information of people in general."

MacFirbis, in his *Book of Genealogies,* just described, after giving a long list, say twenty or more names of famous builders in stone— such as *Casruba,* stone-builder of Ailinn, the palace of the Kings of Leinster already named ; *Troigh Leathan* or Broad-foot, the rath-builder of Tara ; *Bolc,* the son of *Blar,* the rath-builder of Cruachain, the palace of the Kings of Connacht, *Bainchre,* or Fair Face, the builder of Emania, writes :—

" We could find a countless number of the ancient edifices of Erinn to name besides these above, and the builders who erected them, and the kings and noble chiefs for whom they were built, but that they would be too tedious to mention. Look at the *Book of Conquests,* Leabhar na n-Gabhala, if you wish to discover them ; and we have even besides that, evidence of their having been built like the edifices of other kingdoms of the times in which they were built ;— and why should they not ? For there came no colony into Erinn but from the Eastern World ; and it would be strange if they should not have the sense to form their residences and dwelling after the manner of the countries from which they originally went forth, and through which they travelled. . . . And if those colonists of ancient Erinn erected buildings in the country similar to those of the countries through which they came, as it is likely they did, what is the reason the fact is doubted ?"

Compare, then, the buildings erected hundreds and thousands of years ago with these, and it is no wonder, except for the superiority of the ancient building over the modern, that not a stone nor an elevation of the ground should mark their situation ; yet, such is not the case; for, so great is the stability of the old buildings, that there are immense royal *raths* or palaces and forts (*Liosa*) throughout Erinn, in which there are numerous *hewn* and polished stones. . . . .

The only cause of doubt is because lime-cast walls are not seen standing in the place, in which they were erected a thousand and a half, or two thousand, or three thousand and more years since: it is no wonder they should not be; for shorter than that is the time in which the ground grows over buildings, when they are once ruined, or when they fall down of themselves with age. In proof of this, I have myself seen, within the last sixteen years, many lofty lime-cast castles built of limestone; and at this day (having fallen) there remains of them but a mound of earth; and hardly could a person ignorant of their former existence know that there had been buildings there at all.

I leave this, however, to the learned to discuss, and I shall return to prove the fidelity of our national history, to which the ignorant do an injustice.—From O'Curry's *Lectures on the Manuscript Materials of Ancient Irish History*, delivered in the Catholic University of Ireland, pp. 222, 223; translation from MacFirbis's *Book of Genealogies*, the Irish original of which is given in an appendix to the same work.

Q. 4. Describe the Round Towers and tell the probable number still standing, wholly or in part.

A. The probable number is seventy-six. There had been over one hundred Round Towers. Latterly greater care has been taken of these buildings than had been in days now past.

The best description given of these perennial piles is from the pen of Dr. Petrie:—He says of them:—

" These towers are rotund, cylindrical structures, usually tapering upwards, and varying in height from fifty to perhaps one hundred and fifty feet; and in external circumference, at the base, from forty to sixty feet, or somewhat more. They have usually a circular, projecting base, consisting of one, two, or three steps, or plinths, and are furnished at the top with a conical roof of stone, which frequently, as there is every reason to believe, terminated with a cross formed of a single stone. The wall, towards the base, is never less than three feet in thickness, but is usually more, and occasionally five feet, being always in accordance with the general proportions of the building. In the interior, they are divided into stories, varying in number from four to eight feet, as the height of the tower permitted and usually about twelve feet in height. These stories are marked either by projecting belts of stone, sets off, or ledges, or holes in the wall to secure joists, on which rested the floors, which were almost always of wood. In the uppermost of the stories the wall is perforated by 'two, four, five, six, or eight apertures, but most usually four, which sometimes face the cardinal points, and sometimes not. The lowest story, or rather its place, is sometimes composed of solid masonry, and when not so, it never has any aperture to light it. In the second story the wall is usually perforated by the entrance doorway, which is generally from eight to thirty feet from the ground, and only large enough to admit a single person at a time. The intermediate stories are each lighted by a single aperture, placed variously, and usually of very small size, though in several instances, that directly over the doorway is of a size little less than that of the door-way, and would appear to be intended as a second entrance. In their masonic construction they present a considerable variety, but the generality of them are built in that kind of careful masonry called spauled rubble, in which small stones, shaped by the hammer in default of suitable stones at hand are placed in every interstice of the larger stones, so that very little mortar appears to be intermixed in the body of the wall; and thus the outside of spauled masonry, especially, presents an almost uninterrupted surface of stone, supplementary splinters being carefully inserted in the joints of the undried wall. Such also is the style of masonry in the most ancient churches; but it should be added, that in the interior of the walls of both, grouting is abundantly used. In some instances, however, the towers present a surface of ashlar masonry (but rarely laid in courses perfectly regular), both externally and internally, though more usually on the exterior only; and in a few instances, the lower portions of the towers exhibit less of regularity than the upper parts.

" In their architectural features an equal diversity of style is observable, and of these the doorway is the most remarkable. When the tower is of rubble masonry, the doorways seldom present any decorations, and are either quadrangular and covered with a lintel of a single stone of great size, or semicircular-headed either by the construction of a regular arch, or the cutting of a single stone. There are, however, two instances of very richly decorated doorways in towers of this description, namely, those of Kildare and Timahoe. In the more regularly constructed towers, the doorways are always arched semicircularly, and are most usually ornamented with architraves or bands on their external faces. The upper apertures but rarely present any decorations, and are most usually of a quadrangular form. They are, however, sometimes semicircular-headed, and still oftener present the triangular or straight-sided arch. I should further add, that in the construction of these apertures, very frequent examples occur of that kind of masonry, consisting of long and short stones alternately, now generally considered by antiquaries as a characteristic of Saxon architecture in England."

As to the doorways of Irish Round Towers: of the seventy-six towers which remain, only forty-six have got doorways; the others are reduced to their foundations, or else have lost their original entrances.

"Of these forty-six doorways thirty-four are round-headed: the remaining twelve doorways are square-headed. Round-headed doorways generally exhibit a better style of workmanship and materials than are found in the quadrangular specimens."—*Towers and Temples of Ancient Ireland*, Keane, pp. 392, 322.

All dwellings among the pre-Christian Irish were round; oblong buildings were introduced by St. Patrick. See on this subject vols. i. and iii. of O'Curry's *Manners and Customs of the Ancient Irish*. Williams & Norgate. 1873.*

---

* From the term *Cloich-teach*, stone house, applied in ancient times to the pillar-tower in Ireland, an argument has been drawn in favour of the Christian origin of those stately piles. It appears to the author, that from the same term an argument in favour of their *pre-Christian* origin can with logical sequence be drawn.

Let it be borne in mind that the Milesian Irish, as a rule, built in wood not in stone. This is a historical truth. The stone-buildings then are non-Milesian. It was most natural therefore as their own buildings were of wood, that they should call the other buildings "stone-houses." That is precisely what they called the Round Towers. A stone house for them was specially significant—just as they styled the royal stone residence of their predecessors *Aileach* which means high stone-building.

The three terms *Cloich-teach*, *Cloigteach*, bell-house, and *Coilceach*, reed or *Coilgeach*, are phonetic forms of the same term *Cloich-teach*, although they appear different, and each has a distinct and special meaning. *Cloig-teach* does mean "bell-house;" but as applied to the towers, it is a soft pronunciation of *Cloich-teach*, stone house, the guttural *ch*, being sounded like the medial *g*; and although *Coilceach*, means a *reed*, it is in those instances when applied to the towers a ready form by metathesis of articulating the hard consonant *c*, by 'inserting' the vowel sound, *oi*, before the liquid. The argument taken from the three terms is therefore only a single argument and its historical and logical force goes in favour of the pre-Milesian, or pre-Christian origin of the Towers.

In the *Census* of Ireland 1861, there are over one hundred names of places commencing with *tur*, or *tor*, having the meaning of *tower*, at least in most of them, as *Turlough* near Castlebar for *Turloc* that is *tower-place*.

APPENDIX I.

A SUMMARY OF Dr. PETRIE'S HISTORY AND ANTIQUITIES OF TARA HILL,

(IRISH QUOTATIONS OMITTED.)

The locality to which this paper relates is the well-known hill of Tara—a spot which has been celebrated by native as well as foreign writers, as the chief seat of the Irish monarchs, from the earliest dawn of their history, down to the middle of the sixth century, at which period it was deserted. But, though its ancient splendour has been the theme of most modern Irish antiquaries and historians, their labours have thrown but little light either on its past state or existing remains, and have made but little impression on the minds of the learned. Nor could a different result have been anticipated from the careless and inaccurate notices of its ruins, and conclusions drawn from vague references to Irish authorities. The progress of the Ordnance Survey at length afforded an opportunity for a more satisfactory, because a more accurate, investigation; and by a scientific plan of the remains of Tara, joined to an examination of such ancient descriptive notices of its former state as are still remaining, we are put into possession of all the information now likely to be obtained in any way leading to its successful illustration. Before, however I lay the result before the public, it may not be uninteresting to give some detail of the mode of investigation adopted on this occasion.

While this survey was in progress, a careful search was made in all the ancient Irish manuscripts accessible, for such documents of a descriptive or historical character as would tend to identify or illustrate these existing vestiges. The success which had already attended this mode of investigation in respect to the ancient fortress of the kings of Ulster on the hill of Aileach, near Derry, led us in the present instance to anticipate an equally fortunate result, and we were not disappointed. In the same ancient Irish topographical work—the *Dinnseanchus* in which the account of Aileach was discovered, we found several ancient documents relating to this spot, some of which describe, with considerable distinctness and accuracy, the remains existing on Tara hill at the periods of their composition.

Our first labour was to go over the ground with the map, in order to be satisfied of its accuracy, and that no vestige of any ancient remain had been omitted. The propriety of this examination was soon apparent: in our progress many important features were discovered, not previously noticed, and which required the aid of antiquarian science to appreciate; and some interesting traditional information was obtained respecting objects now changed or obliterated.

This examination, fortunately, we were able to make with little difficulty, as the first object mentioned was one in the identification of which we could not be mistaken, namely, a remarkable spring, whose locality on the side of the hill is distinctly pointed out, and which is stated to be the source of a stream which *turned the first watermill ever erected in Ireland.*

The hill of Tara, though undistinguished either for altitude or picturesqueness of form, is not less remarkable for the pleasing and extensive prospects which it commands, than for the associations connected with it, as the site of the residence of the Irish monarchs from the earliest times. In both these circumstances it bears a striking similitude to the hill of Aileach, near Derry—the residence of the kings of Ulster—and to the hill of Emania, near Armagh, another residence of the Ulster kings, but who were of a different race. All these localities have shared a similar fate in the destruction of their monuments at distant periods, and all equally present striking vestiges of their ancient importance.

According to the Irish Bardic traditions, the hill of Tara became the chief residence of the Irish kings on the first establishment of a monarchical government in Ireland under Slainge, the first monarch of the Firbolgs or Belgae, and continued so till its abandonment in the year A.D. 563.

The Bardic history of Ireland states, that there reigned within these periods one hundred and forty-two monarchs, viz., one hundred and thirty-six Pagan, and six Christian.

It is stated in the Annals of the Four Masters, from the book of Clonmacnoise, that Ollamh Fodhla, the fortieth monarch of Ireland, according to the lists, first instituted the triennial assemblies, and erected the Mur Ollamhan or house of Ollamh at Tara.

The additional facts of importance stated by the Four Masters are three. Firstly, that Cormac was the author of the ancient tract called—Teagasc na Riogh, or Instruction of the Kings; secondly, that he was the author or compiler of laws which remained in force among the Irish down to the seventeenth century to be compiled in one volume, which was afterwards called the Psalter of Tara. On each of these facts a few remarks may be permitted. The work called Teagasc na Riogh, has been ascribed to Cormac by the Irish universally from a very remote period, and whether it be his or not it is certainly one of the most ancient and valuable documents preserved in the language.

In concluding this notice of the most important facts connected with Tara during the reign of Laoghaire, it may be briefly stated that it will be shewn from very ancient historical evidences, that Laoghaire was interred after the manner of the pagans, within his own rath on the hill of Tara.

The existing remains on Tara hill, though but time-worn vestiges, are the best evidences of the original character and extent of the works which the Keltic people, not far advanced in civilization, raised in distant ages; and whatever claims to truth the ancient accounts of the place may have, they must now rest on their agreement with these vestiges. And it will also appear, from an examination of the ancient Irish accounts of these remains, that their origin is not assigned to a period which may properly be regarded as beyond the limits of true Irish history. It should not indeed be expected that such accounts would be wholly free from fable, particularly in whatever relates to the earlier national traditions; but it should be anticipated that the names and particular descriptions of the state of the monuments at the time would necessarily have the character of truth, as there could be no inducement for fable in such matters; and, that they really have this veracious character, will appear quite manifest from their agreement with the present vestiges of the monuments to which they refer.

The principal ancient Irish tracts written in illustration of the origin and names of Tara, and describing the localities &c., of the hill and its monumental remains, are preserved in the ancient topographical work called *Dinnseanchus*, a compilation of the twelfth century. Most of the documents found in this work are, however, evidently of an earlier age, though in many instances not of the antiquity ascribed to them; and though some of them are of little value to the present investigation.

THE REMAINS OF ANCIENT MONUMENTS TO BE SEEN ON TARA HILL.

Taking the ancient documents as a guide, the remains on the hill have been identified with the descriptions given on them, in the following order:—

First.—The Well *Neamhnach* (Heaven-Spring). This is marked in the poem as lying east of the *Mur Tea* (Tea's House) which is within the principal rath of Tara; and more accurately in the prose tract, as north-east, and supplying the stream on which the first mill was erected in Ireland. This well was at once identified, as it is the source of a stream which has turned a mill on the site of the ancient one to the present day.

Second.—The next grand feature indentified was *Rath na Riogh* (Fort of the Kings), the most important inclosure on the hill, which is clearly pointed out by its locality in relation to the well *Neamhnach*.

Third.—These two points being ascertained no doubt remained of the situation of *Rath Laoghaire*, (Lowry's fort), which was situated immediately south of *Rath na Riogh*. Having ascertained beyond question these three grand features, the smaller monuments within the enclosure of *Rath na Riogh*, were at once indentified. These are described in the prose only, and are as follows:

Fourth.—*The ruins of the House of Cormac*, in the south-east of the Rath, facing *Rath Laoghaire*, which is to the south.

Fifth.—*The ruins of the Forradh* (meeting) beside the House of Cormac which is to the east.

Sixth.—*Tea-Mur* the ruins of which were, according to the prose, as given in the Book of Glendalough, situated between the *mur* of the *Forradh*, or meeting house and the House of Cormac.

Seventh.—*The Mound of the Hostages*, which according to the prose, lies to the north-east of the ruins of the *Forradh*.

Eighth.—The *Mound of Glas Teamrach* (*glas* means stream), which according to the prose, lies to the west of the mound of Hostages.

Ninth.—The *Lia-Fail* (stone of destiny) which lies by the side of the mound of the hostages.

Tenth.—*The Rath of the Synods*, was the monument next clearly identified. This according to both verse and prose, was situated immediately to the north of the *Lia-Fail*, and the mound of the hostages, and within it were the remains of *Adamnan's pavilion*.

Eleventh.—*The Cross of Adamnan*, which, according to the prose, was situated to the east of this rath, is found in the situation pointed out, but in a mutilated state.

Twelfth & Thirteenth.—South of these was the *Mound of Adamnan*, but this as well as the *House of Mariseo*, to the north of the Well *Neamhnach*, have long been destroyed, and their site occupied by the church dedicated to St. Patrick, and erected since the time of the writers of these ancient documents.

Fourteenth.—However clearly the preceding remains were identified, they were less distinctly pointed out than the next grand monument now to be noticed—namely, the *Teach Miodhchuarta*, or banqueting house, which is described with a remarkable accuracy as an oblong structure, having its lower end to the north, and higher end to the south, with walls to the east and west. In these walls, according to the prose account, there were twelve or fourteen doors, six or seven on each side; and it is a curious fact, that there is a difficulty in ascertaining, at the present moment, whether the number was twelve or fourteen.

Fifteenth.—The next important feature is the *Sheskin*, or Marsh of Tara, which is described as lying to the north-west of *Teach Miodhchuarta*. This spot though now dry, was a marsh, within the memory of the present inhabitants, one of whom, by stopping the well and cutting a drain below it, has changed its ancient character. The ancient name of the well is however, still preserved, namely, *Tobar Finn*. This feature being ascertained, the few which remain were at once identified.

Sixteenth.—*Rath Graine* which, according to the verse and prose lies west of the *Sheskin*, on the height of the Hill.

Seventeenth.—*Fothath ratha Graine* (foundation, or declivity of

Graine's rath) which, according to the same authorities, lies to the south of the preceding.

Eighteenth.—The *Rath of Caelchu*, which, according to the prose, was near the northern head of *Long na m-ban*, the stronghold of the women.

The monument of first importance, both as to size and antiquity of construction, seems unquestionably to be the great Rath, or enclosure, marked in the description by the name *Rath na Riogh* or the Rath or Fortress of the Kings. This great enclosure seems to have been formed of two *murs*, or parapets, having a ditch between them, as described in the prose account. The great or external diameter, taken north-west and south-east is eight hundred and fifty-three feet, the interior seven hundred and seventy-five. It encircled the southern brow of the hill; the northern side being on its top, and the eastern, southern, and western, on its slopes. The rings in most parts have been removed; and, it is to be regretted, that the proprietor is yearly removing more of them to spread on his land. A portion of the outer ring still remaining is two and a-half feet above the natural hill; and the ditch, or bottom, four feet below it so that from the bottom of the ditch to the top of the outer ring is six and a-half feet.

The Bardic etymology of the name *Teamur*, may, at all events, be very well rejected as legendary: nor is it necessary to adopt the mere conjecture of Cormac of Cashel, and other ancient writers respecting its Greek derivation, as a more probable origin of the name appears to be found in the Irish words, *teach*, a house, and *mur* a wall—*Teachmur* = house of the walls, or enclosures for defence; a name particulary applicable to the place. As it is obvious then that *Tea-mur* and *Rath na Riogh* are but different and equally appropriate names of the same fortified regal habitation, there can be no rational doubt of the priority of origin to be assigned to this work above all others circumjacent to it. But, though its great antiquity is thus established, it would be a useless labour to endeavour to assign a period to the foundation of a work erected so long anterior to the dawn of chronological history. That it was considered by the Irish as of the most remote age is clear from their historical tradition which assigns its first erection to the Fir-bolg and the Tuatha De Danann colonies, the predecessors of the Milesians or Scots, and by the latter of whom it was called *Cathair Crofinn*, a name explained by the bards, as signifying the city of Crofinn, a Tuatha De Danann queen, but the most obvious interpretation of which appear to be " the circular *stone*-fortification of the fair house" or enclosure. It may, indeed, be objected to the truth of this historical tradition, and to the interpretation here given of the name, that no remains of a *Cathair*—a term never applied by the Irish to any but a circular stone fortification, without cement—are now to be found on the hill; but a negative objection of this kind should have but little weight in reference to a monument so long subjected to every

P

destructive influence, and, if it were allowed, it would equally apply to all the stone monuments described as existing on the hill in the twelfth century, and of which but few vestiges can now be found.

PUBLIC ROADS.

There were five principal roads leading from Tara to the provinces, according to the Irish Topographical work—called Dinnseanchus. They were called by the following names viz., Slighe Dala, Slighe Asail, Slighe Midhluachra, Slighe Cualann and Slighe Mor.

Slighe Dala was the great south-western road of Ireland which extended from the southern side of Tara Hill in the direction of Ossory.

Slighe Asail was a western road extending from the Hill of Tara towards Mullingar.

Slighe Mor was the great western road, the lie of which is defined by the Eiscir Riada, a line of gravel hills from Dublin to Galway.

Slighe Midhluachra a northern road passing by way of Dundalk.

Slighe Cualann extended from Tara by way of Dublin and Bray.

"Stoney-Batter" in Dublin, and "Booterstown" point out the direction of Slighe Cualann for "Batter" in the one and "Booter" in the other, are broken forms of the Irish term for "road" namely Bothar (*pr.* Bōhar). Like most roads in the olden time the "Slighe" Cualann was paved with large stones. Hence the name "Stoney-Batter." At Booterstown a portion of the old high road is still to be seen.

For a fuller account see *Book of Rights*, (Leabhar na g-Ceart) translated by Dr. O'Donovan—introduction, pp. 58, and 59,—also—Dr. Petrie on the History and Remains of Tara Hill, p. 228, and Dr Joyce, *Irish Names of Places.*—

There are ten or more names in Irish for "road:" *Set* (not in use) like the Latin *Semita*, a path of one animal, *Ro-shĕt*,—(*sh,* has the sound of *h* alone) contracted into *roat*, and *rōt* a great path, wider than a *set*.

Rōt, is pronounced with ō long like the English term *road,* and is perhaps, its root.

Ramhat,—wider again than a *rōt*; an open space before a house,—an area.

Lamh-rōta, a hand-road, that is a road joining two public roads.

Tuagh-rota, a farm road.

Cāsan from *cos,* a foot, a foot-path.

Bealack, a way, or line of road as "fag an Bealach" "clear the way" battle-cry of the 88th Connacht Rangers.

Bōthar (*pr.* Bōhar) from *Bō,* a cow and *tar,* over, athwart, "two cows fit upon it,—one lengthwise, the other athwart."

Bothar-mōr, a high-road; *Bōthairín,* a small road, a path, a bridle road.

Caoi, a way, the direction to a place.

Slighe, a public road.

APPENDIX II.

THE BEST HUNDRED IRISH BOOKS.

CANON ULICK BOURKE, P.P., M.R.I.A.

TO THE EDITOR OF THE FREEMAN.

Claremorris, March, 29th, 1886.

DEAR SIR—Accept my best thanks for having sent me an advanced proof of the able essay by "Historicus" on the subject "The Best Hundred Irish Books," or, rather, as I must take it from his own views—the hundred best books relating to Ireland and to her people.

Its publication in the pages of the *Freeman's Journal* has been earlier than I had expected.

His Lordship the Bishop of Achonry has given expression to the thought that came to my mind directly on reading the praise lavished on Lecky's writings in reference to Ireland—that what he did write has been over-estimated. The rarity of such honest writing by pro-English historians in treating of Ireland and her children in the past has, like water in a desert land, added immensely to the literary and historic value of Lecky's views in his "History of England in the Eighteenth Century," and his "Leaders of Public Opinion in Ireland." With some of your distinguished contributors I largely share surprise at the very ample extension given by "Historicus" to the complex term "Irish Books"—meaning books, or parts of books, written, no matter by whom, about Ireland or the Irish. For my own part, I am pleased with the definition, for it enables one to haul with his literary net all sorts of books relating to Ireland and her people, and then he can sit leisurely on the shore of his own home, and select, according to taste, a hundred which he sets store by, and make them the nucleus of a good Irish library. I see that one critic in the issue of Saturday last (27th March) is quite out of sorts when "Historicus" has not named the valuable work, "Spicilegium Ossoriense," a series of extracts relating to Ireland during the "Cromwellian Campaign," copied from documents in the Vatican Library, Rome, and other sources, and edited by Cardinal Moran. This work, so lauded by the critic, does not, after all, say much that is not already known regarding Ireland and things ecclesiastical. The readers of the "Spicilegium" should be familiar with Latin, Italian, Spanish, mediæval French, and Queen Anne English, or rather the quaint language spoken and written connected with the Elizabethan period.

It appears, at all events, that parts of books written no matter by whom and in any language fell, in the opinion of the writer or critic, under the definition of "Irish books," as expounded by "Historicus." Others, who have written, claim as "Irish" books those regarding Ireland or her people, though the works be in Latin, French, German, Italian, Old English, or Irish of the early, middle, or modern periods. Judge Barry well observes some of the works named by "Historicus," treat of propositions once disputed, but not so any longer. Those works were accordingly of only ephemeral interest. Mere knowledge of the title and purport of such works is enough; take for instance much of what has been written by Swift. "Controversial" details regarding the "Union" or "Emancipation," are now of no value. All that has passed away. The events remain. Able writings like those of Edmund Burke, or the speeches of Grattan, will always be read with pleasure, not for the events recorded so much as for the beauty and the grace of the language in which they have been clothed. The able essay of "Historicus" has received praise on the score that it is impartial. On this head I too wish to bestow praise; nevertheless I should not like to recommend Dr. Todd's Life of St. Patrick without telling my readers to purchase a copy of Dr. Gargan's able critique of that work—or the volume, "St. Patrick, Apostle of Ireland," by my friend, Father William Bullen Morris, Priest of the Oratory. I should not like to see "Hibernia Expugnata"—written by Cambrensis in the twelfth century—recommended for a place amongst any hundred books, good or bad, and the able work "Cambrensis Eversus," from the pen of our countryman, Rev. John Lynch, Archdeacon of Tuam (Born A.D. 1600), so full of real history, denied a place. One of the best books in its way than can be put into a student's hands is "Cambrensis Eversus," translated by Rev. Dr. Matthew Kelly of Maynooth, and edited with original text by him, in the years 1849-52 (3 vols, price 30s). Along with the Life of Bishop Bedel, I should like to have that of the Lord Primate, Dr. Oliver Plunkett, written by Cardinal Moran, a small volume, yet, like the Life of Hugh O'Neill, by Mitchell, one replete with interest. Bedel and Plunkett, flourished in the same century. and are symbols of opposing interests and of religious life in the seventeenth century. Miss Charlotte O'Brien will, I feel convinced, thank me for telling the title of the "Very Old Irish Dictionary," full of curious old English words and country phrases, "which in her copy has been lost." It is "The English-Irish Dictionary," compiled by Father Connor Begley, and edited by Hugh Buidhe MacCurtin, published in Paris, Anno 1732. It is commonly known as MacCurtin's "English-Irish Dictionary," the first ever published.

Sir Charles G. Duffy suggests that the lists of the best Irish books be formulated—one for the Students' Irish library, the other of works for general reading. I have made a selection of the best hundred Irish books, not for general reading, but for the student of Irish history, or the young historian. The works in this list will show what Ireland has been in the days before Niall the Great, and during the golden age of Catholic Ireland from A.D. 432 to 800, and during the incursions of the Lakemen or the Norsemen ; again in the period of the renaissance from A.D. 1014 to 1172 ; and next to the penal period ; and from the commencement of the penal period to the present.

The thanks of Irishmen at home and abroad, and of Irishmen unborn, are due to the *Freeman's Journal*, and in their name I offer the grateful thanks of a people whose history has hitherto been to a great extent neglected.—I remain your faithful servant,

U. J. CANON BOURKE, P.P., M.R.I.A.

A LIST OF THE BEST HUNDRED IRISH BOOKS.

Ancient laws of Ireland, known as the Brehon laws, the Seanchus Mor; the Book of Aichill, 4 vols.
Dr. Keating's Ireland, edited with notes by John O'Mahony. Haverty, New York. 1857.
O'Curry's Manners and Customs of the Ancient Irish, edited by W. K. Sullivan, 3 vols. The first volume as introduction is from the pen of W. K. Sullivan, 1873.
Lectures by O'Curry on the M.S. Materials of Ancient Irish History. Dublin : James Duffy, 1861.
Sir William Wilde's Beauties of the Boyne and Blackwater. In this work the writer gives an account of the pre-Christian mounds situate on the banks of the Boyne. They present an antiquity considerably beyond three thousand years.
Sir William Wilde's Loch Corrib. The fight between the Fir-Bolg and the Tuatha De Danann is recorded in this volume.
Sir Henry Maine's Lectures on the Early History of Institutions. London : Murray, 1875.
Dr. Petrie's Tara Hill—Tranactions of the Royal Irish Academy ; vol 18, Part 11, 1839. Every Irish scholar should have a copy.
Dr. Petrie's Round Towers of Ireland—The Ecclesiastical Architecture of Ireland. Hodges and Smith, Dublin, 1845.
The Four Masters—The Annals of the Kingdom of Ireland, translated, with notes, and edited by Dr. O'Donovan, 6 vols.
A Series of County Maps, say that by Philips or that by Dr. Joyce.
Sir William Wilde's Catalogue of the Royal Irish Academy. A week's study of all that is to be seen in the Royal Irish Academy will add much to the knowledge of any student of Irish Antiquities.
The Transactions (some volumes) of the Royal Irish Academy.
The Transactions of the Kilkenny Archæological Society.
The volumes published by the Ossianic Society.
Transactions of the Gaelic Society.

The Celtic Society and Archæological Society volumes.
The Ulster Archæological Society. One volume of the work done by the Ordance Survey of Ireland—The County of Londonderry. Colonel Colbey, superintendent; Hodges and Smith, 1837. This is the only volume of the rich mine of literary and antiquarian wealth dug up by the staff of the Ordnance Survey of Ireland. The History of the County Londonderry was too good to have it published. The landed proprietors at the time felt the bitterness of the truth told in its pages, and contrived by Parliamentary pressure to put a stop to the publication of the MS. records connected with the other thirty-one counties. But are these records to be had? Certainly. In the Royal Irish Academy there are about one hundred MS. volumes in quarto, three, and in some instances four volumes, relating to each county, containing an account of the past history of each townland and barony in each district in Ireland. No Irish Scholar, no historian can know thoroughly the history of any townland without having had a peep into the pages of this thesaurus of Irish native lore.
The Book of Rights.
The Book of Fenagh, edited by William M. Hennessy.
Lives of Illustrious Irishmen, by James Wills; 12 vols.
The same in another form—The Irish Nation, its History and its Biography; 4 vols. J. Wills.
Chronological account of Irish writers and a descriptive catalogue of their works by Edward O'Reilly, a volume published by the Iberno-Celtic Society
Compendium of Irish Biography; Alfred Webb. Dublin: Gill.
The Genealogies, Tribes, and Customs of Hy-Fiachrach; edited by O'Donovan; one of the Archæological Society publications.
Battle of Magh Rath.
Archdall's Monasticon Hibernicum; edited by Cardinal Moran and his literary associates, with notes.
Loca Patriciana, by Father John F. Shearman.
History of Ireland, by Haverty.
History of Ireland, by Miss Cusack.
History of Ireland, by Thomas Moore.
History of Ireland by MacGeoghegan.
Lays of the Western Gael, by Sir Samuel Ferguson.
Romances connected with this period.
The Three Sorrows of Story-Telling; found in Atlantis from the pen of O'Curry; narrated by Dr. Joyce in his Celtic Romances. Lay of the Children of Lir; Lay of the Children of Tuirenn and Deirdre. The Tale of Deirdre is told in prose in the transactions of the Gaelic Society and in verse by R. M. Joyce, M.D. To these may be added—
Queen Meave, and other Legends of the Heroic Age, by Aubrey de Vere; also the Fair of Carman, The Fight of Ferdiad, and the Feats of the Heroes of the Red Branch.

Works on Keltic Philology throw much light on the early history of the Gaelic race. Of this class are—
Pritchard's Eastern Origin of the Keltic Race.
The Aryan Origin of the Gaelic Race and Language.
Some of Max Muller's Lectures.
Ancient Rome, by Newman.
Zeuss' Grammatica Celtica (preface and prosody).
Les Origines Indo-Européenes, ou les Aryas Primitifs, par Adolphe Pictet.
Language and Literature of the Scottish Highlands.
Harris's Ware 2 vols.; price £6.
Lhuyd's Archaeologia Britannica. 1707. Oxford; price £2.
Census of Ireland.
Irish Manuscript publications. Every volume from the able pen of J. T. Gilbert, author of the History of the City of Dublin, should have a place in an Irish student's library.
Irish MSS. Edited by Professor Zimmer. By Whitley Stokes.
Irish MSS. By Constantine Nigra.
W. M. Hennessy's Works and Translations from the Irish, such as that found in Miss Cusack's St. Patrick.
Romance, The Last Monarch of Tara. By Eblana. Gill, Dublin. In this work the manners, way of living, learning, and civilization of the Ancient Christian Irish are painted with a graphic pencil.
Battle of Magh Leana.
Feast of Dun-na-gedh.
Halliday's Scandinavian Kindgom of Dublin.
Joyce's Names of Places.
Irish Version of the History of the Britons. By Nennius.
The Battles of the Gael with the Gaill. Translated and edited by Dr. Todd.
Lanigan's Ecclesiastical History, 4 vols.
The Trias Thaumaturga and Acta SS. By Colgan.
The Life of St. Patrick, large edition. By Miss Cusack.
The Life of St. Patrick. By Father Morris.
The Life of St. Patrick. By Dr. Todd.
Critique. By Dr. Gargan, Maynooth.
Lives of Irish Saints. By Canon O'Hanlon; by Rev. John Colgan.
Life of St. Columba. By Adamnan. Edited by Reeves.
Life of St. Columbanus.
Aubrey De Vere's Legends of St. Patrick.
Monks of the West. By Montalembert, 7 vols.
Irish Saints. By the Bollandists.
Life of Caius Coelius Sedulius the Elder and his Writings. Published in the Abbé Migne's Volumes of Patristic History and Writing.
O'Neill's Irish Crosses.
Gilbert's Fac-similes of National Manuscripts.
Life of St. Brendan. By Cardinal Moran.
Life of St. Brendan. By Canon O'Hanlon.

Christian Schools and Scholars, vol. i, c. ii. Schools of Ireland.
Lives of Duns Scotus : of Marianus Scotus ; of Dungal.
It would be well to read the lives of some at least of the three hundred missionary clerics, who left Ireland and preached the Faith in Germany, France, Belgium, Italy, Switzerland—such as SS. Killian, Gall, Livinus, and Saints like Benedict and Martin of Tours, whose teaching moulded, as it were, the religious life of Ireland.
Ecclesiastical Antiquities. By Father O'Laverty, Belfast.
The Diocese of Meath By Father Cogan, 4 vols,
Collections on Irish Church History. By Very Rev. Dr. Renehan, President of Maynooth. Edited by Bishop M'Carthy.
Brennan's Ecclesiastical History of Ireland.
St. Bernard's or Canon O'Hanlon's Life of St. Malachy, Archbishop of Armagh.
Life of St. Laurence O'Toole. O'Hanlon.
Cambrensis Eversus. Edited by Dr. M. Kelly.
Annals of Loch Ce (2 vols.). Edited by W. Hennessy.
Richey's Lectures on Irish History.
Life of Raleigh. By Pope Hennessy.
Life of the Poet Spenser.
Spenser's Fairy Queen.
Burke's Hibernia Dominicana.
History of Galway.
History of Iar-Connacht.
M'Gee's History of Ireland.
Mitchel's History of Ireland.
Sullivan's Story of Ireland.
The Succession of Irish Bishops. By Mazicre Brady.
Life of Dr. O'Gallagher. By Bourke.
Spicilegium Ossoriense.
People's History of Ireland. By T. Mooney.
Ecc. History of Ireland. By Father Walsh. Published in New York, 1855.
Life of Cromwell.
Carte Papers.
Molyneux' Case Stated.
Mahony's Reliques of Father Prout.
Tales by Miss Edgeworth, of G. Griffin, Banim, Carleton.
La Verte Erinn. By the Abbé Domenech.
Hayes' Ballads.
Ballad Poetry of Ireland.
The Spirit of the Nation.
The Songs and poems of T. D. S.
Moore's Melodies.
Hardiman's Minstrels.
O'Daly's poets and poetry of Munster.
Poems by Speranza (Lady Wilde), by D'Arcy Magee, Mangan, Davis, Sir Samuel Ferguson.

Basil's Wearing of the Green.
Legends by Matthew Archdeacon, author of " Connacht in '98."
Miss Mulholland's Works.
Dr. Molloy's Geology and Revelation.
Lord Dunraven's Ecclesiastical Architecture.
Sir Robert Kane's Resources of Ireland.
Miss Stokes's able work.
Lewis's Topographical Dictionary.
Castlereagh's Memoirs.
Cornwallis's Correspondence.
Mr, Fitzpatrick's Works.
Grattan's Memoirs by his Son.
Teeling's History of Ireland—Close of Last Century.
Jonah Barrington's Rise and Fall of the Irish Nation.
Curran and his Contemporaries.
Goldsmith, by Washington Irving.
Lives of Distinguished Marylanders, 1775. By Miss Esmeralda Boyle.
Moore's Life of Sheridan.
Swift's works.
Edmund Burke's works.
Goldsmith's works.
Froude's English in Ireland.
Father Tom Burke; his Life by Fitzpatrick. His Lectures and Sermons.
Letters by Dr. MacHale, Archbishop of Tuam.
Mrs. Atkinson's Life of Mary Aikenhead.
Dr. M'Ginn's Life. By D'Arcy Magee.
Life of Dr. Doyle. By Fitzpatrick.
Maguire's Life of Father Mathew.
" Irish in America.
Life of Catherine MacAuley.
Lecky's Leaders of Public Opinion.
New Ireland. By A. M. Sullivan
Young Ireland. By Sir C. G. Duffy.
Luby's Life of O'Connell.
Life of O'Connell. Edited by Mullany.
Justin M'Carthy's History of Our Own Times.
Duffy's Irish Catholic Magazine.

MUSIC.

Moore's Melodies set to music by Sir John Stephenson.
Edward Bunting's Irish Musical Melodies.
The Spirit of the Nation set to music.
Ancient Irish Music. By Dr. P. W. Joyce.
Ancient Irish Song picked up by Dr. Petrie and set to music.

INDEX.

Abernethy, in Scotland, 193
Abhan mhor, 61, 62, 163
Abhcan, God of Music, 45ᴎ, 65
Abraham, 2, 93, 118, 130, 143, 168, 183
Absolom, 28, 174
Abyssinia, 28, 35
Academy, Royal Irish, 32, 33, 34, 58, 62, 69, 72, 82ᴎ, 84, 89, 103, 106ᴎ, 107ᴎ, 111
Achadh-Aldai, Cave of, 86
Achab, 101ᴎ
Achilles, 28, 151, 153, 174
Adamnan, 208
Adleo, 25
Aedh or Hugh, son of Daghda, 78, 84
Aengabla, 27
Aenghus Ceilé Dé, 12
——— son of Daghda, 88
——— Dun, 36
——— Og or Young Aeneas, 152
Africa and African, 34, 120, 127, 131, 134, 157, 173
Agamemnon, 151, 174
Agenor, King of Phœnicia, 127
Agnon, 134
Ailbé, daughter of Bodhbh Dearg, 153
Aileach, or Aily, 37, 39, 70, 72, 75, 77, 78, 79, 81, 82, 87, 139, 148, 171, 200, 201, 205, 206
Aillinn, Stone builder of, 201
Ailm, or Fir, 109
Airgead-lamh, or Silver-hand, 42, 88, 156
——— Ross, 163, 165
Air-lis, or Area, 123, 124
Airmed, 121
Airmedh, son of Dianccacht, 59
Aladdin, 157
Alba, 4, 14, 51, 137, 176, 188
——— Longa, 184
Aldai, 86, 88
Alder, Ruis, or Fearn, 109
Alexander, 166
Alexandria, 166
Alfred, King, 119
Allen, 71ᴎ, 153, 176
——— Lough, 39, 55
Allod, or Lear, King, 47, 65, 88, 134
Alphabet, 109, 110, 111
Alps, 9, 131, 176
Amergin, the Bard, 136, 137, 140, 143, 144, 145, 147, 148, 161, 163, 165
America, United States of, 8, 13, 166
Amhan-choll, or river-hazel, 110
Ammon, 100
Ana, wife of Kermaith, 65
Andalusia, Women of, 191
Anglo-Normans, 188, 189, 192, 193
Anglo-Saxon, 141
Animals, Small, in Ireland, 189
Annals of Ireland, 23, 126, 132, 146

Annals of the Four Masters, 30, 35, 58, 75, 81, 135, 170, 206
——— ——— Ulster, 87
Antiquities, 87, 106, 147, 196, 200, 205
Antrim, 39, 54
Aobh, daughter of Bodhbh Dearg, 153, 154
Aodh, or Hugh, son of Lir, 154
Aoife, 153, 154, 158
Aonach, or Fair, 43, 84
Apollo, 45
Apple-tree, or Queirt, 109
Ara, 1, 35, 51
Arabia and Arabs, 93, 102, 118, 119, 160
Ararat, Mount, 1
Arcadh, 134
Archimedes, 116ᴎ
Architecture, 117, 121, 193, 195, 198, 199, 202, 203, 204
"Architecture, Ecclesiastical, of Ireland," 193
Ardagh, 153, 169
Ardilaun, or Ard-Oilean, 22
Ard-Righ, or Supreme King, 5, 14, 16, 17, 22, 27, 42, 43, 44, 52, 56, 57, 61, 78, 92, 118, 143, 164, 168, 169, 170, 171, 172, 173, 174, 177, 178, 205, 206
Arech Februadh, 136, 137, 140, 145
Argos, 39, 55, 66
Argyle, 188
Aria, 1
Aridh Alainn, King of Munster, 155
Ariosto, 68
Arklow, 163
Armagh, 71ᴎ, 148, 152, 154, 166, 175, 206
Armenia, 1
Armies directed by ladies (Danann), 121
Army, Standing, 14
Armoric Gaul, 176
Arannan, son of Milesius, 137, 140
Aran, Islands of, 35, 36, 51, 153
Arrow, Lough, 55, 58, 59, 61, 63, 199
Arts, 16ᴎ, 128
Arts, Danann, 113, 121, 124
——— Keltic, 198
Aryan, 7, 8, 11, 13, 36, 47, 49, 67, 68, 89, 91, 92, 94, 95, 97, 104, 105, 114, 116ᴎ, 119, 120, 123, 125, 128, 129, 130, 131ᴎ, 157, 159, 180, 181, 182, 188, 193, 194
"Aryan Origin of the Gaelic Race and Language," 193, 194, 197, 201
Asail, Slighe, see Slighe
Ash, or Nion, 109
Ashford, 22, 25
Asia, 13, 17ᴎ, 30, 34, 77, 94, 100, 105, 120, 127, 131
——— Minor, 67, 86, 87, 116ᴎ, 123, 131, 135
Aspen, or Eabhadh, 109, 110
Assaroe, 55
Assuerus, King, 93, 184

Assyrians, 93, 101, 111
Astarte, 108N
Astyages, grandfather of Cyrus, 184
Atheus and Athenians, 17N, 23, 55, 104, 130
Atlantic, 2, 5, 6, 14, 18, 54, 62, 117, 141, 142, 144, 145, 156N
Atlantis, 74, 145, 150, 156N
Attila, 68N
Aughrim, or Eac Druim, 163
Augustus, Emperor, 67, 169, 184
Aurones, or Auruncans, 8N
Austria, 4, 87, 183
Authors who support Christian origin of Ogham writing, 105
——————————Pagan origin of Ogham writing, 106
Author's own opinion, 104

Baal, 108N
Baath, 134
Babel, Tower of, 135
Babylon, 44N, 95, 98, 102, 158
Badbh, Goddess of War, 47, 65
Baile-an-tocher, or Ballytogher, 164
Bainchré, or Fair Face, 201
Balkan Range, 4
Ballina, 81, 167
Ballinahinch, 169
Ballinasloe, 163
Ballymote, Book of, 30, 58, 78, 84, 97, 98,
Bally O'Douda, 81
Ballysadare, 23, 24, 39, 61, 62, 63N, 70, 72, 157, 199
Ballyshannon, 3, 54, 59N, 71N, 152
Ballytogher, 164
Balor of the Evil Eye, 24, 43, 53, 54, 55, 56, 58, 60, 61, 63, 65, 67
Baltic, 52N
Baltra, 61
Banba, Queen, 143, 147, 148
Banquet, The Smith's, 160
Banqueting House of Tara, 208
Ban-shee, or Bean-sidhe, 71N
Bantry Bay, 162
Ban-tuathach, or Lady Chief, 48, 49
Bards, 124, 144, 178
Baring-Gould, 107N, 108N, 159
Bastarnæ, The, 14
Battle of Magh Tura, 23, 24, 37, 39, 42, 46, 53, 56, 199
—— Eve of, 24
—— Ladies in, 88
—— of Geashill, 161
Bealach, a road, 210
Bealtaine, 46
Beathach, 18
Beathaigh, Druim, 163, 165
——————Rath, 163, 165
Beatrice, 159
"Beauties of the Boyne and Blackwater," 69, 74
Beds of the Big Men, 64N
—————— Fenians, 64N
Behistun, 101
Being, Supreme, 40, 49
Beith, or Birch, 109
Beith-luis-nion, 106, 109, 110

Bel, or Beal, 15
Belcek, 54
Belfries, or Bell-houses, 193, 194, 195
Belgae, see Firbolg
Belgedan Mount, or Benlevi, 20, 21, 22
Belgium, 4, 6, 10, 191
Bells, Mass, 155, 156, 195
Bellona, see Badbh
Belus, 135
Benen, Saint, 160N
Benjamin, son of Rachel, 154
Benn Edair, 163
Beogamhain, 134
Bhering's Straits, 131, 134
Bible, Modern Hebrew, 100N
Bill, father of Milesius, 134, 137, 138
Birch, or Beith, 109
Biscay, Bay of, 137, 139
Blackie, Professor, 68, 68N, 118
Black Foreigners, 4
————— Sea, 3, 4
Bladh, uncle of Milesius, 138
Bladhma, Sliabh, 166
Blar, father of Bolc, 201
Bobel-Loth, or Common Alphabet, 109, 111
Bodhbh-Dearg, or the Red, 70N, 71, 88, 148, 152, 153, 154, 158
Bohemia, 14, 87
Boinn, wife of Neckthann, 84
Book of Ballymote, 30, 58, 78, 84, 89, 97, 98, 107N, 110, 111, 126
—— Clonmacnois, 206
—— Conquests, or Leabhar na n-Gabhala, 201
—— Fermoy, 151, 159
—— Genealogies, 41, 70, 201, 202
—— Glendalough, 208
—— Hymns, 161N
—— Invasions, 89, 149
—— Kells, 197
—— Lecan, 29, 30, 46, 58, 78, 89, 98, 110, 111, 112, 126
—— Leinster, 15, 30, 34, 46, 58, 62, 89, 98, 112, 126
—— Rights. or Leabhar-na-gCeart, 126, 210
Bolc, son of Blar, 201
Bolg, meaning of, 10
Bollandists, The, 90
Bollandus, Father (S.J.), 90
Booterstown, 210
Bothar, a road, 210
—— mor, or high road, 210
Bothairin, or little road, 210
Boyne River, 37, 44, 46, 75, 79, 83. 84, 85, 86, 87, 121, 123, 145, 147, 153, 160, 161, 163, 165
Boyne, Brugh on the, 39, 46, 70, 84, 87, 122, 152, 160
—— —— Great Cemetery of, 84
Bracklin, 165
Brass as a writing material, 99, 102
Bratha, Father of Breogan, 134
Bray, 210
Breas, 15, 19, 42, 43, 53, 54, 57, 58, 60, 61, 88, 107
—— meaning of, 47

Breastplate of St. Patrick, 161N
Brechin, in Scotland, 193
Brefni, 39, 172
Bregia, in Meath, 165
Brehons, or Breitheamh, 15, 29, 48, 119, 120, 122, 125, 139, 178, 179, 180
——— Laws, 177, 179, 180, 181, 182, 183, 184
Brendan, St., 155
Brennus, 48
Breogan, son of Bratha, 134, 137, 138, 140, 141, 162, 163
Brian, 65, 88
——— King of Hy-Many, 126
Bri-damh, or Ox Mount, in King's County, 164, 165
Brigantes, 134, 135, 140, 141
Brighit, meaning of, 47, 65
Bri-leith, 152
Briotan Mael, 5
Britain, 4, 5, 6, 10, 14, 51, 106, 120, 125, 126, 132, 137, 176, 181, 188, 194
British Law, 181
——— Museum, 59N, 102
Bró, or Handmill, 124
Broad-foot, or Troigh-Leathan, 201
Bron River, 161
Brownson, Dr., on the Irish, 191
Brugh on the Boyne, 39, 46, 70, 84, 122, 152, 160
——— of Burra, 79
——— or Town of the Dead, 79
Bruidne, 60, 61
Buan, 24, 51
Bute, Saint, 111
Burial of the Dead, 122
Burra, 79, 87
Burron, 169
Burta, 75

Cadmus, 66, 127, 130
Caelchu, Rath of, 209
Caen Druim, 44
Caesar, 9, 13, 65, 67, 96, 121, 166, 179
Caesarea, 166
Caherduff, 26
Cahers, or Cashels, 36, 62, 63, 76, 78, 121, 122, 124, 149, 163, 198
Caicher, 148, 163
Cailte Mac Ronain, 176
Cairbre, the Poet, 43, 83, 84
——— Cinn Chait, 170
Caithness, 35
Caledonia, 13, 14, 39, 53
Calmel, 60, 61
Cambrensis, Giraldus, 189, 193
Canaan, son of Cush, 7, 166
Canaanites, 7, 10
Caoimhghin, Giolla, Poet, 112
Caoin, The, 113, 121
Capa-Cirant, near the Red Sea, 128
Cape Clear, 145
——— Comorin, 158
Carbory, West, 162
——— East, 162
Carinthia, 14

Carlingford, 148
Carman, or Wexford, 72, 73, 122, 142
Carns, 21N, 30. 31, 33, 62, 76, 85, 121
Carn-an-aoin-Fir, or of the One Man, 31, 33
——— Eochaidh, 27
——— na Cluithe, 23
Carthage, 36
Cas, son of Rory, 174
Casan, a footpath, 210
Cashel, King Cormac of, 12, 46, 126, 134, 209
Caspian Sea, 1, 131
Casruba, stone-builder of Ailinn, 201
Castleconnell, 143
Castleconnor, 81
Castlelyons, 164
Castlemaine, 143
Castlepollard, 154
Castletown, 143
Cathair an Nair, 163
——— Crofinn, 200, 209
——— of Aileach, 201
Cavan, 39, 172
Cave, Fingal's, 54
——— of Achadh Aldai, 86
Caves, 36, 63, 84, 103
Ceantire, Mull of, 155
Cerastes, The, 95
Cermet Milbeol, 45N
Cesh Corainn, 63
Cesnola, General, 68, 77, 83, 92
Cethe, 88
Ceylon, 133
Chaldea and Chaldeans, 2, 93, 94, 100N, 101, 128, 129, 131
Cham, or Ham, 7, 10, 52N, 94, 129, 135, 137
Champollion, 108
Character, Chaldaic, 100N
——— Phoenician, 100N, 101
——— Ogham (secret), 98, 106N
Charlemagne, 40, 66
Children of Lir, 150, 151, 153, 154
——— Turenn, 72, 156, 157, 158
——— Rory, 173
China, 131, 178
Christian, 3, 6, 9, 10, 12, 13, 14, 21, 33, 39, 41, 43, 51, 52, 62, 64N, 72, 75, 80, 81, 87, 89, 90, 92, 93, 94, 95, 96, 97, 99, 100, 102, 103, 104, 105, 106, 107N, 108, 112, 113, 116, 117, 125, 128, 129, 130, 132, 133, 135, 150, 155, 160N, 167, 168, 169, 170, 171, 173, 174, 175, 176, 178, 179, 181, 186, 187, 189, 192, 193, 194, 195, 196, 199, 204, 206
Christian Theory of Round Towers, 194
Church, Early Irish, 35, 195, 196
——— Catholic, Laws of, 180
Chus, 166
Cian, a Danann Chief, 61, 88
Cinerary Urns, 32
Cingris, King of Egypt, 128
Ciun Drom Sneachta, The, 126
——— Chait, Carbry, 170
Circell, 8
Circles, 62, 63, 64, 84
Cirr and Cuirrell, wives of Daghda, 84
Clan Ruadhraidh, 168, 169
Clan System, 113, 117, 118, 177, 183, 184, 185
Clanna Morna, 41, 175

Clanna Deagha, 175
——— Baolsgne, 175
Clare, 153, 188
——— River, 143
Clasagh, Druim, 163, 165
Clear, Cape, 145, 161
Clety, or Cleitigh, 70, 71ɴ, 153
Cleopatra's Needle, 82
Cloghelea, 85
Cloig-teach, or Clogad, 195, 204ɴ
Clonmacuois, 84, 172, 196
——————— Tighearnach of, 33, 172
——————— Book of, 206
Clontarf, 5, 52ɴ, 62
Cnoc Meadha, 153
Cohhthach, 155
Cogadh Gaedhil re Gallaibh, 4
Coilgeach, 195
Colchis, 135
Colgan, Father, 161ɴ
Coll, or Hazel, 109
Colla Uais, 170
Collooney, 61
Colman, son of Cohhthach, 155
Colours, Knowledge of, by Danauns, 121
Colpa, son of Milesius, 137, 140, 145, 166
——— Inver, 145, 166
Columbia, 166
Columbus, 166
Colum Cnuellemeach, 44ɴ'
Columkille, or Columba, St., 29, 30, 197, 198
Comorin, Cape, 158
Conaing's Tower, 38
Conaire, King, 170, 171
Conal Kearnach, 168, 174, 175
Conang, 86
Conga, son of Rory, 174
Cong, Cumang or Cuing, 20, 21, 22, 23, 25, 31, 36, 37, 39, 58, 63ɴ, 88, 178
Conmac, son of Queen Meav, 169
Commacné, 169
Conmaic-ne Culaid Tolad, 22
Conn, Lough, 3, 166
Conn of the Hundred Fights, 29, 167, 175
——— son of Lir, 154
Connacht, 21ɴ, 29, 35, 41, 48, 55, 71ɴ, 78, 153, 155, 162, 165, 166, 167, 168, 169, 170, 175, 176, 178, 189, 191, 201, 210
Connemara, 169
Connell Maceochegan, 25
Connor, Dun, 36
Conquests, Book of, 201
Conor MacNessa, King, 150, 166, 168, 169, 171, 174, 175, 176
Cooley, or Cuailgne, 148
Cootestown, 164
Corann, the Harper, 63
Corca Lughaidh, 162
Corc, son of Queen Meav, 169
——— Lughaidh, 98, 99
Corcomroe, 169
Corgenn, a Connacht Chief, 78
Cork, 5, 103, 106ɴ, 117, 162, 164
Cormac, Cas, 167
——— House of, 208
——— King of Cashel, 12, 46, 134, 209
——— Mac Airt, 15, 30, 175, 176, 179, 206

Cormac O'Cuirnin, 59ɴ
Cornwall, 17, 188
Corrib, or Orbsen, Lough, 22, 24, 25, 28, 31, 32, 35, 39, 47, 48
Corr-sliabh,or Curlew Mountains,56,56ɴ,57
Corunna, 137, 140
Craobh-Ogham, 106ɴ
Credne, the Artificer, 27, 45ɴ, 47
Cremation early practised, 122
Cremthain, 84
————————Sciath Beul, 162, 165
————————Naidh Nair, 170
Crete, 134, 135
Croatia, 183
Crofinn, Cathair, 200, 209
Cro-Ghaile, 27
Crom Cruach, 172
————Sunday of Black, 172
Cromleachs, 30, 39, 62, 63, 64ɴ
Cross, Village of, 22, 25, 26
——— and Circle, 108ɴ
——— of Adamnan, 208
Cruachan, 39, 74, 84, 122, 169, 176, 201
Cruach Patrick, 78
————Crom, 172
Crux Ansata, The, 108ɴ
Cu, 88
Cuaileann, Sliabhtha, 166
Cuailngi, Sliabh, 148, 166
——— Tain-ho, 174
——— uncle of Milesius, 138, 148
Cnala, ————————, 138
Cualann, Slighe, see Slighe
Cuan O'Lochain, Poet, 44
——— or Strangford Lough, 3
Culge, or Fifth, 5, 14
Culgeadh Sreing, 29
Cuchullan, 64ɴ, 174
Cullen, Lough, 3
Cumhal, Finn Mac, 123
Curchog, Lady, 149, 150, 151, 159, 160
Curium, 77, 86
Curlew Mountains, 56, 56ɴ, 57
Curraidhe na Craoibhe Ruaidhe, 175
Cush, son of Cham, 7
Cuthites, 7
Cyprus and Cypriote, 68, 77, 82, 83, 86, 87, 89, 92, 93, 95, 102, 103, 116ɴ, 122
Cyrus the Great, 44ɴ, 65, 116ɴ, 184

Da Chich Danainne, 75
Dacia, 50
Dada (Father), Origin of, 67
Dagda, 25, 26, 42, 45, 46, 48, 49, 58, 59, 60, 61, 65, 67, 70, 77, 78, 81, 84, 88, 92, 121, 139, 148, 152, 201
——— meaning of, 44
——— Mór, 44, 57, 64, 67, 84, 88, 89, 121
Dair, or Oak, 109
Dairbreach, Loch, 154, 155
Dala, Slighe, see Slighe
Dal-Aradian, 168
Dalkey, 163
Dalmatia, 14
Dalton on the Round Towers, 193, 194, 197
Damnonii, Domhna, 17

Dana, 49, 50, 65, 91
Danae, mother of Perseus, 66, 158
Danai, or Dani, 18, 50
Danann, Tuatha de, 2, 4, 5, 6, 15, 18, 19, 20, 22, 23, 24, 25, 26, 27, 28, 29, 30, 31, 36, 37, 38, 39, 40, 41, 42, 44, 45N, 46, 47, 48, 49, 50, 51, 52, 53, 54, 55, 56, 58, 59, 60, 61, 62, 63, 64, 65, 66, 67, 68, 69, 70, 71, 71N, 72, 73, 74, 75, 77, 78, 79, 80, 81, 82, 83, 84, 85, 87, 87N, 88, 89, 90, 91, 97, 102, 103, 104, 107, 111, 112, 113, 116, 117, 118, 119, 120, 121, 122, 123, 124, 125, 126, 127, 139, 142, 143, 144, 145, 146, 147, 148, 149, 150, 151, 152, 153, 154, 155, 156, 157, 158, 159, 162, 165, 170, 177, 178, 186, 187, 189, 193, 197, 198, 199, 200, 201, 209
Danann, Character of, 40, 113, 127, 166, 187
——— Dress and Ornaments of, 55
——— Meaning of, 48, 50
——— Respect for Female sex, 83, 121
——— Stories, 149, 150, 151, 152
——— Warlike Weapons of, 56
Danes, 4, 5, 52, 62, 87, 90, 91, 104, 114, 122, 189, 193
Danesfield, 48
Danube River, 4, 11, 14, 50, 65, 87, 131
Dathy, King, 170, 175, 176
D'Avèze, Count, on the Irish, 191
David, King, 28, 101, 119, 136, 185
Davies, Sir John, 182, 190
De, meaning of, 49
Dead Sea, 100
——— Towns of the, 32, 37, 83, 84
Decies, 164
De Domnand, 53
Deirdre, 169, 174, 175
Delbeth, 47, 58, 88, 89
——— Daughter of, 50
Delt and Drucht and Daithe, 45
Demotic, 95, 98, 101
Denmark, 4, 156
Deoch, daughter of King Finghin, 155
Derg-Dian-Scothach, 70N, 152, 153
——— son of Daghda, 70N, 148, 152, 153
Derry, 5, 75, 76, 78, 171, 201, 205, 206
Destiny, Island of, 6, 137, 142, 193
Devonshire, 17, 188
Diancencht, the Physician, 27, 45N, 57, 59, 65, 67, 88
Diarmaid, 176
——— meaning of, 27, 47
Dibon, in Moab, 100
Dictionary, Dr. O'Brien's, 132
Digamma, The, 95
Dinnseanchus, 75, 84, 205, 207, 210
Dionysius, 8N, 131
Dixon, Most Rev. Dr., 100
Doah, two rivers, 50N
Doinn, Teach, 166
Donagh M'Gillapatrick, 72
Domhnach Crom Duabh, 172
Domhnachs, or Churches, 198
Donegal, 5, 29, 54, 71N, 75, 126, 138, 147, 159
Donn, Heber, son of Milesius, 136, 137, 140, 145, 145N, 166
Dowth, 39, 75, 83, 85, 86
Dress and Ornaments of the Firbolg, 56

Dress and Ornaments of the Fomorians, 55
——————————————— Tuatha de Dananns, 55
Drogheda, 75, 85, 103, 147
Drucht and Delt and Daithe, 45N
Druids and Druidism, 9, 15, 32, 72, 73, 83, 98, 104, 105, 106, 113, 119, 120, 139, 143, 150, 160, 178, 179, 187, 195
Druim Beathaigh, 163, 165
Druim Clasach, 163, 165
Druim Dian, 71N, 153
——— Finghin, 164, 165
Drumligheau, or Drumleen, 70N, 144, 147, 148, 151, 159
Duach Temen, 88
——— Gallach, 126
Duald Mac Firbis, 29, 40, 106, 187, 201
Duan Gireannach, The, 126
Dubhaltach, or Duald, 201
Dublin, 210
Dumhacha, or Sandhills, 145N
Dumhas, or Tumuli, 28
Dun Aenghus, 36
Dun Connor, 36
Dundalk, 210
Dun Deilginnis, 163
Dun Edair, 163
Dungarvan, 111N, 147, 163
Dun Inn, 163
Dun Sobhairce, 163
Dunmore, 169
Duns, 16, 121, 122, 149, 152, 153, 160, 163
Durrow, 165
Dwellings of Dananns, 113
Dyeing, Knowledge of, by Dananns, 121

Eac-Druim, or Aughrim, 163
Eadhadh, or Aspen, 109, 110
Ealadan, 47, 51, 88, 89
Eas-Aodha-ruaidh, or Assaroe, 55, 71N, 152
Eas-Dara, or Dara's Waterfall, 63, 70
East, The, 1, 6, 38, 45, 96, 99, 101, 102, 105, 106, 117, 119, 120, 123, 158, 184
Eastern Origin of the Irish, 1, 2, 74, 102, 121, 158, 159, 177, 201
Eber Fionn, 134, 135, 140, 142
——— Glunfinn, 134
——— Scot, 134
Ebleo, uncle of Milesius, 138
Ebhleon Sliabh, 166
Echtach, 88
Edana, the Poetess, 25, 43, 83, 84, 121
Edan, 148
Edenderry, 165
Ederlamh, 88
Eily, O'Carrolls of, 167
Eiscir Riada, 210
Egypt and Egyptians, 82, 86, 89, 92, 94, 95, 98, 102, 108N, 111, 128, 129, 133, 134, 136, 137, 158, 186
Eire, or Erin, 1, 3, 10, 13, 14, 16, 19, 28, 29, 34, 36, 38, 39, 41, 42, 45, 46, 50, 51, 54, 57, 62, 69, 70, 72, 73, 78, 81, 82, 83, 89, 90, 92, 95, 96, 99, 102, 111, 116, 117, 119, 120, 127, 137, 140, 141, 142, 143, 146, 147, 150, 153, 156, 157, 158, 160, 166, 169, 171, 172, 176, 179, 187, 188, 189, 192, 200, 201

—— Queen, 143, 146, 147, 148
—— Ulle, 21, 22
Erimhon, or Heremon, 134, 137, 138, 140
Elthlenn, 44, 51, 61, 65, 70
Elatha, father of Breas, 53, 54, 55, 58, 60, 61, 107N
Elbe, River, 39, 50
Ellas, 101
Elijah, 101
Emania, 169, 171, 172, 175, 176, 201
Emperor Augustus, 67, 169, 184
—————— Charlemagne, 40, 66
—————— Julius, 67, 174
—————— Peter of Russia, 44, 124
—————— Trajan, 184
Empress, or Great Mother, 184
En, son of Ethoman, 45N, 163
England, 13, 21N, 85N, 94, 115, 171, 180, 182, 188, 190, 191, 194, 198, 201, 204
English, 47, 67, 70, 87, 90, 94, 97, 109, 114, 132, 141, 155N, 164, 180, 186, 188, 189, 190, 194, 210
Enna Airgetheach, K., 171, 172
Enniskillen, 70
—————— meaning of, 55
Eochaidh, Carn, 27
—————— Garbh, 88
—————— or Ollamh Fodhla, 172
Eochy Feidhleach, 171, 174
—————— King, Mac Erc, 18, 19, 20, 21, 22, 23, 24, 25, 26, 27, 28, 29, 31, 42, 43, 44 48, 63N, 200
—————— Mór, 167
Eoghamhan, 134
Eoir, or Nore, 165
Eothail, 62
Epic of Aryan Nations, 114, 115
Erc, 18, 21
Erne, Lough, 3, 54, 55, 57
Ernin, son of Duach Gallach, 126
Eros, 159
Erris, or Iarros, 17, 41, 155
Esau, 143
Esclann, Brehon of Dagda, 84
Eserg, son of Neid, or God of Slaughter, 65, 88
Esker Riada, 165, 210
Esru, 134
Essay on the History and Antiquities of Tara Hill, 200
Etan, wife of Ogma, 65
Ethoman, 45N
Etrurians and Etruscan, 8, 9, 32, 37, 39, 82, 83, 94, 95, 122, 123, 129
Ethiopians, 93, 137, 184
Ethnea, daughter of Tureun, 157
Euêmeros and Euemerism, 68
Euphrates, 6, 94, 158
Europa, 128, 158
Europe and European. 5, 6, 7, 10, 12, 18, 23, 34, 39, 40, 41, 50, 77, 82, 85, 89, 92, 94, 95, 96, 100, 106N, 117, 118N, 120N, 124, 125, 126, 127, 131, 157, 173, 176, 177, 181, 182, 198
Euxine, 14, 135, 136
Eve of Battle, 24
Eye, Evil, 53, 54

Factna the Wise, 174
Fag-an-Bealach (clear the way), 210
Fair Hill, 20, 22, 25
—— of Carman, 73
—— Ridge, or Caen Druim, 44
—— of Tara, 73
Fairy Mount, or Sidh Neunta, 71N, 153
—————— Seat or Sidhe, 71N, 149
—————— Hills, 82, 149
Faise, Glean, 166
Family or Clan, The, 118, 183
—————————— Honourable position of women in the, among the Dananns, 121
Fas, Milesian Heroine, 146, 147
Fathach, the Poet, 24
Fathan, Maolmuire of, 112, 126
Fate of the Children of Lir, 150, 151, 153, 154
—————————— Turenn, 72, 156
Feal, Queen of King Lughaidh, 146
Feale, River, 146
Fearainn, Rath, 25
Fearn, or Alder, 109
Febal, son of Lodan, 63
Febric Glas, 134
Februadh, Arech, 136, 137, 140, 145
Fe Fiad, 160, 161N
Feis, or Parliament, 14
Felim, or Eblind, Sliabh, 143
Fenian Language and Militia, 131
—————— Period, 175, 176
Fenius Farsa, 127, 128, 129, 130, 131, 132, 133, 134, 135, 136
Feradach, King of Scotland, 98, 99
Fergus Mac Roigh, King of Ulster, 168, 169, 171, 174, 175
Ferguson, Lady, 174
—————— Sir Samuel, 174, 175
Fermanagh, 71N
"Fermoy, Book of," 151, 159
Ferthas, or Graves, 28
Fiachra, son of Lir, 154
Fiadh, 160, 161N
Field of Columns, 26
Fingal's Cave, 54
Finghin, 155
—————— Druim, 164, 165
Finn, River, 138
—————— Tobar, at Tara, 208
Finland, 62N
Finnbar, 70N, 152, 153
Finneachaidh, Sidh, 152, 154
Fionn, 64N, 128N
—————— Eber, or Heber, 134, 135, 136, 161, 162, 166, 167, 168
—————— ghuala, or fair shoulder, 154, 155, 159
—————— Mac Cumhal, 128, 176
—————— Traigh, or White Strand, 62
Fintan, King of Leinster, 26
Firbolg, or Belgæ, or Belgians, 2, 4, 5, 6, 8, 9, 10, 11, 12, 13, 14, 15, 16, 17, 18, 19, 20, 21, 22, 24, 25, 26, 27, 28, 29, 30, 32, 35, 36, 36N, 38, 39, 40, 41, 42, 44, 47, 51, 52, 57, 58, 63N, 64, 67, 71N, 88, 120, 125, 147, 150, 162, 165, 170, 171, 177, 178, 179, 186, 187, 188, 189, 193, 198, 199, 200, 206, 209
Firbolg, Character of, 10

Firbolgs as Colonists, 10
—— Derivation of, 9, 10, 11
—— Dress and Ornaments of, 56
—— Intelligence of, 14, 67
—— Warlike Weapons of, 56
Fir-Domnnan, or Domhna, 17, 187, 188
——Gael, 188
——Gaileonn, 17, 187, 188
Fir, or Ailm, 109
Fire God, 45
—— and Sun Worship, 46
Fitzpatricks of Ossory, 167
Five Great Roads, The, 210
Flanders, 188
Flann, of Monasterboice, 77, 78, 79, 111, 112
—— son of Conang, 86
Fleadh Goibhneann, 160
Fleasg Fili, or Wand of the Poet, 162
Flemings, 186, 188, 191
"Flight of the Earls," 183
Fodla, or Ireland, 143, 157, 172
—— Ollamh, 171, 172
—— Queen, 142, 147, 148
Foghmarach, meaning of, 11, 156
Fomorians, 2, 4, 5, 7, 8, 14, 18, 23, 24, 36, 38, 42, 43, 51, 52, 53, 54, 55, 56, 57, 58, 59, 60, 61, 62, 63, 63ᴎ, 64, 65, 67, 72, 78, 87ᴎ, 125, 150, 156, 165, 171, 199, 201
——, Dress and Ornaments of, 55
——, Warlike Weapons of, 56
"Foray of Queen Meav," 174
Foreigners, Black, 4
————White, 4
Forradh, or Meeting Place, 208
Fort of Heroes, 25
—— of fold-like defense, 25
"Forus Feasa" (Keating's), 129
Fothadh ratha Grainé, 208
"Four Masters," 4ᴎ, 30, 35, 58, 75, 81, 85ᴎ, 87, 111, 134, 135, 165, 170, 206
Foxes, The, 167
Foyle, or Feball, Lough, 63, 78, 139
———————— River, 70ᴎ, 138, 139, 140, 162
France, 137, 173, 198
Franks, The, 40
Frenchmen, 191
French people, 40, 114, 186, 188, 189, 191
Froude, James Anthony, 90, 91
Fuad, Uncle of Milesius, 138, 148, 166
———— Sliabh, 148, 152, 166
Fulman, Milesian leader, 163

Gabhaltas of the Kinné, 185
Gabhar, The, 73
Gadelus and Gadelians, 131, 132, 133, 134, 135, 183, 184, 185
Gaedhil re Gallaibh, Cogadh, 4, 7
Gaelic, 2, 7, 9, 11, 19, 37, 38, 39, 42, 43, 46, 48, 49, 50, 51, 52, 54, 63, 70, 87, 90, 94, 96, 104, 111, 112, 116ᴎ, 117, 118, 124, 125, 128, 131, 133, 136, 138, 149, 150, 172, 173, 174, 179, 183, 185, 193
Gaetulia, 134
Gail, or Pillar Stones, 195, 199, 200
Gaileun, or Leinster, 18

Galamh, or Milesius, 6, 126, 134, 135, 136, 137, 138, 140
Galatians, 13, 14
Galenii, 17
Gallacia, 9, 135, 138, 140, 141
Gallia, 6, 14, 173
Gallic, 94, 95, 100
Gallicia, 4, 5, 6
Galway, 20, 21, 22, 39, 48, 70, 71ᴎ, 153, 156ᴎ, 163, 167, 188, 191, 201, 210
Gaodhal-Glas, 128, 134, 136
————— meaning of, 128ᴎ, 131
Gaul and Gauls, 4, 6, 48, 95, 96, 97, 120, 123, 125, 179
Gavel-kind, 177, 183, 185
Gamanraidhi, 41
Gamh Mountains, 63, 63ᴎ
Gara, Lough, 3
Garaidh Mac Morna, 176
Garbhan, 79
Garmen, or Carmen, 142
Geashill, Battle of, 161, 164, 165
"Genealogies, Book of," 41, 70, 201, 202
Geoffry of Monmouth, 132
German, 53, 68, 96, 114, 115, 120ᴎ, 125
Germany and German, 6, 8, 36ᴎ, 50, 64, 189
Giant's Causeway, 54
Gill, Lough, 63
Giolla, Caoimbghin, Poet, 112
———— Isa Mór Mac Firleisigh, 201
Giraldus Cambrensis, 189, 193
Gladstone's (Rt. Hon. Wm. E.) Views on, Mythology, 114, 116
Glas-Teamhrach, 208
Glean-Faise, 166
———— mo Ailleam, or Glen-of-men-athletes, 23
———— Scotin, 166
"Glendalough, Book of," 208
Glei and Glan, and Gleise, 45
Glnaire, Inis, or Inishglory, 155
Gobain Saora, 193
Gobhnenn, 47, 51, 160, 161ᴎ
God, The True, 83, 115, 119, 128, 136, 160ᴎ
Gold in Wicklow, 171
Golden Age of Irish History, 175, 176
———— Collar, 175
Goliath, 136
———— of the Fomorians, 63
Goll, son of Morna, 41
Gomer, 166
Gort, or Ivy, 109
Gostinn, a Milesian leader, 163
Gospel, The, 104, 193
Government, 113, 117, 119, 183, 184
Graine, Princess, 176
———— Rath, at Tara, 208, 209
Graves, Dr., 104
Great House of the 1,000 Soldiers, 15
Grecian, 43, 47, 49, 50, 51, 66, 67, 77, 82, 94, 95, 105, 151, 158, 186
Greece, 6, 7, 14, 66, 74, 82, 86, 87, 91, 94, 96, 97, 98, 100, 103, 117, 122, 127, 130, 131, 151
Greek, 8ᴎ, 11, 13, 32, 40, 89, 114, 116ᴎ, 127, 128ᴎ, 129, 130, 131, 151, 157, 177, 179, 209
Greisa, 44ᴎ

Q

Grianan of Aileach, 37, 39, 69, 70, 72, 75, 139
Grimm, 115
Grote, 115
Gruibne, Poet, 98

Habits, Social, of Dananns, 113
Ham, or Cham, 7, 52N, 94, 129, 135, 137
Hamitic. 94
Harun of Mesopotamia, 4
Haverty's "History of Ireland," 132
Hawthorn, or Huath, 109
Hazel, or Coll, 109
Healing Bath, or Sanative Pool, 24
Heap of the Game, 33
―――― One Man, 31
Heath, or Ur, 109
Heber Donn, 136, 137, 140, 145
―――― Finn, 134, 135, 136, 137, 138, 140, 145, 147, 148, 150, 161, 162, 163, 164, 165, 166, 167, 168, 170, 173
―――― Gluntinn, 134
―――― Scot, 134
―――― son of Ir, 162, 165, 166, 168
Hebrew, 93, 94, 100, 101, 118N, 121, 127, 129, 130, 138, 181, 185, 186
Hebrides, 35, 52, 53, 54
Hector, 121
Helen, 159
Hellas, 159
Hellenes, 10, 11, 50
Hellespont, 157
Helvetia, 14, 125
Hem, or Sem, 7, 130, 135
Henry II., 178
Henschinius, Father, 90
Heptarchy, 171
Herakloos, 157
Hercules, 97, 134, 135, 157
Heremon, 134, 137, 138, 140, 145, 147, 148, 150, 161, 162, 163, 164, 165, 166, 167, 168, 169, 170, 171, 172, 178, 186
Hermes, 97
Herodotus, 7, 50, 68, 77, 131
Hibernia, 14, 107N
Hieratic Letter, 94, 95, 98
Hieroglyphics, 94, 95, 100, 101, 108
Highlanders, 19
Highlands of Scotland, 183
Hill of Uisneach, 44
―――― Emania, 44
―――― Tara, 44
Hindu Kush Mountains, 1
―――― Temples, 96
―――― Laws, 180, 182
Hindus River, 1, 2, 6, 158
Hindus, Language of, 114
Hindustan, 184
Hissarlik, Mound of, 116N
Hogan, Rev. E., on the Irish, 191N
Homer and Homeric, 28, 30, 114, 121, 128N, 146, 151, 174
Hostages, Mound of the, 208
House Communions, 184
―――― of Conn, 208
―――― of Marisco, 208

Houses of the Dananns, 123
Howth, 3, 163
Huath, or Hawthorn, 109
Hugh, Red, 55
Hugony Mór, or The Great, 171, 173
Human Sacrifices, The Irish did not offer, 120
Humber River, 176
Hurling, 23
Hy Falgia, or Offaly, 165
Ily Mani, 163, 167
Ily, the Tower of, in Kent, 194

Iar-Connacht, 167
Iarros, or Errus, 17N, 155
Iberia, 1, 3, 6, 9, 125, 135
Icelanders, 114, 157
Idols of Dananns, 119
Ifin, or Gooseberry, 110
Ilbreach, 70N, 71N, 88, 152
Iliad, 30, 68, 68N
Illumination, Irish, 96, 197, 198, 199
Illyria, 14
Imcheall, or Circuit Builder, 79
Inch, Island of, 75
Indai, son of Aldai, 88
Indech, 53, 54, 58, 60, 61
India, 92, 93, 108N, 120N, 184
Indus, or Hindus, 6N, 94, 117, 158
Inisfail, 6, 9, 53, 125, 135, 137, 138, 140, 142
Inis Gluaire, 155
―――― Kethlen, or Enniskillen, 55
―――― na bh-fuinedhach, 2N
―――― Righ, 166
―――― Saimher, 3
Innes, Rev. J. (M.A.), 90, 106N
Intelligence of Firbolg, 14
"Introduction to Greek Classic Poets" (Coleridge), 180
Invasion of Ireland, 111, 193
"Invasions, Book of," 89, 149
Inver Skené, 3, 143, 144, 145, 166
―――― Slainghi, 142, 144
―――― Colpa, 145, 166
―――― Mhor, 163
Iobath, or death-healer, 18, 38
Iohadh, or Yew, 109
Iol-Dana, or many arts, 42, 47
Ir, son of Milesius, 137, 140, 145, 162, 165, 166, 167, 168, 169, 170, 171, 173
Irené, 137
Ireland, 1, 3, 4, 5, 7, 11, 17, 18, 19, 21N, 24, 25, 29, 30, 34, 35, 36, 38, 39, 41, 42, 43, 45, 46, 47, 52, 58, 62, 66, 67, 70, 71, 71N, 72, 75, 76, 77, 80, 82, 83, 85, 87, 89, 90, 91, 92, 94, 95, 98, 99, 103, 104, 105N, 106, 106N, 111, 112, 116, 117, 120, 121, 122, 123, 125, 126, 127, 128, 130, 132, 134, 135, 136, 138, 141, 145, 146, 148, 149, 150, 152, 155, 158, 159, 160, 161, 163, 165, 166, 167, 168, 170, 172, 173, 174, 175, 176, 178, 179, 180, 181, 182, 183, 184, 186, 187, 188, 189, 190, 191, 192, 193, 194, 195, 198, 201, 202, 204, 206, 207, 210
Ireland, Annals of, 23, 126
―――― Story of, 34

Irish, 1, 2, 5, 6, 7, 10, 13, 17, 18, 23, 30, 31, 32, 34, 35, 37, 38, 40, 41, 44, 45, 46, 47, 48, 49, 50, 51, 52, 55, 57, 58, 59N, 62, 63, 63N, 64N, 67, 69, 70, 71, 71N, 72, 74, 75, 76, 77, 78, 79, 80, 81, 82, 83, 84, 87, 89, 90, 91, 92, 93, 95, 96, 97, 98, 103, 104, 105, 106, 106N, 107, 108, 109, 110, 111, 112, 114, 118N, 120, 121, 122, 124, 125, 126, 127, 128, 129, 130, 131, 132, 133, 134, 135, 141, 145, 148, 149, 150, 155N, 160, 160N, 161N, 163, 169, 170, 171, 172, 174, 175, 176, 179, 180, 181, 183, 185, 186, 187, 188, 189, 190, 191, 193, 194, 195, 196, 197, 198, 199, 200, 202, 204, 205, 206, 207, 209, 210
Irial Glunmhor, 168
Iron Mountain, 39
Isidore, Saint, 90
Island of Burra, 87
——— Destiny, 6, 137, 193
——— Dalkey, 163
——— Kethlen, 55
——— Kings, 166
——— the Remote, 2
——— Towers, 5, 200
———Noble, 5, 22, 42, 117
———Tory, 5, 18, 38, 52, 54, 200
Islands of Aran, 35, 36, 51, 153
——— Archipelago, 157
Isle of Man, 14, 35, 47, 51, 71N, 194
——— Staffa, 34, 35
——— the West, 3, 4, 21
Isles British, 85
———Giant of the, 60
———King of the, 54
———Northern, 43
Israel, 5, 42, 100, 119, 128, 136
Ister, 50N
Isthmean, 122
Italy, 6, 14, 94, 125, 198
Ita, Sleamhna, 166
Ith, uncle of Galamh, 137, 138, 139, 140, 162, 170
Inchar, 65, 88
Iucharba, 65, 88
Ivy, or Gort

Jacob, 39, 121, 148
Japhet, 4, 7, 8, 88, 130, 134, 135
Japhetic, 7, 10, 180
Jarlath, Saint, 169
Jeremias, Prophet, 121
Jeroboam, 170
Jerome, Saint, 13, 130
Jews, The, 100, 101, 167, 168, 187
Job the Just, 102, 118, 119
Joseph, Brother of Benjamin, 154
Josephus, 99
Jove, 186
Joyce, Dr. R. D., 174, 210
Judges, 119, 178
Julius, 67, 174
Jupiter Tonans, 64
Jutland, 18

Karnac, 82, 102, 116N
Kavanaghs, 167
Keane on Round Towers, 193, 204

Keann, or Head King, 183
Kearnach, Conul, 168
Keating, Dr., 12, 18, 30, 42, 45, 48, 49, 58, 126, 127, 129, 130, 131, 161
Keish Curran, 199
Kells, 44, 70N
——— Book of, 197
Keltic, 4, 5, 6, 7, 8, 8N, 13, 36, 39, 40, 45, 48, 56, 64, 65, 66, 67, 71, 85, 89, 95, 96, 97, 98, 100, 102, 105, 109, 111, 114, 117, 119, 121, 124, 125, 126, 127, 128, 129, 135, 138, 139, 151, 157, 158, 159, 177, 178, 179, 181, 184, 186, 188, 193, 197, 198, 199, 200, 207
Kelts, 4, 9, 10, 11, 14, 38, 42, 48, 95, 99, 111, 116, 117, 119, 120, 121, 123, 124, 125, 140, 141, 166, 183, 187, 195, 197, 199, 200
Kenmare, 3, 143, 144, 145
Kennfaelad, 127
Kerb, son of Buan, 24
Kermaith, 65, 139, 143
Kerry, 3, 75, 126, 145, 145N, 146, 147, 162
Kerry O'Connor, 169
Kesair, Lady, 21N
Kethlen, King of Balor, 55, 56, 60, 61, 65
Kian, father of Lugh, 157, 158
——— son of Oltal Olom, 167
Kildare, 44, 71N, 153, 176, 204
Kilgefin, 153
Killein, 70
Kilkenny, 163, 182
Killower, 28
Kiar, 169
Kilmactraney, 57, 58, 59, 63
Kilmaine, 21, 22, 23, 169
Kimbaeth, King, 33, 34, 171, 172
Kimric, 11, 18, 30N
King Core of Munster, 98, 89
——— Eoghan Mór, 167
——— In-Chief, or Ardrigh, see Ardrigh
——— Keann, or Head, 183
——— — Connacht, 155, 201
——— — Cashel, see Cormac
——— — Egypt, 128, 136
——— — Hy Many, 126
——— of Ireland, 43, 168, see Ardrigh
——— Men (Agamemnon), 174
——— — Offaly, 73, 165
——— — Phœnicia, 127
——— — Troy, 125, 151
——— — Tuatha de Danann, see Danann
——— — Ulster, 168, 173, 205
——— — the Firbolgs, see Firbolg
——— — Danann, see Danann
——— — Orgiallians, 170
——— or Great Father, 184
Kings, 119, 143, 148, 149, 150, 151, 152, 155, 156, 170, 172, 176, 177, 178, 184, 201
Kings, Fort of the, or Rath na Riogh, 207, 209
Kings, Instructions of, 206
King's County, 59, 147, 164, 165, 166
Kinsale, Old Head of, 145, 162
Kirkwall, 79, 87
Knight of the Swan, 159
——— Red or Royal Branch, 168, 169, 174, 175
Knighthood, Five Orders of, 175

Knock Aine, 75
—— Gréine, 75
Knocks, or Hillocks, 28, 64
Knock Ma, or Meadh, 21, 22, 23, 71N, 153
—— na g-Cuach, or "Hill of the Cuckoos," 27
Knocknarea, 62, 63, 64N
Knowledge, 14, 116, 119, 121, 126, 127, 128, 130, 149, 180, 187
Knowledge and Training of Women among the Dananns, 83, 121
Knowth, or Cnoghda, 39, 75, 83, 84, 85, 86

Laisach Lanmor, 168
Laban, 143
Labhraidh Loingseach, 18, 171, 173
Lactantius, 13
Lady Physicians, 83
——Curchog, 151
Laighean, or Leinster, 18
——————Origin of the name, 18
Lairgnen, King of Connacht, 155
Lakes, 3, 154, 155, 156
Lake of Oaks, 154
Lamh Finn, 134
——Rota, 210
Land of Promise, 118
———— Prophecy, 71N
———— Youth, 71N
Language, 117
—————— Irish, 150, 155N, 180
"Language, Aryan Origin of Gaelic," 104, 116, 193
Lauigau, Dr., on Round Towers, 194, 196, 197
Laoghaire, or Leary, King, 207
Laoighis, or Leix, 168
Lastoyric, Dr., on the Irish, 191
Latham, Dr., on the Kelts, 14, 125
Latin, 47, 67, 89, 92, 97, 127, 128N, 129, 130, 157, 177, 179, 210
Latins, 8, 105, 114, 177
Latium, 8, 37
Law, Breton, 179, 180, 181, 182, 206
—— Catholic Church, 180
—— English, 180
—— God's, 182
—— Hindu, 180, 182
——— Man's, 182
—— Natural, 182
——— Roman, 180, 181, 182
—— Spartan, 181
—— Statute, 180
——— Tables of the, 180, 181
—— Written, 182
Laws, Code of, 14, 113, 117, 118, 122, 125, 177, 178, 179, 180, 181, 182, 206
Leabaidh na bh-Fian, 64N
Leabaidh na bh-Fear-mór, 64N
Leabhair-na-h-Uidhre, 83, 83N, 98
———————— g-Ceart, 126, 210
———————— n-Gabhala, 201
Leaca Mac Nemedh, 28
———— or Flagstones, 28, 30
Lead as a writing material, 99, 102
"Lecain, Book of," 29, 30, 46, 58, 78, 98, 112, 126

Leda, 158, 159
Ledwich, Dr., 90, 105N, 122
Legends, The World's, 114
Leinster, 18, 21, 73, 92, 102, 162, 165, 166, 170, 175, 186, 201
"Leinster, Book of," 15, 20, 34, 46, 58, 62, 98, 112, 126
Leinster, Knights of, 175
Leitrim, 20, 39, 54, 169;
Leix, 168
Leoghaire, or Leary, King, 92
—————— Children of, 72
—————— son of Lughaidh, 70N
Letters, 92, 94, 95, 96, 97, 101, 105, 109, 110, 121, 128, 179, 198
Levi, Tribe of, 161
Lewis, 115
Lia-Fail, or Stone of Destiny, 83, 208
"Liber Hymnorum," 161N
Liberator, The (O'Connell), 194
Lifford, 70N, 138, 159
Ligurians, 14
Limerick, 70, 75, 143, 147
Linen as a writing material, 99, 102
Liogair-né, 188
Lios, or Fort, 123, 124, 149, 202
Lir, or Lear, or Allod, 54, 65, 67, 88, 150, 151, 152, 153, 154, 155, 158
Literature, Ancient Irish, 121, 179
—————— Danann, 121
Livy, 7
Lombardy, 8N
Londonderry, 75
Long Arm, Lugh of the, 156
Long-na-m-ban, or Stronghold of the Women, 209
Lot, 143
Lough Allen, 39, 55
—— Arrow, 55, 58, 59, 61, 63, 199
—— Conn, 3
Lough Corrib, 20, 22, 24, 25, 28, 31, 32, 35, 36, 39, 47, 48
—— Cuan, 3
—— Cullen, 3, 48
—— Derg, 152
—— Erne, 3, 54, 55, 57
—— Feball, or Foyle, 63, 70, 78, 139
—— Gara, 3
—— Gill, 63
—— Glynn, 153
—— Mask, 3, 20, 24, 35, 27, 28, 31, 39, 42, 63, 200
—— Ree, 161
—— Swilly, 70, 75
Loughrea, 103
Louth, 70, 84, 148, 166
Louvain, Library of, 90
Louvre, The, 109
Lowry's Fort, or Rath Laoghaire, 207
Lucanian Coast, 9
Luchta, son of Luchad, 44N
Lucian, 97, 98
Lugh, or Lughaidh, King, 42, 43, 44, 44N, 46, 48, 51, 56, 58, 59, 60, 61, 63, 65, 67, 81, 84, 88, 92, 98, 124, 139, 140, 146, 156, 157, 158, 162, 170
Lugh, meaning of, 47

Lugh Nosa, or August, 43
Luge, or Lewis, 70
Luireach Patruic, 161ₙ
Luis, or Mountain Ash, 109
Lus-mhagh, or Herb-field, 59
Luxor, 116ₙ
Lycia, 92
Ma, meaning of, 21, 97
Mab, or Mabhbh, 21, 21ₙ, 64ₙ
Mac Alny, 70
—— Alrt, Cormac, 175
—— Allod, or Loid, 70
—— Aonguls, 168
—— Auleys, 167
—— Carthys, The, 167
—— Coill,or Coll, 44, 45ₙ, 47, 70, 139,147,148
—— Conn, 70
—— Connemara, 167
—— Cuilleanan, Cormac, 134
—— Cumhal, Finn, 128, 176;
—— Dermotts, 167
—— Donnells, 167
—— Dowdals, 167
Macedonia, 3, 14
Mac Elthlenn, or Mac Ellen, 70
—— Engus, 70
—— Erc, 43
—— Firbis, Duald, 29, 30, 40, 41, 70, 81, 82, 106, 149, 127, 188, 201, 202
—— Geoghegans, 25,167
—— Gennis, 168
—— Gillapatrick, 72
—— Govan, 70
—— Grime, 47. 70, 147,148
—— Guires, 167
—— Gunn, or Gunn, 70
Macha, a Lady Chieftain, 60
—— Queen, 170
Mac Hugh, 70
—— Iceacht, or Ceacht, 47, 147, 148
Mac Kean, 70
—— Lachlins, 167
—— Lir, or Manannan, 47, 65, 88
—— Mabons, 167
—— Mnrraghs, 167
—— Morna, 176
—— Namaras, 167
—— Neid, 70
—— Nessa, Conor, King, 150, 166, 171, 174, 175, 176
—— Rannall, or Reynolds, 169
—— Roigh, Fergus, 168, 171, 174, 175
—— Ronain, Cailte, 176
—— Shethor, 70
Madel, 166
Maen Magh, 163, 165
—— or Labhraidh Longseach, 173
Magh Cullen, or Magh Uillin, 48
—— Danaan, or Danesfield, 43, 48
—— Enne, 59ₙ
—— Itha, 138, 139
—— Leana, or Moleana, 165
—— Maen, 163, 165
—— Mór, 43
—— Murthemne, 166
—— n-Ealta, 3
—— n-Eithrigh, 26

Magh Nevy, 21
—— Réln, 19, 20, 39
—— Sleacht, 172
—— Tuireadh, 14ₙ, 15, 23, 24, 55, 146, 150, 157
———————— Conga, 18, 23, 24, 37, 39, 42, 46, 58, 59ₙ, 146, 150, 199
————————Battle of, 18, 36, 43, 44, 53, 56, 60, 65, 72, 150, 150, 157, 199
—— Tura, meaning of, 26, 30, 31, 32, 35,199
—— Tura of the Fomorians, 23, 24, 37, 42, 43, 45ₙ, 46, 59ₙ, 65, 72, 78, 146, 150, 157, 199, 201
Magi, The, 120
Magog, 88, 134
Maine, Sir H. Sumner, 119, 179, 180, 181, 182
Maini, Hy, 163, 165
Mainistreach, Flann, 111
Malachy II., King, 44
Maliu, 54
Man, Isle of, 14, 35, 47, 51, 71ₙ, 194
Manannan Mac Lir, 47, 65, 67, 70ₙ, 71ₙ, 88, 150, 152, 160
Mangan, Clarence, 161ₙ
"Manners and Customs of Ancient Irish" (O'Curry), 15, 55, 72, 78, 80, 111, 117, 121, 200, 204
Mantan, 163
Maolmuire of Fathan, 112, 126
Marathon, 23, 57
Marcus, 172
Maria Teresa, Queen, 141
Marisco, House of, 208
Marriage among the Danauns, 113, 121, 122
Marsh of Tara (Sheskin), 208
Mars, 131
Marseilles, 96
Mask, Lough,3, 20, 24, 25, 27, 28, 31, 39, 42, 63ₙ, 200
Masinissa, King of Africa, 173
Mass, 68ₙ, 155
————Bell, 155
Matabrune, Queen, 159
Matarra, 128
"Materials, MS." (O'Curry), 34, 57, 96, 98, 100, 102, 105, 117, 149, 202
Mauritania, 134
Max Muller, 93, 94, 115, 117, 125
Mayo, 3, 17, 20, 21, 22, 33, 36, 37, 39, 41, 42, 58, 59ₙ, 70, 121, 153, 155, 156ₙ, 188, 188, 189
"Mayo, a Plea for the Evicted Tenants of," 183
Mean-Uisge, 27, 31
Meath, 16, 44, 70ₙ, 72, 75, 147, 149, 152, 157, 161ₙ, 165
Meab, Queen of Connacht, 168, 169, 171, 174, 175
Meave's Butter-roll, 64ₙ
Media, 101, 102
Medicine studied by ladies (Danann), 121
Mediterranean, 3, 134, 135, 137, 157, 173
Memnomium, Ruins of, 116ₙ
Memphis, 102, 128, 136
———— The Irish, 84
Menelaus, 28, 151
Men's work among the Dananns, 124

Mercury, 64
Mesopotamia, 4
Messianic Traditions, 114
Meuse, 13
Michol, daughter of Saul, 136
Midhir, 70ɴ, 71ɴ, 88, 152
Midhluachra, Slighe, *see* Slighe
Milbeoil, Kermad, 139
Miledh, Milesius or Gallamh, 6, 126, 134, 135, 136, 137, 138, 140, 141, 142, 144, 145ɴ, 150, 161, 163, 187
Milesius, 2, 5, 6, 8, 9, 18, 29, 41, 64ɴ, 70, 71ɴ, 74, 80, 81, 83, 87, 91, 92, 112, 116, 120, 124, 125, 127, 128, 132, 134, 135, 136, 137, 138, 140, 141, 142, 143, 144, 145, 146, 147, 148, 149ɴ, 150, 152, 160, 161, 162, 163, 165, 166, 167, 172, 177, 178, 183, 186, 187, 188, 189, 200, 209
Military Orders, 178
Mills, 124
Mioch, son of Dianceacht, 59
Miodhchnarta, Teach, of Tara, 208
Mioscau Meldhh, 64ɴ
Mis Slieve, 143, 144, 145, 146, 147
Moah, 100
Moabites, 100
Moabite Stone, 99, 100, 101
—— Letter, 94
Modern Hebrew Bible, Letters of, 100
Mogha Nuadhat, 167
Moleana, or Magh Leana, 165
Moore, Thomas, 33, 34, 38, 46, 96, 142, 155, 193, 194, 196, 197
Moravia, 87
Morna, Clauna, 41
Mor Righan, or Great Queen, 64, 84, 121
—— Slighe, *see* Slighe
Moses, 5, 48, 66, 93, 101, 116, 121, 128, 130, 132, 133, 138
Monasterboice, 78, 78, 79, 111
Monks, Irish, 194, 197
Monmouth, Geoffry of, 132
Monolith, the, 82
Monuments, 69, 77, 82, 84, 88, 106ɴ, 199, 206, 207, 208
Mound of the Hostages, 208
Mounds, 30, 31, 37, 62, 64ɴ, 84, 85, 86, 88, 103, 106, 116ɴ, 152, 153, 159, 206, 207, 208
Mountains, Old Cuckoo, 58
Mount Brahlieve, 58
Mourne Mountains, 86, 163
Moy River, 81
Moyle River, 54, 155, 156
Moytura Conga, 33, 146, 199
"MS. Materials" (O'Curry's), 34, 57, 96, 98, 100, 102, 106, 149ɴ, 202
Mucca Mhanannain, 160
Muin, or Vine, 109
Muintir Eoluis, or People of Knowledge, 169
Muir Icht, 145
Mull, 154
—— of Cantyre, 155
Mullingar, 210
Munster, 21, 51, 92, 98, 99, 102, 103, 155, 164, 165, 166, 167, 170, 175

Munster, Knights of, 175
Mur Ollamhan at Tara, 172, 206
Murthemni, uncle of Milesius, 138, 166
Museums, 59, 102
Music, 113, 121, 187
Mykenae, 32, 39, 55, 66, 68
Mythology, 68, 113, 114, 115, 158, 159
Myths of the Early Ages, 113, 114

Nachor, grandsire of Abraham, 2
Napoleon I., 40, 66, 67
—— III., 40
Nar, uncle of Milesius, 138, 163
Nas, or Naas, 39, 44, 81
Naul, or Nel, son of Fenius, 128
Navan, 103, 147, 175
Neale, The, 25, 26, 27, 36
Nearchu, 24
Neamhnach, Well of, 207, 208
Necropolis, 32, 37, 83, 84
Nechthann, 84
Neid, or Niat, 60, 65, 70, 78, 88, 139, 200
Neimheidh, 4, 5, 21, 38, 120
Nemedians, 2, 4, 6, 9, 15, 19, 38, 39 40, 42, 52 162, 165
Nemedius, 4, 6, 18, 47, 125
—— Flags of the Sons of, 28
Nemed Mac Badhrai, 27
Nennius, 12ɴ, 49, 50, 126, 132, 140
Nenual, son of Fenius, 128, 134
Nessa, mother of Conor, 168, 174
Netterville, 84
Nevy's Plain, 21, 22
Newgrange, 39, 75, 79, 83, 85, 86, 87, 103
Newport, Co Tipperary, 143
Newtown-Hamilton, 71ɴ, 148, 152
Ngedal, or Reed, 109
Nia, Plain of, 22
Niagh Nasc, or Knights of the Golden Collar, 175
Niall of the Nine Hostages, 167, 170
Nibelungen Lied, The, 68ɴ
Nicholas, Saint, 201
Nichbur, 36ɴ
Nile, River, 34, 40, 87, 94, 116ɴ, 131, 136
Nimrod, 101, 135
Niniveh, 98, 101, 102
Nion, or Ash, 109
Niul, 128, 129, 130, 131, 132, 133, 134, 136
Noah, 7, 88, 134
—— daughter of, 21ɴ
Nore, River, 163, 165
Normans, 29, 90, 126
Northern Isles, 43
Norwegians, 4, 52ɴ, 114
Norway, 156
Nuada, King, 22, 25, 26, 27, 29, 42, 43, 47 49, 53, 56, 58, 60, 88, 134, 156]
Nuadhat, 153, 167
—— Queen of, 56
—— meaning of, 47
Nymphfield, 23, 25

Oak, or Dair, 109, 120
Oaks, Lake of, 154
O'Boyles, 167
O'Brien, Dr. (Most Rev.), 198, 195

O'Briens, The, 167
O'Byrnes, The, 167
O'Carrolls of Ely, 167
Ocean, German, 53
Ochtriuil, daughter of Dianceacht, 59*
O'Connell, the Liberator, 194
O'Connell, Bishop of Kerry, 126
O'Connors of Corcomroe, 169
O'Conor, Charles, of Belanagare, 132, 193, 196
——— Roderick, 43, 178
——— Don, 167
——— Kerry, 169
O'Cuirnin, Cormac, 59N
O'Curry, Eugene, 12, 15, 16, 23, 29, 30, 34, 38, 52N, 55, 56, 57, 59, 62, 63, 73, 74, 75, 78, 80, 81, 83, 89, 91, 95, 96, 98, 100, 102, 106, 111, 120, 121N, 145N, 149N, 150, 151, 156N, 159, 160N, 161, 168, 175, 179, 180, 187, 198, 200, 202, 204
O'Davoren, 12
Oder, 10
Odin, or Woden, 64
O'Donnells, 167
O'Donovan, Dr., 23, 29, 34, 35, 37, 59N, 62, 63, 74, 75, 85N, 91, 103, 111, 120, 133, 165, 180, 210
Oe, 84
Oenach Colmain, 84
O'Fallons, 167
O'Farrells, 169
Offaly, 73, 165
O'Flaherty (Ogygia), 7, 32, 91, 106, 107, 110, 170, 178
O'Flahertys, The, 167
O'Flynn, Eochy, 111
O'Gallaghers, 167
O'Garas, 167
Ogham, 89, 92, 93, 94, 95, 96, 97, 98, 99, 100, 103, 104, 105, 106, 107, 108, 109, 110, 119, 133, 146, 147
Ogma, 26, 44, 47, 51, 57, 58, 60, 61, 65, 67, 84, 88, 89, 92, 97, 98 107N
Ogmius, 97, 98
O'Grady, Standish, 16, 34, 132
Ogygia (O'Flaherty's), 32, 106N, 107, 165, 170
O'Hanlon, Very Rev. Canon, 172
O'Haras, 167
Oldhe, 98
——— Cloinne Lir, 156N
Oidheam, 98
Olgh, 97
Oileli, or Olchell Arann, 153, 154
Olr. or Spindle-Tree, 110
Oirib, or Orbsen, 20, 47, 48
Ollial Olom, 167
Oisin, 176
O'Kanes, 167
O'Kellys, 167
O'Kennedys, 167
Ollam, 84
Ollamh Fodhla, 168, 171, 172, 206
Ollamhs, 29, 45N, 98, 119, 120, 172, 178
Oll-Athair, or Great Father, 42, 44, 48, 64, 65
O'Lochan, Cuan, the Poet, 44
O'Loughlinns, 167, 169

Olympian God, 158
Olympic Games, 43, 122
Olympus, 62, 160
O'Maddens, 167
O'Mahony, 11, 42, 45, 49, 50, 132N
O'Malleys, 167
O'Maolconaire, Tanaidh, 111
O'Malones, 167
O'Moores, 168
O'Mulconry, John, 78
O'Mulloys, 167
O'Murphys of Hy Many, 167
——— Leinster, 167
O'Neills, 167
Onn, or Furze, 109
Opinions, Author's, 115
——— Coxe's, 114
——— Gladstone's, 114
——— of Irish Scholars, 132
——— Three Leading, on Round Towers, 192
O'Quinns, 169
Orbsen, or Corrib, Lough, 20
Ordal, son of Aldai, 88
Ordnance Survey, 15, 16, 62, 75, 78, 205
Orgiallians, 170
"Origin and Development of Religious Belief," (Baring Gould,) 107N
O'Reillys, 167
Orkney Islands, 35, 52N, 53, 54, 79, 87
O'Rourkes, 167
Oscar, 176
Oscans, 8, 9, 94, 95, 129
Ossianic, 68N
Ossory and Ossorians, 73, 163, 167, 210
Othian, or Fahan, 126
O'Tooles, 167
Oughterard, 48
Oxford, 90
Ox Mountains, see Gamh
Ox Mount, or Bri-damh, 164
Oxus, 92, 94

P, The Letter, 107
Pagan Origin of Ogham Writing, 106
——— Theory of Round Towers, 194, 195, 196, 197
Pagan Kelts, 200
Painting, Knowledge of, by Dananns, 121
Palace, Crystal, 103
Palm-branch, Writing in the form of, 103
Papebroke, Father, 90
Pap Mountains, 75
Parchments as Writing Material, 99
Parliament, Ancient Irish, 14, 178
———————Kilkenny, 182
Partholan, 2, 3, 4, 5, 6, 21, 52
Patrick, Saint, 22, 30, 43, 80, 92, 95, 96, 104, 108, 111, 160N, 161, 192, 193, 195, 198, 204, 208
Patroclus, 28
Paul, Saint, 104, 115
Peel, Tower of, in Isle of Man, 194
Pelasgic, 11, 39, 50, 65, 67, 82, 94, 95, 117, 129, 131
Peloponnesian War, 63

Peninsula, Spanish, 14
Pentarchy, 14, 35, 174, 177
Pentateuch, 100, 101, 131
Persepolis The Pillars of, 116N, 158
Perseus, 66, 157
Persia and Persians, 1, 23, 40, 68, 87, 92, 93, 111, 114, 171, 184
Perth, 118
Petrie, Dr., 15, 34, 46, 62, 75, 77, 78, 80, 81, 84, 91, 161N, 177, 191, 192, 193, 194, 195, 196, 197, 198, 199, 200, 201, 202, 205, 210
Pethboc, or soft B., 110
Phaleg, 135
Phallic, 107N, 108N
Pharaoh, King of Egypt, 128, 130, 132, 136, 137, 158
Philipstown, 165
Phoenicia and Phoenicians, 7, 89, 92, 94, 95, 100, 101, 105, 106, 111, 127, 128N, 129, 131N, 132N
Physicians, Danann Ladies, 121
Pictet, Adolphe, 2N, 117, 120N, 125
Picts and Scots, 176, 188
Picture-Writing, 94, 95
Pillars of Persepolis, 116N
Pillar-Stones. 30, 84, 92, 102, 104, 105, 106, 195, 199, 200, 201, 202
Plague, 3
Plain, Hill of the, 21N
—— of Flocks, 3
—— of Nevi, 21, 22
—— Nia, or Magh Tura, 22
—— of the Shield-shell, 26
—— of Towers, or Magh Tura, 26, 30
Pliny, 131
Poets and Poetry, 119, 120, 122, 131, 179, 200
Poland, 4
Pompey, 174
Portumna, 152, 153, 154
Pre-Christian Irish History, 112
Preservation of Irish Language, Society for, 150, 155
Priam, King of Troy, 30, 125, 151
Prichard, 125
Primitive Inhabitants of Ireland, 106
Promise, Land of, 118
Proofs of Character in Firbolg and Danann, from MSS. and Ruins, 15, 82, 125
Proofs of Pagan Origin of Ogham, 97, 107
—— of Burial of the Dead, 122
—— that Dananns knew the Arts, 125
Propaganda College, 127
Proverbs, Solomon's, 101
Psalms, David's, 101
Psyche, 159
Ptolemais, 169
Ptolemy, 131
Public and Periodic Gatherings, 122
—— Roads, 210
Punch Cartoons, 189
Punjaub (five rivers), 50N, 158
Pyramids, 82
Pythian, The, 45

Queen Cuirrell, 84
—— Cleopatra, 82
—— Crofinn, 200, 209
Queen Elizabeth, 170
—— Great, or Mór Rigban, 64, 84, 121
—— Kothlenn, 55
—— Matabrune, 159
—— Meab, 64N, 168, 169, 171, 174, 175
—— Michol, 136
—— Saba, 167
—— Tea, 162, 164, 207, 208, 209
—— of Tuatha de Danann, 209
—— of Connacht, 168
—— of Ireland, *see* Eire and Ireland
——, or Great Mother, 184
Queen's College, Cork, 117
—— County, 168
Queirt, or Apple-tree, 109

"Race, Aryan Origin of the Gaelic," &c., 104, 116N, 133, 177
Races, Earliest, 1
Rachel, wife of Jacob, 154
Rainhat, or area, 210
Raleigh, Sir W., 190
Rangers, Connacht, 210
Rannall, or Mac Rannall, 169
Raphoe, 70N, 147, 151, 159
Raths, 16, 36, 39, 59, 81, 84, 118N, 121, 122, 123, 124, 198, 201, 202
Rath Beathaigh, or Beagh, 163, 165
—— Builder of Tara, 201
—— Cro-porta, 25
—— Conrath, 143
—— Caelchu, 209
—— Fearainn, 25
—— Graine, 208, 209
—— Laoghaire, 207, 208
—— na-Riogh, 14N, 15, 16, 20, 36, 207, 208, 209
—— Molicatha, 81
—— of the Synods, 208
—— Uin, or Rahoon, 163
Rathlin, 35
Rawlinson, Sir Henry, 93, 101
Red Hugh, 55, 152
—— or Royal Branch Knights, 168, 169, 174
—— Sea, 100, 128, 133
Reed, or Ngedal, 109
Ree, Lough, 161
Refloir, King, 136
Religious Rites, 15, 178, 187
Remus, 36, 37, 131
Respect of the Dananns for the Weaker Sex, 83
Revelation, 114
Reynolds, or Rannall, 169
Rhaetia, or The Tyrol, 14
Rhea Sylvia, 65, 131
Rhine, River, 13, 14
Rich, Barnaby, on Ireland, 189
Righ, or King, 118
"Rights, Book of," 126
Rinuccini, the Nuncio, 190
River Large, or Abhan Mhor, 61
—— Small, or Abhan bheag, 61
Roads, Public, 210
Roigh, mother of Fergus, 174
Roboam, 164
Roland, 68

Roman, 100, 105, 106, 109, 111, 176, 180, 181, 182, 198
Romans, 8, 28, 40, 96, 115, 123, 129, 173
Rome. 8, 9, 16, 32, 36, 37, 65, 90, 96, 116N, 127, 129, 131, 169, 171, 181, 182, 198
Romulus, 36, 37, 131, 184
Rory, Children of, 173
Rosa and Rose, 128N
Roscommon, 3, 17N, 58, 122, 153, 169
Rosetta Stone, The, 101
Rosg-Catha, or Eve of Battle, 24.
Ro-shet, or Road, 210
Ross, son of Rory, 174
Rōt, or Road, 210
Ros, meaning of, 17N
—— Airgead, 163, 165
—— in England, 17N, 35
—— in Munster, 17N
—— in the Highlands, 17N
—— Nair, 166
—— na Riogh, 84
Rostrevor, 17N
Roumelia, 4
Round Towers, 180, 192, 193, 194, 195, 196, 198, 199, 200, 202, 203, 204
Round Towers as Signal Turrets, 195, 197
Royal Irish Academy, 32, 34, 37, 58, 62, 69, 72, 82N, 84, 89, 107N, 111
Ruadh-raidh, or Roory, King, 168
Ruis, or Alder, 109
Rurai, or Roderick O'Conor, K. I., 43, 178
Rnadraidh Clan, 169, 173
—————— Mor, 171, 173, 174, 175
Russia, 117

Saba, wife of Olial Olom, 167
Sabines, 8, 9, 28, 129
Sabh Ildanadh, The, 44
Sacrifices, Human (none), 120, 171
Sail, or Willow, 109
Saimher, 3
Samaritan, 94, 100, 127
Samhain, or November, 172
Samnites and Samnium, 8, 116N
Samuel the Prophet, 101, 119, 185
Sand Hills, 145
Sanative Pool, or Healing Bath, 24
Sanskrit, 93, 95, 97, 102, 118N, 120, 128
Saul, King of Israel, 42, 119, 136, 185, 187
Saxons, 96, 141, 188, 204
Scandinavia, 5, 54, 90, 103, 104, 114
Scáthall, or Scell, meaning of, 26
Sceiné (gen. Skené), wild beauty, 3
Schliemann, 68
Science, or Ealadhan, 97, 114, 116N
Scota, Lady, 128, 128N, 131, 132, 134, 136, 137, 141, 144, 145, 146
Scotch, 106, 186, 188, 189, 191, 209
Scoti, 10, 35, 91, 107N, 131, 132, 133, 134, 135, 136, 172, 176
Scotin, 166
Scotland, 14, 90, 98, 106, 137, 155, 183, 191, 193, 194, 201
Scriptures, Sacred, 100, 107, 158
Sculpture (Danann), 122
Scythian, 7, 60, 127, 128, 130, 131, 132N, 134, 136, 157

Sea Black, 34
—— Northern, or German Ocean, 53, 54, 137
Seafield, 62
Seanachaidh, 12, 106N, 119, 131, 135, 140, 142, 149, 178
Sean Chuach, or Old Cuckoo, 58
Seancus Mór, 105
Sean Mhagh, or Old Plain, 3
Secret Character of Ogham, 98] 119
Sedga, Chieftain, 163
Seilg, meaning of, 11
Sem, son of Noah, 7, 130, 135, 166
Semiramis, Queen, 93, 149
Semita, or Path, 210
Semitic, 7, 10, 94
Seng, wife of Mileslus, 136
Septs, 184, 185
Septuagint, 4N, 170
Servia, 183
Seth, 99, 130
Set, or Road, 219
Shannon, River, 21, 152, 153, 161, 162, 163, 164
Shenaar, 127, 128, 129, 131, 130, 132
Shetland Isles, 52N, 53
Sheskin, or Marsh of Tara, 208
Sicily, 134, 135, 173
Siculians, 8
Sidh, or Fairy, 39, 71N
Sidhe, or fairy-hills, 88, 144, 149, 152
—— Buidhbh, 71N
—— Droma Deine, 153
—— Cletigh, 71N, 153
—— Finneachaidh, 152
—— Meadha, 71N, 153
—— Trium, 153
—— Neanta, 153
Sigean Shore, 28
Sighmael, 70N, 71N, 152, 153
Silver-hand, or Airgead-lamh, see Airgead-lamh
Simon Breac, or Speckled, 5
Sinai, 93, 95, 100
Siorna, K., 171, 172
Six, The, 23
Skarif, or Scariff, 163
Skellig Rocks, 145, 162
Skené, wife of Amerghin, 3, 145
—— Inver, 3, 143, 144, 145, 166
Skins as writing material, 99
Slainge, 15, 27, 206
————Inver, 142, 144
Slane in Meath, 79, 84, 103, 152, 153, 161N
Slavs, 183
Slaney, River, 18, 85
Slemhna Magha Itha, 138, 166
Sligo, 23, 37, 43, 55, 56, 58, 62, 70, 157, 189, 199
Sliabh, an Iaruin, 39
—— Eblind, or Felim, 143, 166
—— na m-ban, 39
—— Bladhma, or Bloom, 166
—— Mis, 143, 144, 145, 146, 147
—— Cuailgne, or Cooley, 148, 166
—— Fuadh, 148, 152, 153, 166
Slighe, a public road, 210
—— Asail, or Western road, 210

Sligho, Cualann, or Eastern road, 210
—— Dala, or Great South Western road, 210
—— Midhluachra, or Northern road, 210
—— Mór, or Elscir Riada, 210
Sloe-tree, or Strait, 109
Smerwick, 145, 145n, 190
Smith's Banquet, The, 160
Social Habits of Dananns. 113, 122, 177
Solomon, his Proverbs, 101n
—— King, 119
Society for Preservation of Irish Language, 150
South Munster Society of Antiquarians, 103
Spain and Spaniards. 6, 9, 17n, 114, 125, 126, 134, 135, 138, 139, 140, 142, 145n, 161, 162, 163, 166, 198
Spanish Peninsula, 14, 134
Spartan State, Code of the, 181
Spenser, Edmund, 182, 189
Spindle-tree, or Oir, 110
Sreng, 15, 19, 20, 26, 27, 28, 29, 42
Sruth na Maoile, 155
—— meaning of, 19
Sru, the leader, 133, 134
Stackallen Bridge, 39
Staffa, Isle of, 54
Statute Law, 180
St. Columbkille, 29, 30, 197, 198
—— Isidore, 90
—— Jarlath, 169
—— Jerome, 13, 130
—— Patrick, 22, 30, 43, 80, 93, 108, 160n, 170, 172, 192, 193, 195, 198, 204, 208
—— Paul, 104, 115
—— Nicholas, College of 201
Stone as a writing material, 99, 103
—— House, or Ciolgteach, 195, 198
—— Pillars, 30, 84, 92, 99, 102, 199, 200, 201, 202
—— of Destiny, or Lia-fail, 208
—— Monuments, 106, 107, 122, 123
—— Dwellings, 198, 199, 200, 201, 202
Stoney Batter, 210
Strait, or Sloe-tree, 109
Strangford or Cuan Lough, 3
Strabo, 131
Stream of the Maoil, or Mull, 155
Styria, 14
Suir, River, 35
Suirghe, 148, 163
Sullivan (W. K.), 1, 91, 117
—— (A. M.), 34
Supreme Being, 40
Sun and Fire Worship, 46, 205, 119, 171, 173
Sutherland, 35
Swan, Knight of the, 159
Sweden, 52n, 156
Swift, Dean, on the Irish, 190
Switzerland, 14
Synods, Rath of the, 208

Table lands, 1
—— staves, 102
Tables of the Law, 101
—————— Poets, 102

Tables, Twelve, 9
Tablets, Wooden, 102
—— of Wax, 102
—— of Umbria and Samnium, 116n
Tabra-fena, or Wells of Fenius, 133
Tadhg Mór, 70n, 71n, 152, 153
Taoi and Tulom and Trug, 45n
Taibhli Filidh, 102
Tailte, Queen of King Eochy, 43, 44, 51, 121
Taillteann, or Teltown, 43, 46, 70, 70n, 72, 74, 84, 122, 144, 147, 149, 150, 159
Tain-bo-Cuailgne, The, 174
"Tales, The Three Most Sorrowful," 74, 149, 156, 169, 174
Tallacht, or Tallaght, 3
Tamhleacht, meaning of, 41
Tanistry, 177, 183, 184
Tara, or Teamhair, 5, 14, 15, 16, 18, 19, 20, 21, 35, 36, 37, 39, 43, 44n, 45n, 46, 57, 58, 72, 73, 74, 78, 81, 84, 122, 143, 147, 156, 157, 161n, 168, 171, 172, 176, 177, 200, 201, 205, 206, 207, 208, 210
Tara, Psalter of, 206
Tath, 194
Tea, wife of Heremon, 163, 164
Teach Doinn, 145n, 166
—— Miodhchuarta at Tara, 208
—— Mór Millidh Amus, 15
—— Mur, meaning of, 208, 209
Teagasg na Riogh, 206
Tea's House at Tara, 207
Teige, 167
Templemore, 201
Tethmoy, or Tuath da Magh, 164
Tethra, 58
Teutones and Teutonic, 36n, 65, 114
Thebes, 102, 116n
Theistic Traditions, 114
Theodoric, 68n
Thor, or Donar, 64
Thrace, 4, 12, 14, 50, 137
Tighearnach of Clonmacnoise, 33, 34, 172
Tighearnmas, King, 170, 171, 172
Tigh Teamrach at Tara, 15
Tigris, 40, 92, 158
Timahoe, 204
Tinne, 109
Tipperary, 70, 143, 166
Tirawly, 167
Tireragh, 81, 167
TirErril, 23, 43, 55, 56, 199
Tiri, or Tiree, 54
Tir-fiachra, 167
Tir-na-h-oige, 71n
Tir-Tairrgine, 71n
Tlacta, 46
Tobur Finn, 208
Tochur, 163, 165
Todd, Dr., 12, 126, 141
Tonn Cliodhna, 161
Tor, or Tower, 200
Tory Island, 5, 18, 38, 51, 54, 200
Tower Conaings, 38
—— Ilythe, 194
Tower of Babel, 135
—— of Peel 194;

Towers, Island of, 5
——— Round, 69, 72, 79, 80, 81, 87, 180, 192, 193, 194, 195, 196, 197, 198, 199, 200, 203, 204
Towns of the Dead, 32, 83, 87
Traigh Eothaile, or Traigh an Chairn, 63
Trajan, Emperor, 184.
Tralee, 143
Treanmor, 176
Treviri, 13
Tribes and Families, 183
Triennial Parliament of Tara, 172, 206
Trinity College, 35, 59N, 63N, 69, 72, 78, 90, 126, 149N, 151, 161N, 197
Troad, The, 151
Troigh Leathan, or Broad Foot, 201
Troy and Trojan, 25, 30, 32, 67, 68, 116N, 121, 125, 151
Tuagh-rota, or farm road, 210
Tuaith da Magh, or Tethmoy, 164
Tuam, 21, 71N, 153, 169
Tuatha, or Tribes, 49, 50, 72, 74
Tuathach Ban, 48, 49
Tuatha de Danann, *see* Danann
——— meaning of, 48
Tuirin, near Lough Mask, 200
Tuirenn, Fate of the Children of, 72, 156, 157, 158
Tulach an Triuir, 31, 37
Tullaghbeg, 165
Tullamore, 165
Tumuli, or Tombs, 31, 62, 64, 87, 106, 198
Tur, or Tower, 200
Turanian, 127
Tartha, or Columns, 26
Tur Trean Teamhrach, 200
Tuscany, 8N
Twelve Tables, 9, 180, 181, 182
Tyrol, *see* Rhaetia

Ughi, a Milesian leader, 163
Uilleann, or Woodbine, 110
Uillin, 47, 48
Uisneach, 44, 46, 143, 174, 175
Ulla, Ulladh, or Ulster, 21, 51, 150, 162, 165, 167, 168, 169, 170, 174, 205, 206
"Ulster, Annals of," 87
Ulysses, 151, 174
Umbria and Umbrians, 8, 9, 116N, 129
Un, a Milesian leader, 165
——— Rath, called Rahoon, 163, 165
Ur of Chaldea, 2, 4
Ur, or Heath, 109

Valencia, 162
Vallancey, General, on Round Towers, 193, 194, 196
Valley of Sinai, 93, 95, 100
Vedic Poets, 114
Venice, 9
Venus, 108N

Vere, Sir Aubrey de, 174
Vikings, 52N
Vine, or Muin, 109
Vistula, 4, 10, 50
Volscians, or Volsci, 3, 8N, 9

Wales, 17N, 188
Wand of the Poets, or Fleasg Fili, 102
Ware, Sir James, 91, 107N
Warrenstown, 164
Waterfall, Dara's, 63
——— of Red Hugh, 152
Watermill, first in Ireland, 206
Wax as a writing material, 102
Weaker Sex, Respect for, by Tuatha de Danann, 83
Weaker Sex, Knowledge and Training of, 83, 141
Weapons, Warlike, 56
Well of Fenius, 133
——— Neamhnach (Heaven Spring), 207, 208
Wells, 31
Welsh, 9, 11, 13, 188, 189
Western Asia, 100
Western Continent, 14
West, Isle of the, 3
Westmeath 44, 46, 143. 147, 154
Westminster Abbey, 83
Wexford, 18, 72, 122, 142
White Foreigners, 4
Wicklow, 18, 163, 171
"Wideway" Mykenae, 39
Wilde, Lady, 96, 198
——— Sir W., 10N, 28, 30, 31, 32, 33, 36, 37, 59N, 63N, 64N, 69, 74, 75, 85, 86, 87, 91, 106N
Williams, W., 111N, 147
Willow, or Sail, 109
Wilton, Lord Grey de, 190
Windele, on Round Towers, 193, 194, 197
Wolfian Theory, The, 68
Women's Rights and Position among the Kelts, 141
——— among he Dananns, 121
Women's Works among the Dananns, 124
Wood as a writing material, 99, 102
Woodbine, or Uilleann, 110
Wooden Buildings, 200
——— Tablets, 102
Worship of the True God, 15
——— False gods, 15
——— Sun and Fire, 46
Writing Materials (Ancient Irish), 99
——— Secret, 47

Young, Arthur, on Ireland, 190
Youth, Land of, *see* Tir-na-h-oige

Zeuss, 98, 158

Price 7s. 6d.

The Aryan Origin of the Gaelic Race & Language.

BY THE

VERY REV. U. J. CANON BOURKE, P.P., M.R.I.A.

SECOND EDITION.

LONDON:
LONGMANS, GREEN & CO., PATERNOSTER-ROW.
1876.

OPINIONS OF THE PRESS.

(*From the Freeman's Journal.*)

The consummate skill with which the Very Rev. Author has utilised his ponderous materials, the acumen with which he states and supports his own views, the dexterity with which he aids a concurrent or combats an opponent, these, joined to a great force of expression, signal illustrative faculty, and a wonderful range of learning, make this book altogether out of the ordinary category. Its perusal offers the most conclusive answer to those who question the advantage of exploration in the language, literature, and antiquities of Ireland. From this book the sceptical or the ignorant will learn to look with new sentiments upon what is the fashion to contemn or to neglect; to the scientific it will be a welcome auxiliary, and no reader, we venture to predict, but will own that he has never spent his time to better purpose than in gathering from the rich stores here provided for him.

(*From the Irish Times.*)

Canon Bourke shows with admirable skill how, to men learned in the science of languages, a knowledge of the Keltic is a necessary element in their investigation, and he brings a blush to the cheek of Irishmen when he informs them that in France and in Germany that language which they are fast abandoning is studied with much interest and zeal by the great philologists of the day. In his researches, the author shows that there is a great similarity between the Latin and Gaelic letters. The depth of thought displayed in this work must raise it above the level of the ephemeral productions which too frequently in latter times have issued from the Press . . .

(*From the Morning Mail.*)

. . . The work is a most valuable contribution to philological literature; it displays immense erudition and research, combined with a judicial impartiality not always found in the works of enthusiastic writers on controverted questions of race and language. In style it can be compared for clearness, energy, and aptness of illustration with any work in the English language; and we should be glad if we could see more works of the kind as the result of the learned leisure of the higher dignitaries of the Roman Catholic Church.

WORKS BY THE SAME AUTHOR.

Fcap. 8vo, cloth, limp, price 2s. 6d.

The College Irish Grammar. 8th Edition. For the use of Students of Intermediate Schools and Colleges; may be used at the Examinations under the Intermediate Education (Ireland) Act of 1879.

Fcap. 8vo, cloth, price 3s. 6d.

Easy Lessons or Self-instruction in Irish. 7th Edition. A KEY is annexed to the end of each Part.

Crown 8vo, wrapper, price 2s. 6d.

The Bull "Ineffabilis Deus." In Four Languages—LATIN, IRISH, FRENCH and ENGLISH; with a Dissertation on the Art of Illuminating in the Past and Present.

Crown 8vo, price 7s. 6d. (Second Edition).

The Aryan Origin of the Gaelic Race and Language.

8vo, cloth, price 5s. (Second Edition).

Dr. O'Gallagher's Sermons in Irish, English Version; and a Memoir of the Bishop, and a History of his Times.

Crown 8vo, wrapper, price Sixpence.

The Life and Labours of St. Augustin (Bishop of Hippo-Regius). With an Account of the Canons Regular and of the Augustin Friars in Ireland. Second Edition.

People's Edition, price Sixpence.

The Doctrine of the Immaculate Conception of the B.V.M.

The People's Edition.

The Dignity, Sanctity, and Intercessory Power of the Blessed Virgin Mary, Mother of God.

Fcap. 8vo (Second Edition, 210 pages), wrapper 1s., cloth 2s.

Life and Times of the Most Rev. Dr. MacHale, Archbishop of Tuam and Metropolitan.

Life of the Most Rev. Dr. MacHale (in Irish). Published in the *Gaelic Journal.*

Price Sixpence.

A Plea for the Evicted Tenants of Mayo. A Letter addressed to the Right Hon. William E. Gladstone, First Lord of the Treasury and Chancellor of the Exchequer.

www.ingramcontent.com/pod-product-compliance
Lightning Source LLC
Chambersburg PA
CBHW021409230426
43666CB00006B/682